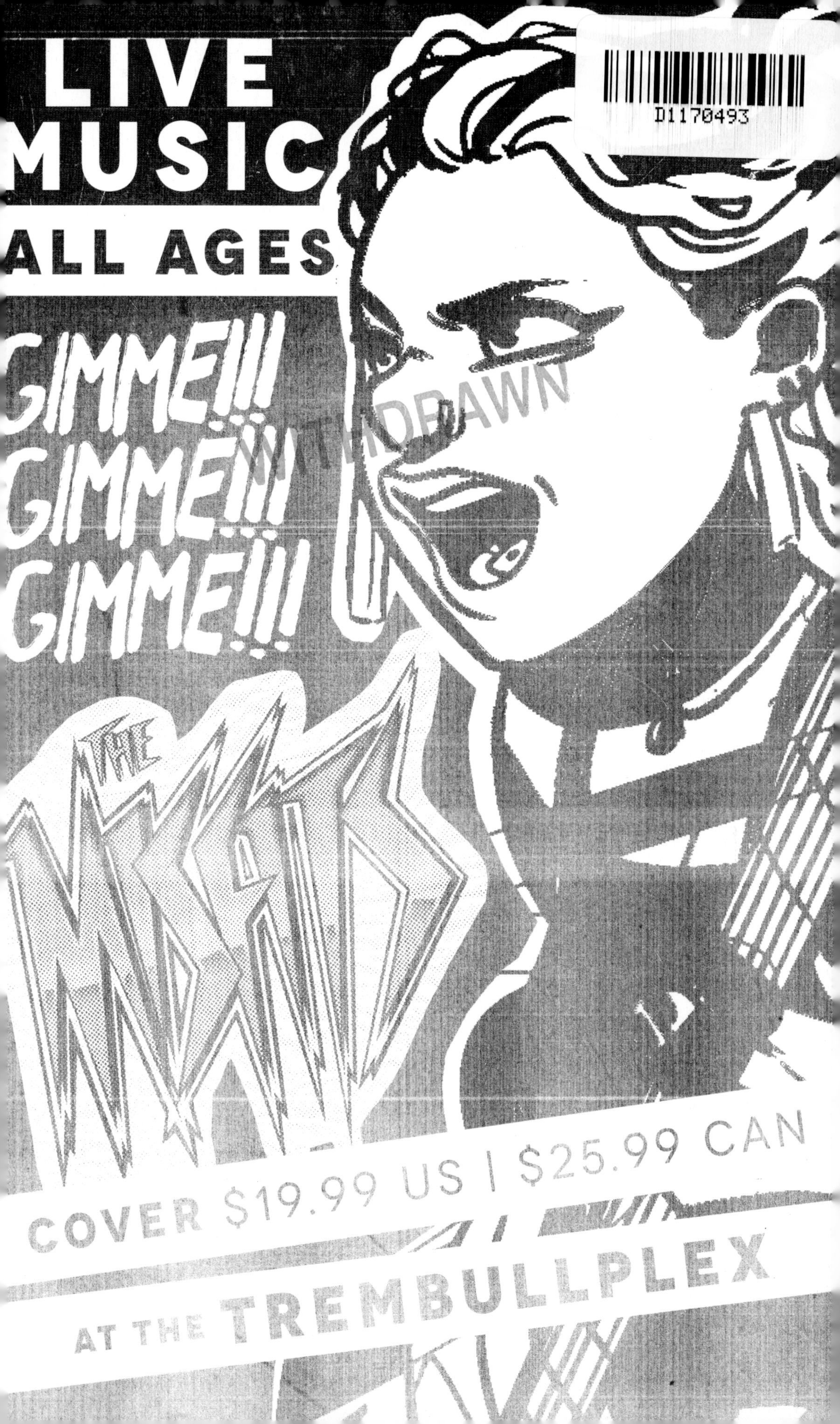
LIVE MUSIC
ALL AGES
GIMME!!! GIMME!!! GIMME!!!
THE
COVER $19.99 US | $25.99 CAN
AT THE TREMBULLPLEX

ISBN: 978-1-63140-930-1   17 18 19 20   1 2 3 4 5

JEM AND THE HOLOGRAMS: THE MISFITS. AUGUST 2017 FIRST PRINTING. HASBRO and its logo, JEM AND THE HOLOGRAMS, and all related characters are trademarks of Hasbro and are used with permission. © 2017 Hasbro. All Rights Reserved. The IDW logo is registered in the U.S. Patent and Trademark Office. IDW Publishing, a division of Idea and Design Works, LLC. Editorial offices: 2765 Truxtun Road, San Diego, CA 92106. Any similarities to persons living or dead are purely coincidental. With the exception of artwork used for review purposes, none of the contents of this publication may be reprinted without the permission of Idea and Design Works, LLC. Printed in Canada. IDW Publishing does not read or accept unsolicited submissions of ideas, stories, or artwork.

Ted Adams, CEO & Publisher • Greg Goldstein, President & COO • Robbie Robbins, EVP/Sr. Graphic Artist • Chris Ryall, Chief Creative Officer • David Hedgecock, Editor-in-Chief • Laurie Windrow, Senior Vice President of Sales & Marketing • Matthew Ruzicka, CPA, Chief Financial Officer • Lorelei Bunjes, VP of Digital Services • Jerry Bennington, VP of New Product Development

Special thanks to John Barber; Hasbro's Andrea Hopelain, Elizabeth Malkin, Ed Lane, Beth Artale, and Michael Kelly for their invaluable assistance.

For international rights, contact
licensing@idwpublishing.com

WWW.IDWPUBLISHING.CO

Facebook: facebook.com/idwpublishing
Twitter: @idwpublishing
YouTube: youtube.com/idwpublishing
Tumblr: tumblr.idwpublishing.com
Instagram: instagram.com/idwpublishing

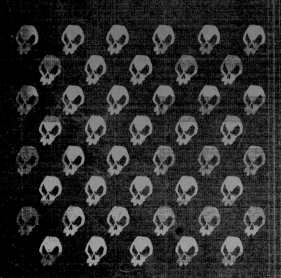

MAKING

WRITER KELLY THOMPSON

ARTIST JENN ST-ONGE

COLORS & LYRICS LETTERING M. VICTORIA ROBADO

LETTERS & DESIGN SHAWN LEE

SERIES EDITORIAL ASSIST CHRIS CERASI

SERIES EDITOR SARAH GAYDOS

COVER M. VICTORIA ROBADO

COLLECTION EDITS JUSTIN EISINGER
ALONZO SIMON

PUBLISHER TED ADAMS

MISCHIEF
WEST COAST TOUR 2017
PHOENIX | SAN DIEGO | LOS ANGELES | SAN FRANCISCO | PORTLAND | SEATTLE

THE STORY SO FAR

THE MISFITS
ARE THE GREATEST
BAND IN THE WORLD,
ACCORDING TO...
THE MISFITS.

BUT AFTER MAKING ENEMIES
OF RIVAL BANDS JEM AND THE
HOLOGRAMS *AND* THE STINGERS
THEY FIND THEMSELVES IN A PRECARIOUS
POSITION, AND ABOUT TO NOT BE A BAND AT ALL!

THE MISFITS, HOWEVER, ARE NOTHING IF NOT
SURVIVORS, AND THEY'LL NEVER GIVE UP,
ESPECIALLY WHEN... THEIR SONGS ARE BETTER!

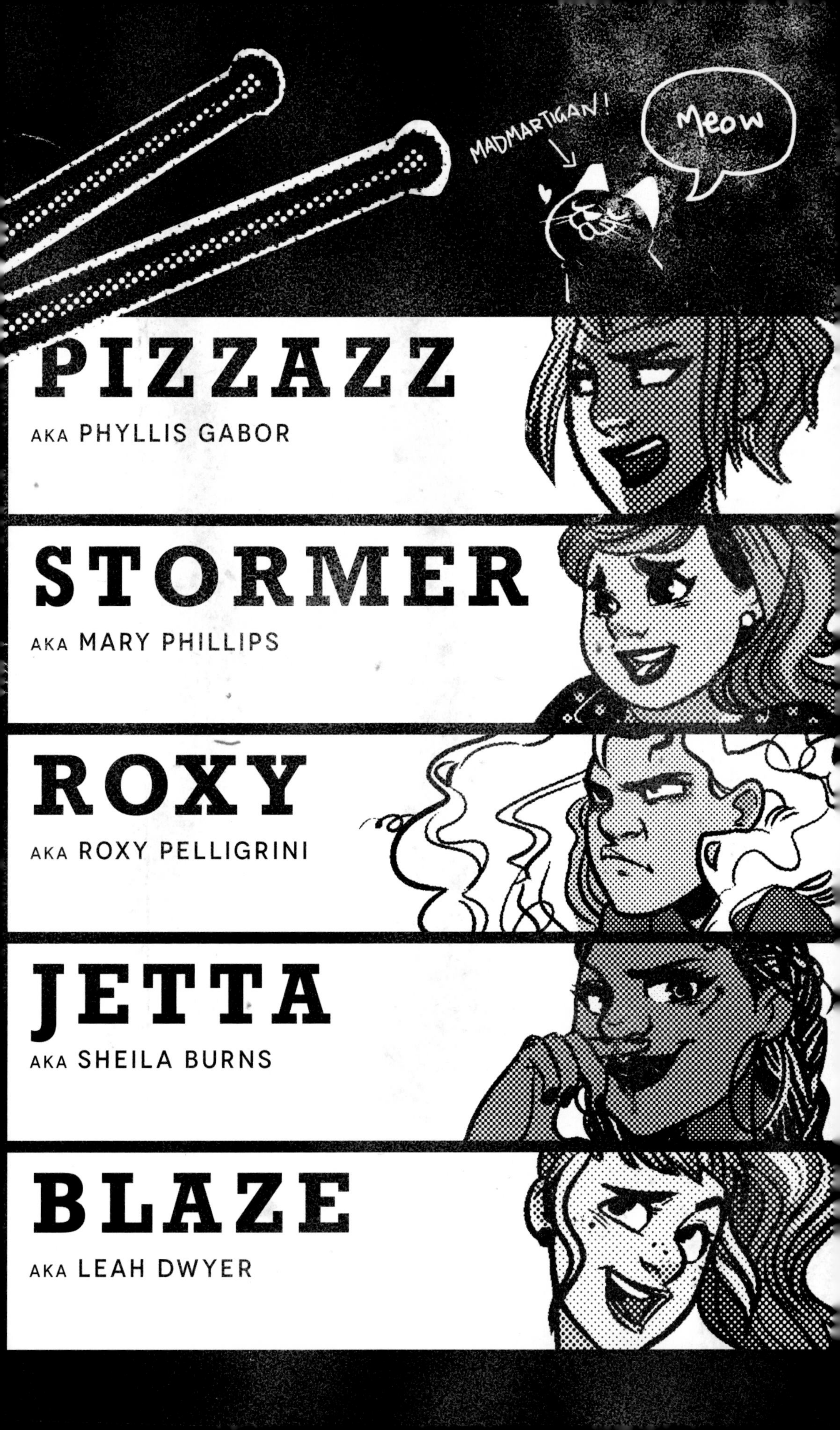
MADMARTIGAN!
Meow
PIZZAZZ
AKA PHYLLIS GABOR
STORMER
AKA MARY PHILLIPS
ROXY
AKA ROXY PELLIGRINI
JETTA
AKA SHEILA BURNS
BLAZE
AKA LEAH DWYER

ART M. VICTORIA ROBADO

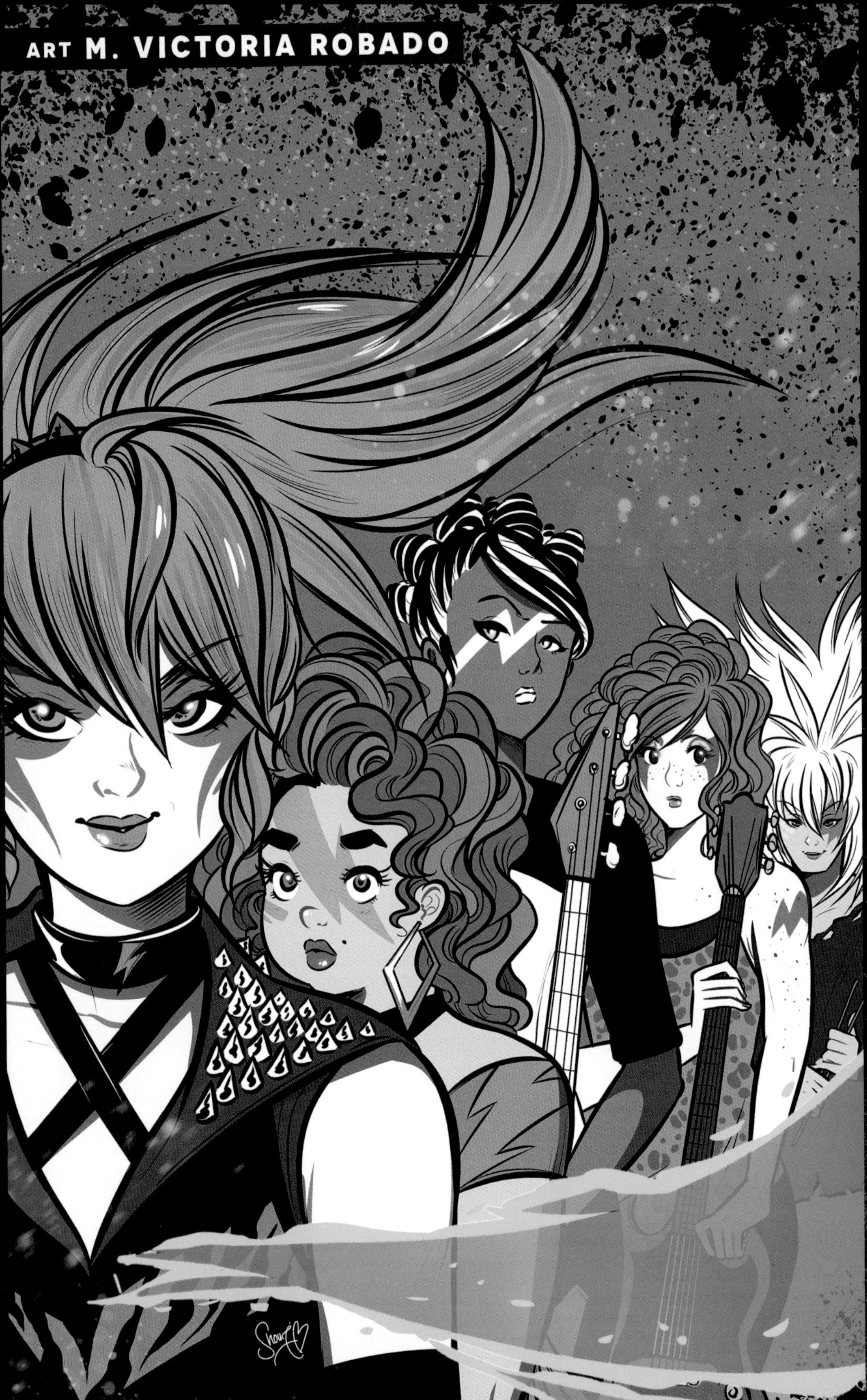

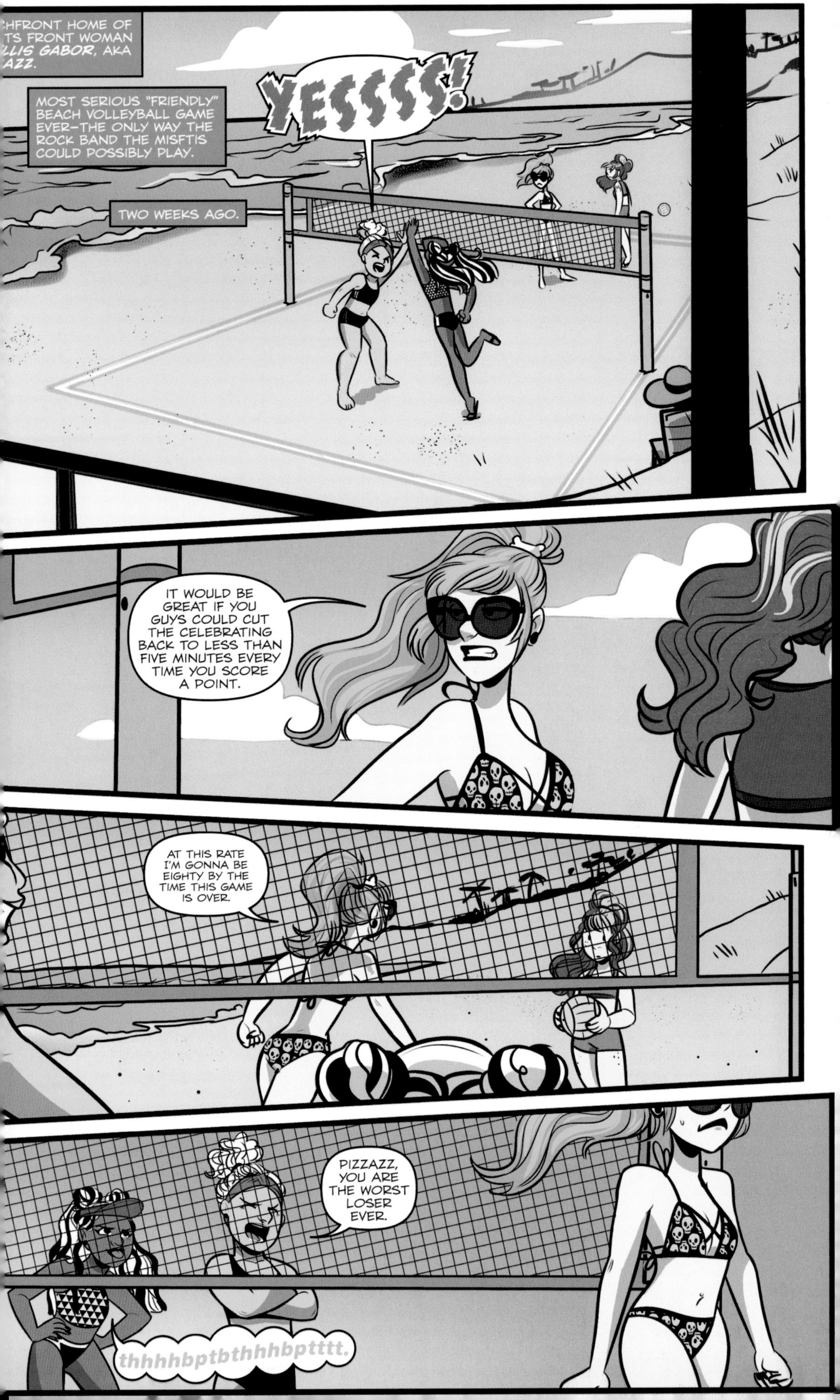

CHFRONT HOME OF
TS FRONT WOMAN
LLIS GABOR, AKA
AZZ.
MOST SERIOUS "FRIENDLY" BEACH VOLLEYBALL GAME EVER—THE ONLY WAY THE ROCK BAND THE MISFTIS COULD POSSIBLY PLAY.
YESSSSS!
TWO WEEKS AGO.
IT WOULD BE GREAT IF YOU GUYS COULD CUT THE CELEBRATING BACK TO LESS THAN FIVE MINUTES EVERY TIME YOU SCORE A POINT.
AT THIS RATE I'M GONNA BE EIGHTY BY THE TIME THIS GAME IS OVER.
PIZZAZZ, YOU ARE THE WORST LOSER EVER.
thhhhbptbthhhbptttt.

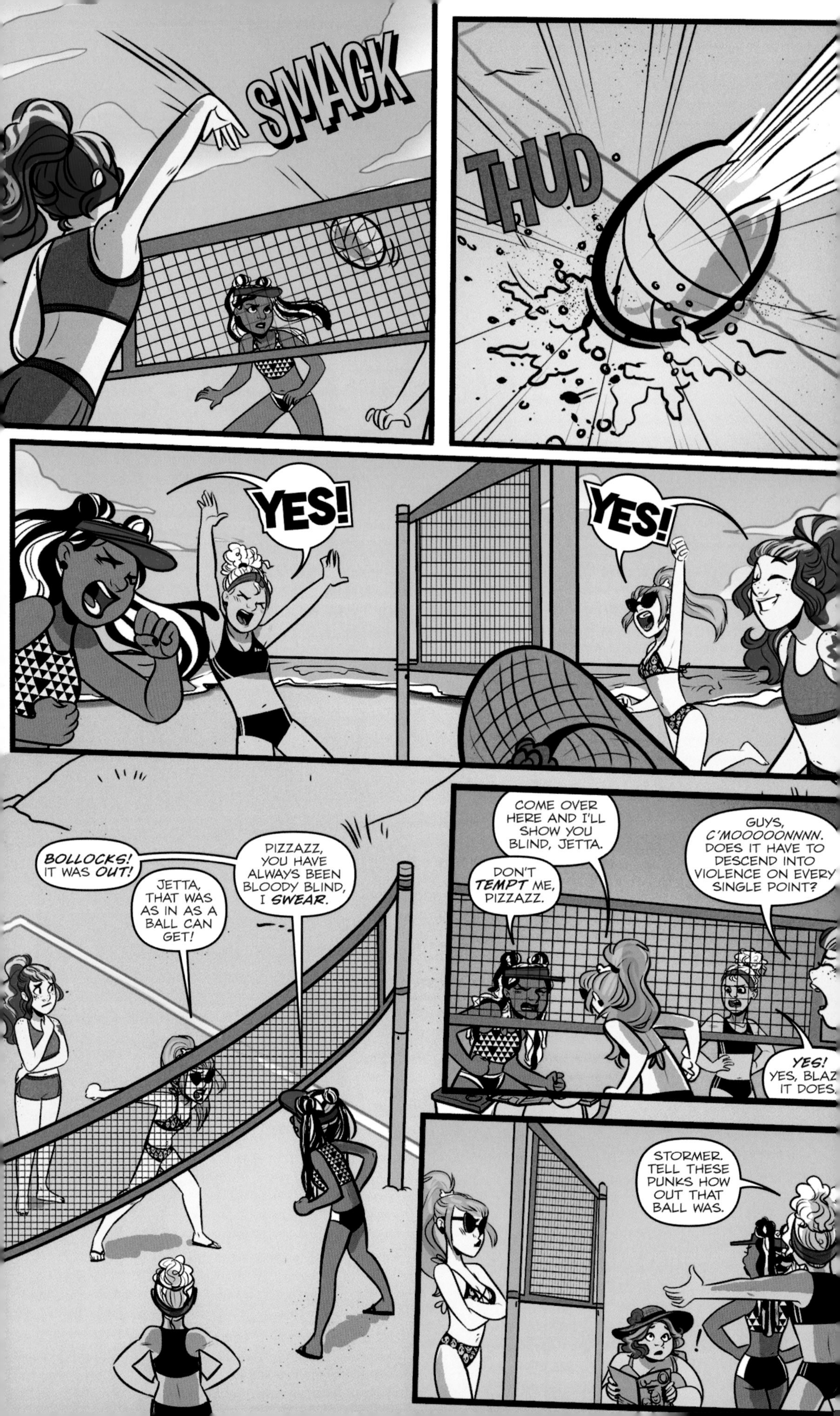
SMACK
THUD
YES!
YES!
BOLLOCKS! IT WAS OUT!
JETTA, THAT WAS AS IN AS A BALL CAN GET!
PIZZAZZ, YOU HAVE ALWAYS BEEN BLOODY BLIND, I SWEAR.
COME OVER HERE AND I'LL SHOW YOU BLIND, JETTA.
DON'T TEMPT ME, PIZZAZZ.
GUYS, C'MOOOOONNNN. DOES IT HAVE TO DESCEND INTO VIOLENCE ON EVERY SINGLE POINT?
YES! YES, BLAZ IT DOES.
STORMER. TELL THESE PUNKS HOW OUT THAT BALL WAS.

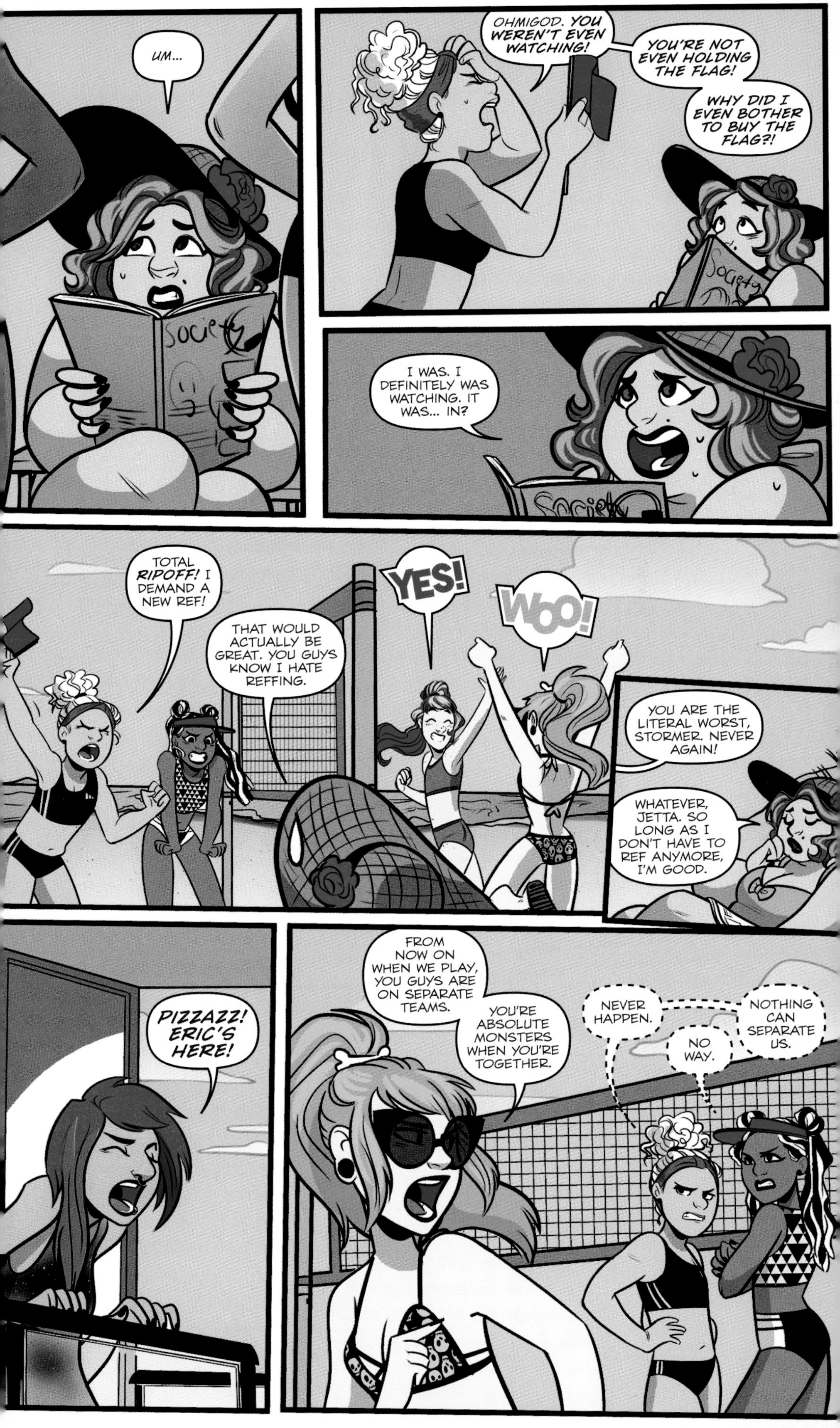
UM...
OHMIGOD. YOU WEREN'T EVEN WATCHING!
YOU'RE NOT EVEN HOLDING THE FLAG!
WHY DID I EVEN BOTHER TO BUY THE FLAG?!
I WAS. I DEFINITELY WAS WATCHING. IT WAS... IN?
TOTAL RIPOFF! I DEMAND A NEW REF!
THAT WOULD ACTUALLY BE GREAT. YOU GUYS KNOW I HATE REFFING.
YES!
WOO!
YOU ARE THE LITERAL WORST, STORMER. NEVER AGAIN!
WHATEVER, JETTA. SO LONG AS I DON'T HAVE TO REF ANYMORE, I'M GOOD.
PIZZAZZ! ERIC'S HERE!
FROM NOW ON WHEN WE PLAY, YOU GUYS ARE ON SEPARATE TEAMS.
YOU'RE ABSOLUTE MONSTERS WHEN YOU'RE TOGETHER.
NEVER HAPPEN.
NO WAY.
NOTHING CAN SEPARATE US.

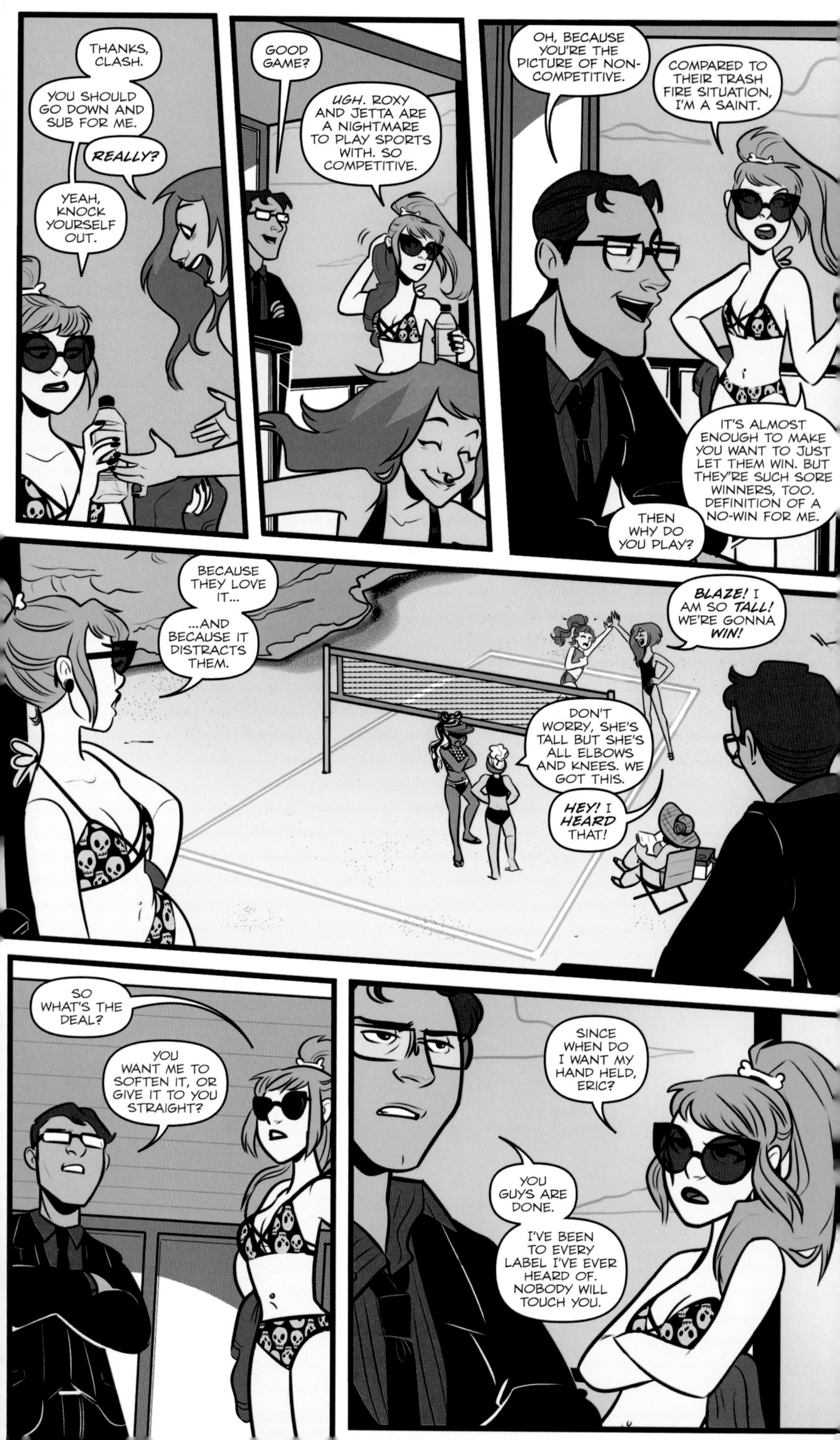
THANKS, CLASH.
YOU SHOULD GO DOWN AND SUB FOR ME.
REALLY?
YEAH, KNOCK YOURSELF OUT.
GOOD GAME?
UGH. ROXY AND JETTA ARE A NIGHTMARE TO PLAY SPORTS WITH. SO COMPETITIVE.
OH, BECAUSE YOU'RE THE PICTURE OF NON-COMPETITIVE.
COMPARED TO THEIR TRASH FIRE SITUATION, I'M A SAINT.
IT'S ALMOST ENOUGH TO MAKE YOU WANT TO JUST LET THEM WIN. BUT THEY'RE SUCH SORE WINNERS, TOO. DEFINITION OF A NO-WIN FOR ME.
THEN WHY DO YOU PLAY?
BECAUSE THEY LOVE IT...
...AND BECAUSE IT DISTRACTS THEM.
BLAZE! I AM SO TALL! WE'RE GONNA WIN!
DON'T WORRY, SHE'S TALL BUT SHE'S ALL ELBOWS AND KNEES. WE GOT THIS.
HEY! I HEARD THAT!
SO WHAT'S THE DEAL?
YOU WANT ME TO SOFTEN IT, OR GIVE IT TO YOU STRAIGHT?
SINCE WHEN DO I WANT MY HAND HELD, ERIC?
YOU GUYS ARE DONE.
I'VE BEEN TO EVERY LABEL I'VE EVER HEARD OF. NOBODY WILL TOUCH YOU.

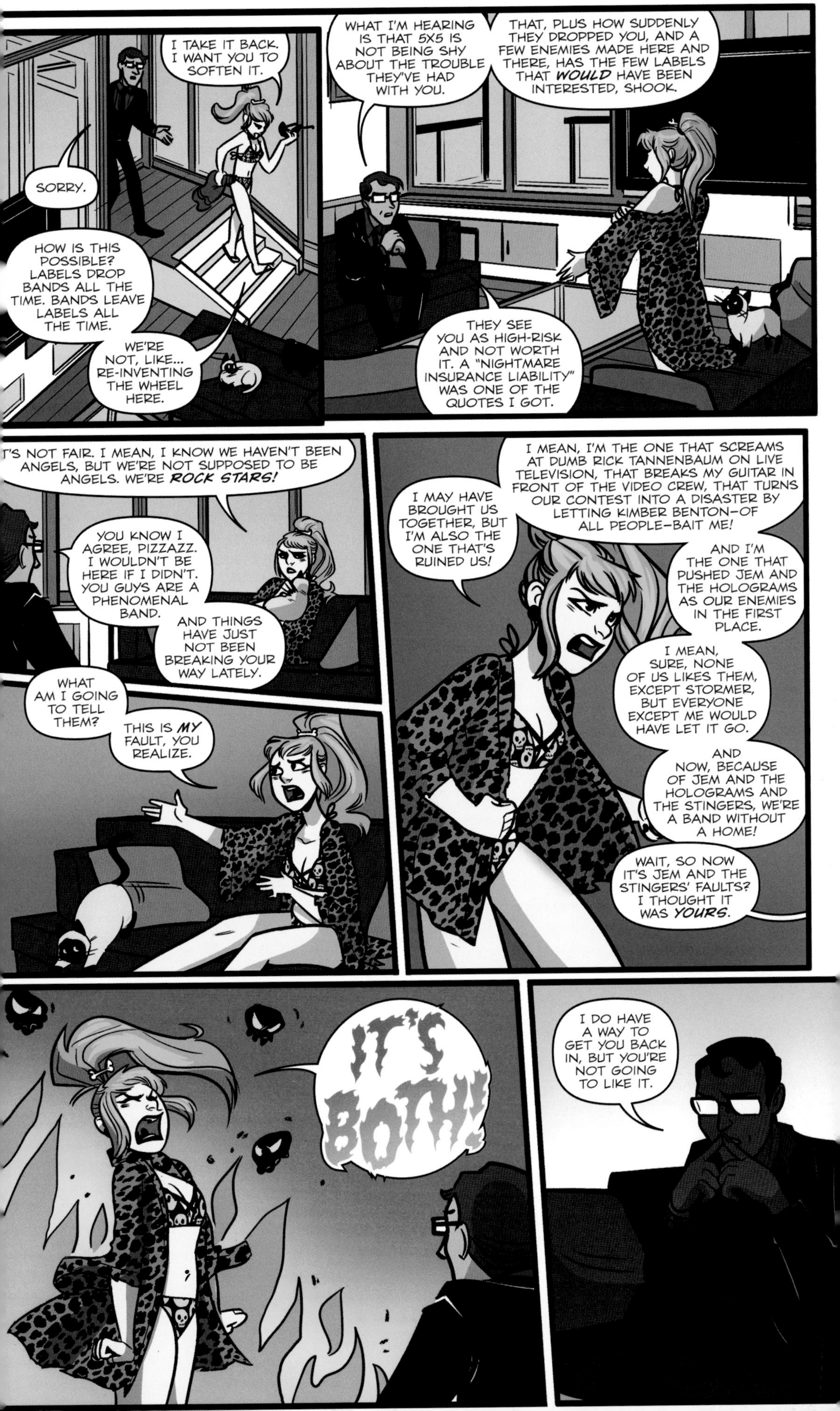
I TAKE IT BACK. I WANT YOU TO SOFTEN IT.
SORRY.
HOW IS THIS POSSIBLE? LABELS DROP BANDS ALL THE TIME. BANDS LEAVE LABELS ALL THE TIME.
WE'RE NOT, LIKE... RE-INVENTING THE WHEEL HERE.
WHAT I'M HEARING IS THAT 5X5 IS NOT BEING SHY ABOUT THE TROUBLE THEY'VE HAD WITH YOU.
THAT, PLUS HOW SUDDENLY THEY DROPPED YOU, AND A FEW ENEMIES MADE HERE AND THERE, HAS THE FEW LABELS THAT *WOULD* HAVE BEEN INTERESTED, SHOOK.
THEY SEE YOU AS HIGH-RISK AND NOT WORTH IT. A "NIGHTMARE INSURANCE LIABILITY" WAS ONE OF THE QUOTES I GOT.
'T'S NOT FAIR. I MEAN, I KNOW WE HAVEN'T BEEN ANGELS, BUT WE'RE NOT SUPPOSED TO BE ANGELS. WE'RE ***ROCK STARS!***
YOU KNOW I AGREE, PIZZAZZ. I WOULDN'T BE HERE IF I DIDN'T. YOU GUYS ARE A PHENOMENAL BAND.
AND THINGS HAVE JUST NOT BEEN BREAKING YOUR WAY LATELY.
WHAT AM I GOING TO TELL THEM?
THIS IS *MY* FAULT, YOU REALIZE.
I MAY HAVE BROUGHT US TOGETHER, BUT I'M ALSO THE ONE THAT'S RUINED US!
I MEAN, I'M THE ONE THAT SCREAMS AT DUMB RICK TANNENBAUM ON LIVE TELEVISION, THAT BREAKS MY GUITAR IN FRONT OF THE VIDEO CREW, THAT TURNS OUR CONTEST INTO A DISASTER BY LETTING KIMBER BENTON–OF ALL PEOPLE–BAIT ME!
AND I'M THE ONE THAT PUSHED JEM AND THE HOLOGRAMS AS OUR ENEMIES IN THE FIRST PLACE.
I MEAN, SURE, NONE OF US LIKES THEM, EXCEPT STORMER, BUT EVERYONE EXCEPT ME WOULD HAVE LET IT GO.
AND NOW, BECAUSE OF JEM AND THE HOLOGRAMS AND THE STINGERS, WE'RE A BAND WITHOUT A HOME!
WAIT, SO NOW IT'S JEM AND THE STINGERS' FAULTS? I THOUGHT IT WAS ***YOURS***.
IT'S BOTH!
I DO HAVE A WAY TO GET YOU BACK IN, BUT YOU'RE NOT GOING TO LIKE IT.

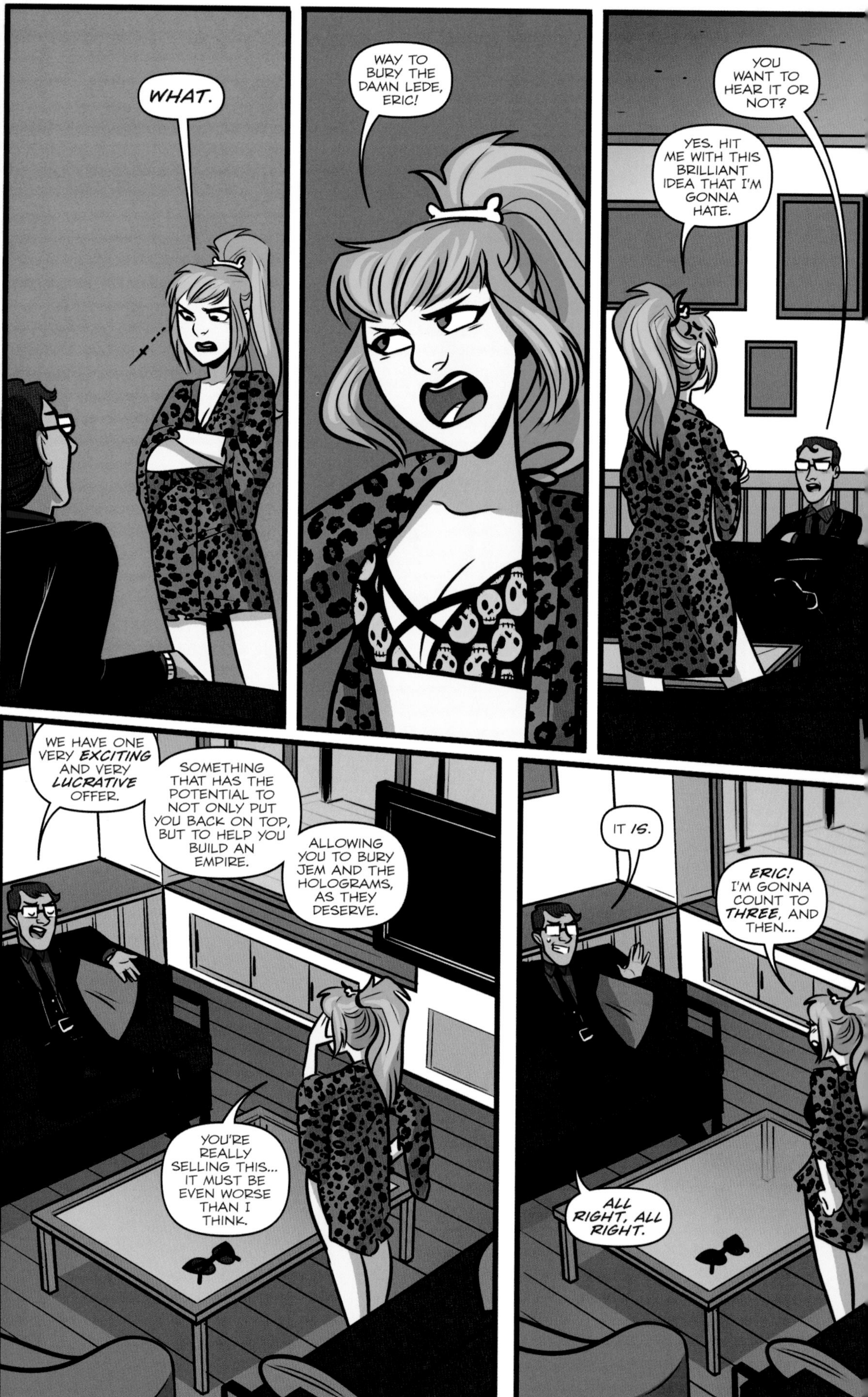

WHAT.
WAY TO BURY THE DAMN LEDE, ERIC!
YOU WANT TO HEAR IT OR NOT?
YES. HIT ME WITH THIS BRILLIANT IDEA THAT I'M GONNA HATE.
WE HAVE ONE VERY EXCITING AND VERY LUCRATIVE OFFER.
SOMETHING THAT HAS THE POTENTIAL TO NOT ONLY PUT YOU BACK ON TOP, BUT TO HELP YOU BUILD AN EMPIRE.
ALLOWING YOU TO BURY JEM AND THE HOLOGRAMS, AS THEY DESERVE.
YOU'RE REALLY SELLING THIS... IT MUST BE EVEN WORSE THAN I THINK.
IT IS.
ERIC! I'M GONNA COUNT TO THREE, AND THEN...
ALL RIGHT, ALL RIGHT.

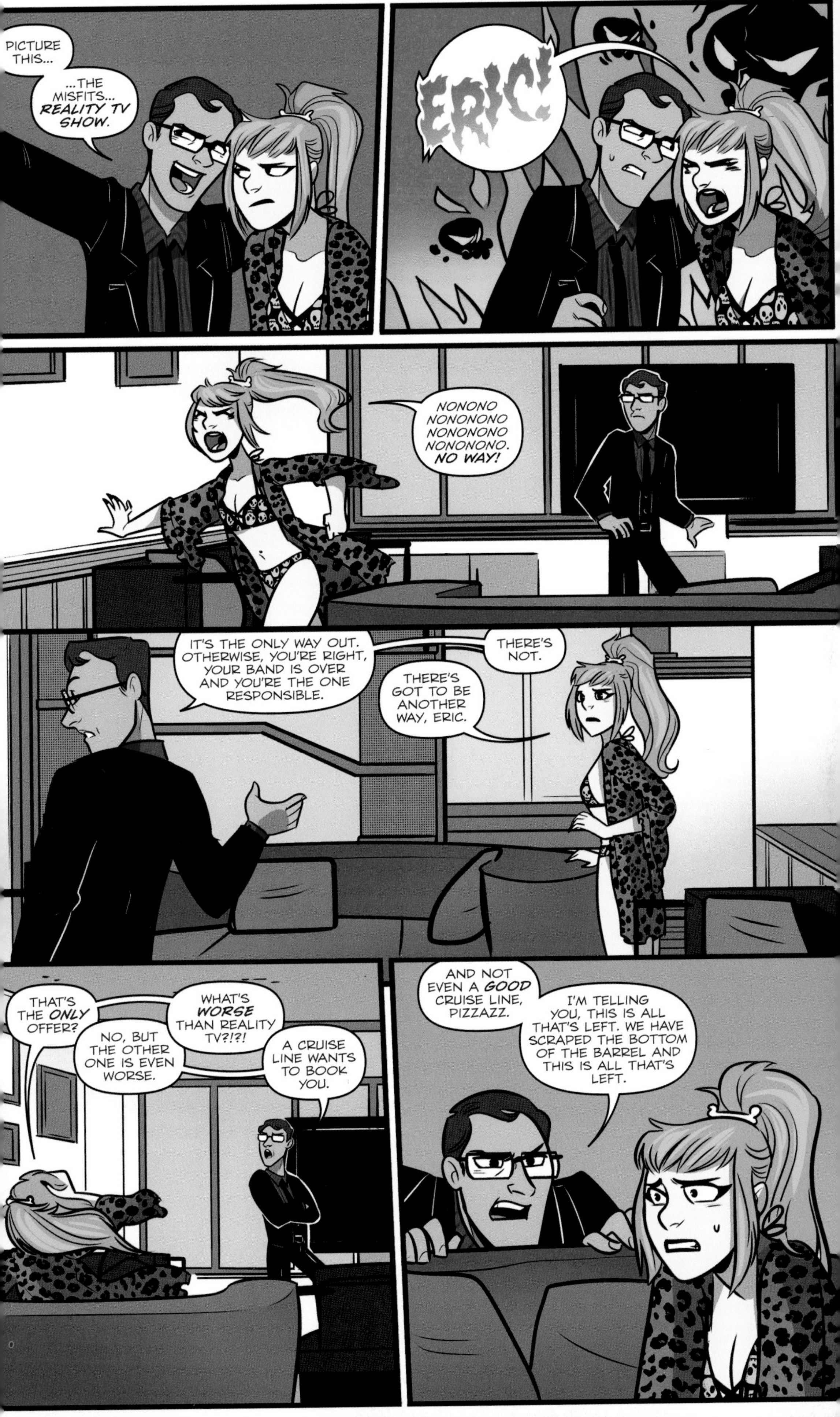
PICTURE THIS...
...THE MISFITS... REALITY TV SHOW.
ERIC!
NONONO NONONONO NONONONO NONONONO. NO WAY!
IT'S THE ONLY WAY OUT. OTHERWISE, YOU'RE RIGHT, YOUR BAND IS OVER AND YOU'RE THE ONE RESPONSIBLE.
THERE'S GOT TO BE ANOTHER WAY, ERIC.
THERE'S NOT.
THAT'S THE ONLY OFFER?
NO, BUT THE OTHER ONE IS EVEN WORSE.
WHAT'S WORSE THAN REALITY TV?!?!
A CRUISE LINE WANTS TO BOOK YOU.
AND NOT EVEN A GOOD CRUISE LINE, PIZZAZZ.
I'M TELLING YOU, THIS IS ALL THAT'S LEFT. WE HAVE SCRAPED THE BOTTOM OF THE BARREL AND THIS IS ALL THAT'S LEFT.

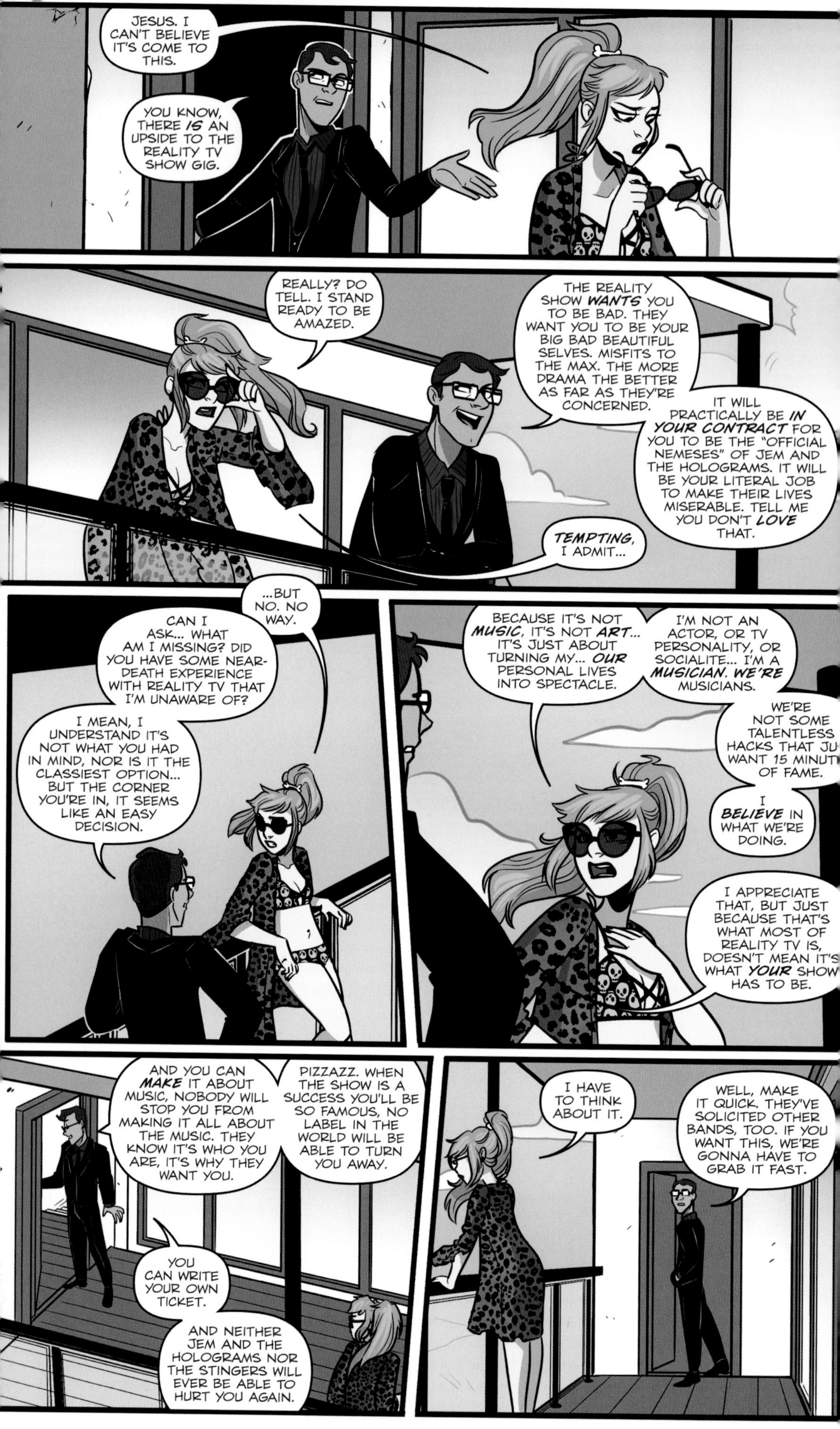

JESUS. I CAN'T BELIEVE IT'S COME TO THIS.
YOU KNOW, THERE *IS* AN UPSIDE TO THE REALITY TV SHOW GIG.
REALLY? DO TELL. I STAND READY TO BE AMAZED.
THE REALITY SHOW *WANTS* YOU TO BE BAD. THEY WANT YOU TO BE YOUR BIG BAD BEAUTIFUL SELVES. MISFITS TO THE MAX. THE MORE DRAMA THE BETTER AS FAR AS THEY'RE CONCERNED.
IT WILL PRACTICALLY BE *IN YOUR CONTRACT* FOR YOU TO BE THE "OFFICIAL NEMESES" OF JEM AND THE HOLOGRAMS. IT WILL BE YOUR LITERAL JOB TO MAKE THEIR LIVES MISERABLE. TELL ME YOU DON'T *LOVE* THAT.
TEMPTING, I ADMIT...
...BUT NO. NO WAY.
CAN I ASK... WHAT AM I MISSING? DID YOU HAVE SOME NEAR-DEATH EXPERIENCE WITH REALITY TV THAT I'M UNAWARE OF?
I MEAN, I UNDERSTAND IT'S NOT WHAT YOU HAD IN MIND, NOR IS IT THE CLASSIEST OPTION... BUT THE CORNER YOU'RE IN, IT SEEMS LIKE AN EASY DECISION.
BECAUSE IT'S NOT *MUSIC*, IT'S NOT *ART*... IT'S JUST ABOUT TURNING MY... *OUR* PERSONAL LIVES INTO SPECTACLE.
I'M NOT AN ACTOR, OR TV PERSONALITY, OR SOCIALITE... I'M A *MUSICIAN. WE'RE* MUSICIANS.
WE'RE NOT SOME TALENTLESS HACKS THAT JU WANT 15 MINUT OF FAME.
I *BELIEVE* IN WHAT WE'RE DOING.
I APPRECIATE THAT, BUT JUST BECAUSE THAT'S WHAT MOST OF REALITY TV IS, DOESN'T MEAN IT'S WHAT *YOUR* SHOW HAS TO BE.
AND YOU CAN *MAKE* IT ABOUT MUSIC, NOBODY WILL STOP YOU FROM MAKING IT ALL ABOUT THE MUSIC. THEY KNOW IT'S WHO YOU ARE, IT'S WHY THEY WANT YOU.
PIZZAZZ. WHEN THE SHOW IS A SUCCESS YOU'LL BE SO FAMOUS, NO LABEL IN THE WORLD WILL BE ABLE TO TURN YOU AWAY.
YOU CAN WRITE YOUR OWN TICKET.
AND NEITHER JEM AND THE HOLOGRAMS NOR THE STINGERS WILL EVER BE ABLE TO HURT YOU AGAIN.
I HAVE TO THINK ABOUT IT.
WELL, MAKE IT QUICK. THEY'VE SOLICITED OTHER BANDS, TOO. IF YOU WANT THIS, WE'RE GONNA HAVE TO GRAB IT FAST.

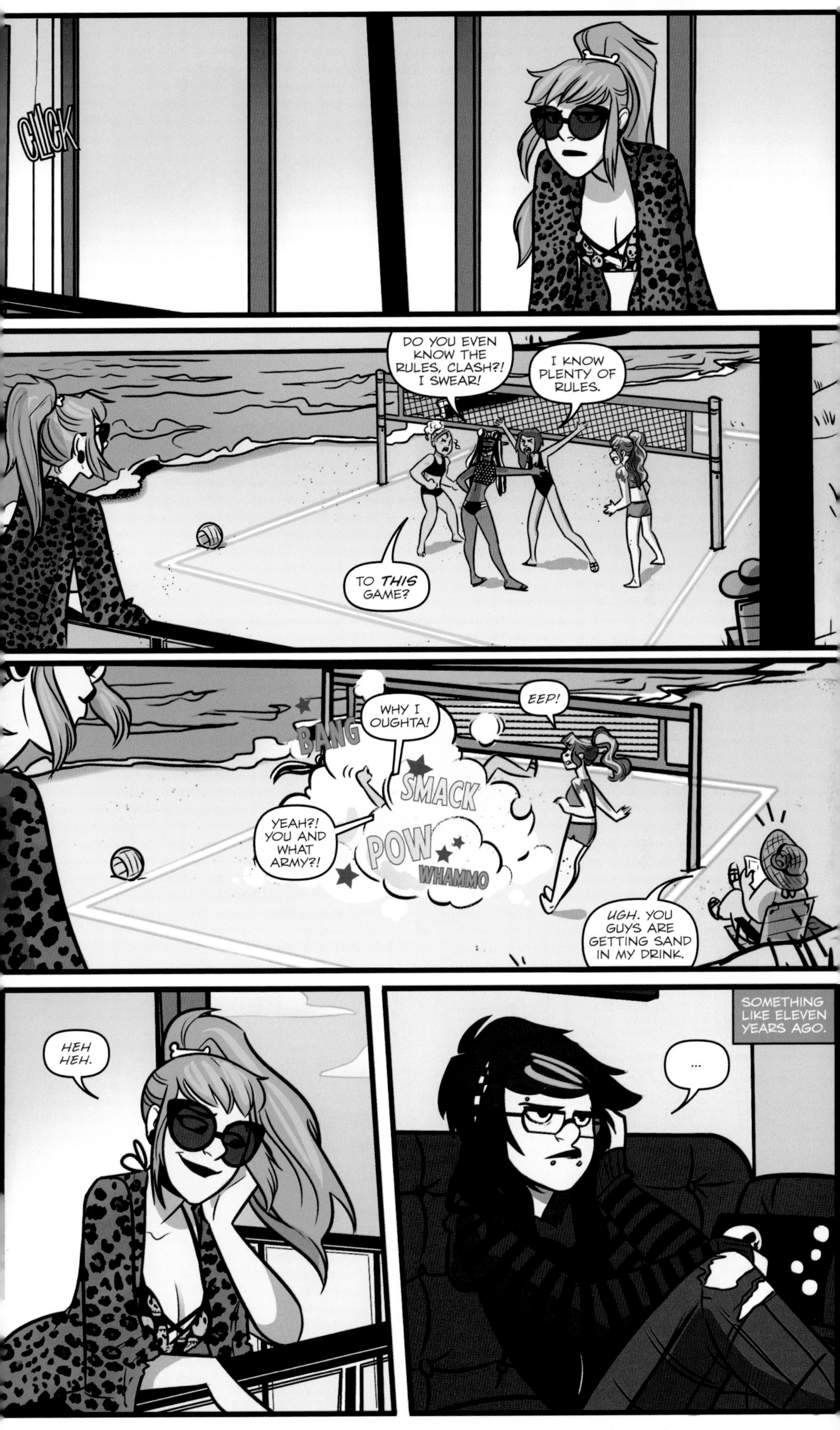
CLICK
DO YOU EVEN KNOW THE RULES, CLASH?! I SWEAR!
I KNOW PLENTY OF RULES.
TO *THIS* GAME?
WHY I OUGHTA!
EEP!
BANG
SMACK
YEAH?! YOU AND WHAT ARMY?!
POW
WHAMMO
UGH. YOU GUYS ARE GETTING SAND IN MY DRINK.
HEH HEH.
SOMETHING LIKE ELEVEN YEARS AGO.
...

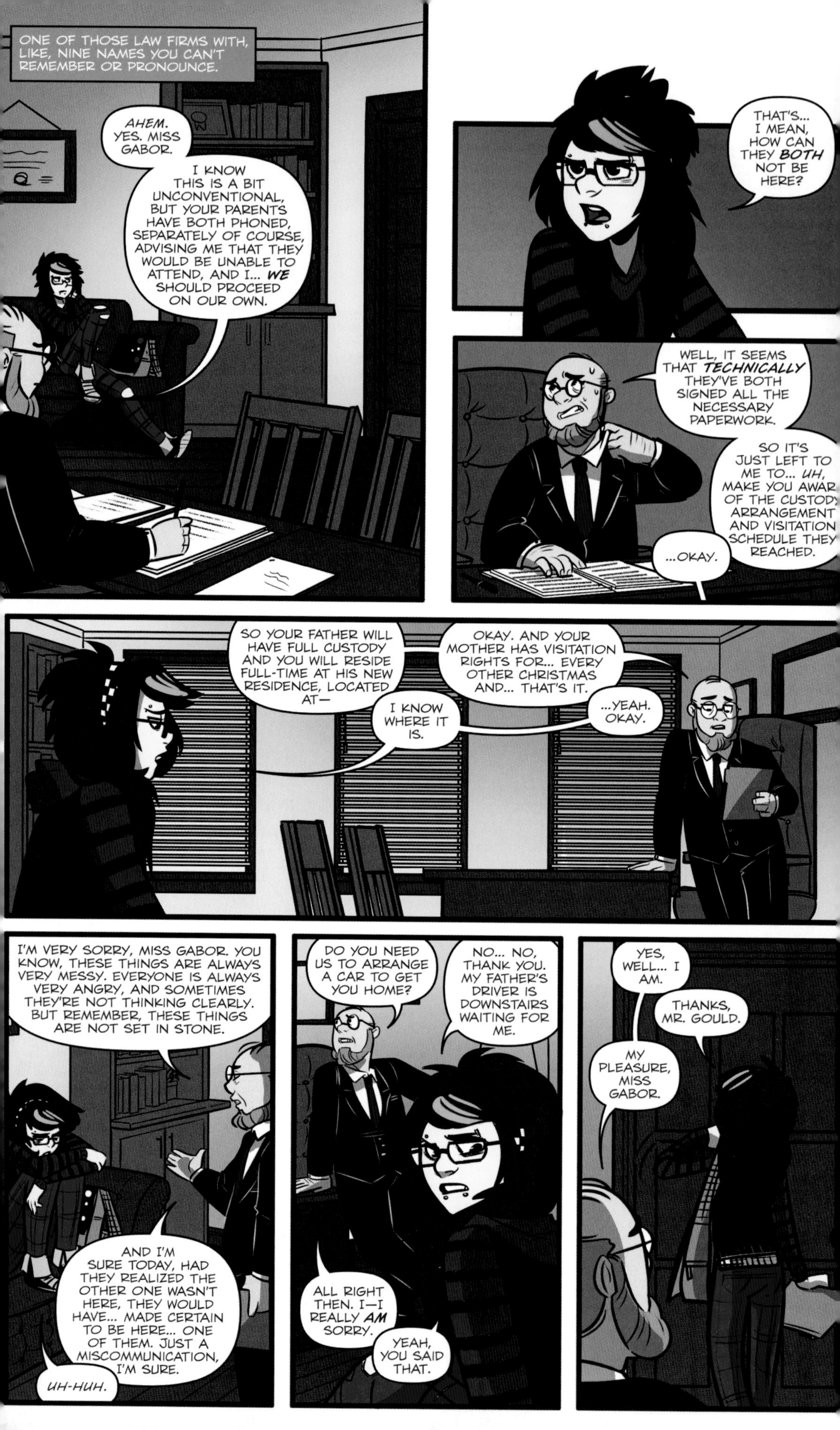
ONE OF THOSE LAW FIRMS WITH, LIKE, NINE NAMES YOU CAN'T REMEMBER OR PRONOUNCE.
AHEM. YES. MISS GABOR.
I KNOW THIS IS A BIT UNCONVENTIONAL, BUT YOUR PARENTS HAVE BOTH PHONED, SEPARATELY OF COURSE, ADVISING ME THAT THEY WOULD BE UNABLE TO ATTEND, AND I... WE SHOULD PROCEED ON OUR OWN.
THAT'S... I MEAN, HOW CAN THEY BOTH NOT BE HERE?
WELL, IT SEEMS THAT TECHNICALLY THEY'VE BOTH SIGNED ALL THE NECESSARY PAPERWORK.
SO IT'S JUST LEFT TO ME TO... UH, MAKE YOU AWAR OF THE CUSTOD ARRANGEMENT AND VISITATION SCHEDULE THEY REACHED.
...OKAY.
SO YOUR FATHER WILL HAVE FULL CUSTODY AND YOU WILL RESIDE FULL-TIME AT HIS NEW RESIDENCE, LOCATED AT—
I KNOW WHERE IT IS.
OKAY. AND YOUR MOTHER HAS VISITATION RIGHTS FOR... EVERY OTHER CHRISTMAS AND... THAT'S IT.
...YEAH. OKAY.
I'M VERY SORRY, MISS GABOR. YOU KNOW, THESE THINGS ARE ALWAYS VERY MESSY. EVERYONE IS ALWAYS VERY ANGRY, AND SOMETIMES THEY'RE NOT THINKING CLEARLY. BUT REMEMBER, THESE THINGS ARE NOT SET IN STONE.
AND I'M SURE TODAY, HAD THEY REALIZED THE OTHER ONE WASN'T HERE, THEY WOULD HAVE... MADE CERTAIN TO BE HERE... ONE OF THEM. JUST A MISCOMMUNICATION, I'M SURE.
UH-HUH.
DO YOU NEED US TO ARRANGE A CAR TO GET YOU HOME?
NO... NO, THANK YOU. MY FATHER'S DRIVER IS DOWNSTAIRS WAITING FOR ME.
ALL RIGHT THEN. I—I REALLY AM SORRY.
YEAH, YOU SAID THAT.
YES, WELL... I AM.
THANKS, MR. GOULD.
MY PLEASURE, MISS GABOR.

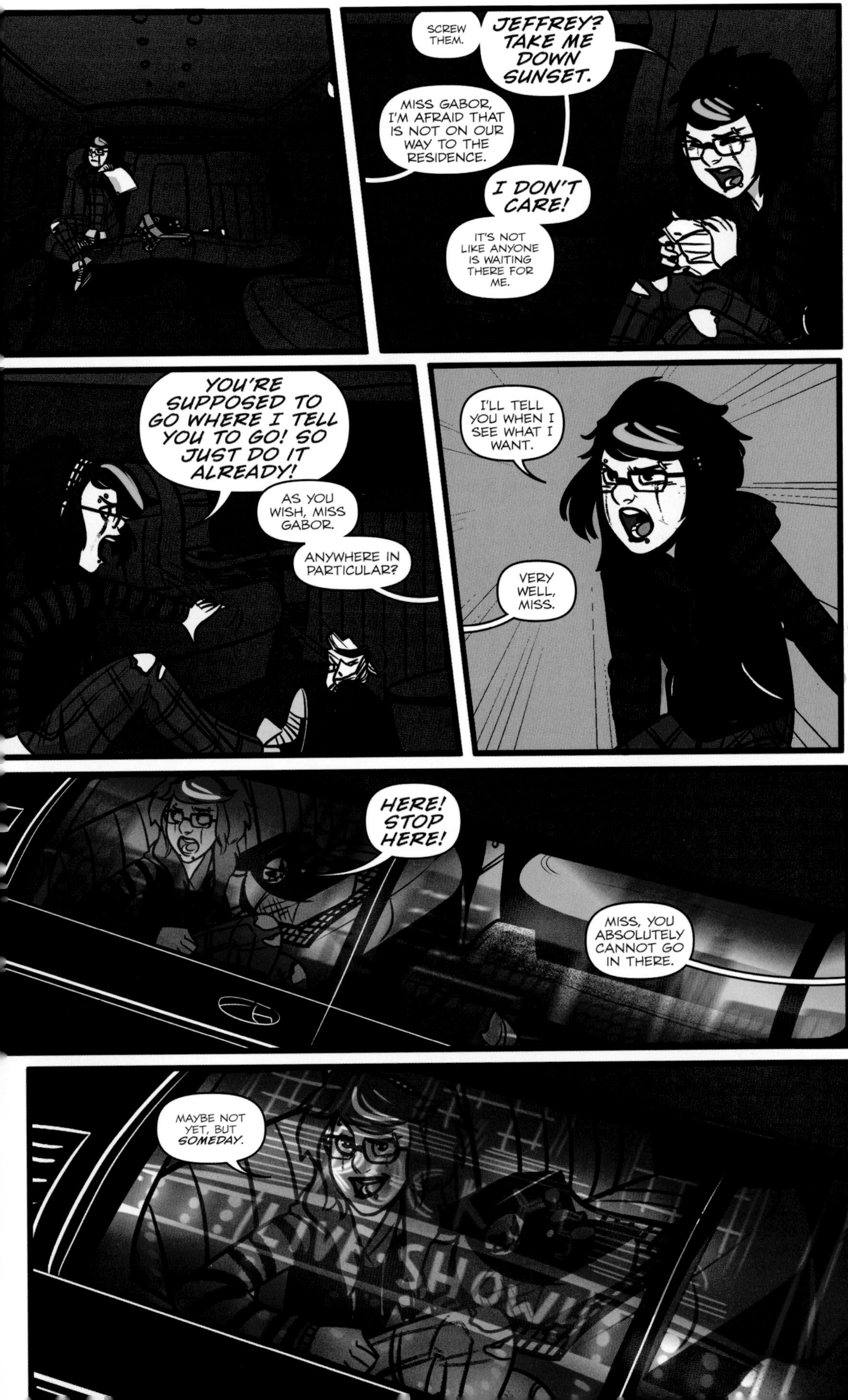
SCREW THEM.
JEFFREY? TAKE ME DOWN SUNSET.
MISS GABOR, I'M AFRAID THAT IS NOT ON OUR WAY TO THE RESIDENCE.
I DON'T CARE!
IT'S NOT LIKE ANYONE IS WAITING THERE FOR ME.
YOU'RE SUPPOSED TO GO WHERE I TELL YOU TO GO! SO JUST DO IT ALREADY!
AS YOU WISH, MISS GABOR.
ANYWHERE IN PARTICULAR?
I'LL TELL YOU WHEN I SEE WHAT I WANT.
VERY WELL, MISS.
HERE! STOP HERE!
MISS, YOU ABSOLUTELY CANNOT GO IN THERE.
MAYBE NOT YET, BUT SOMEDAY.
LIVE SHOW

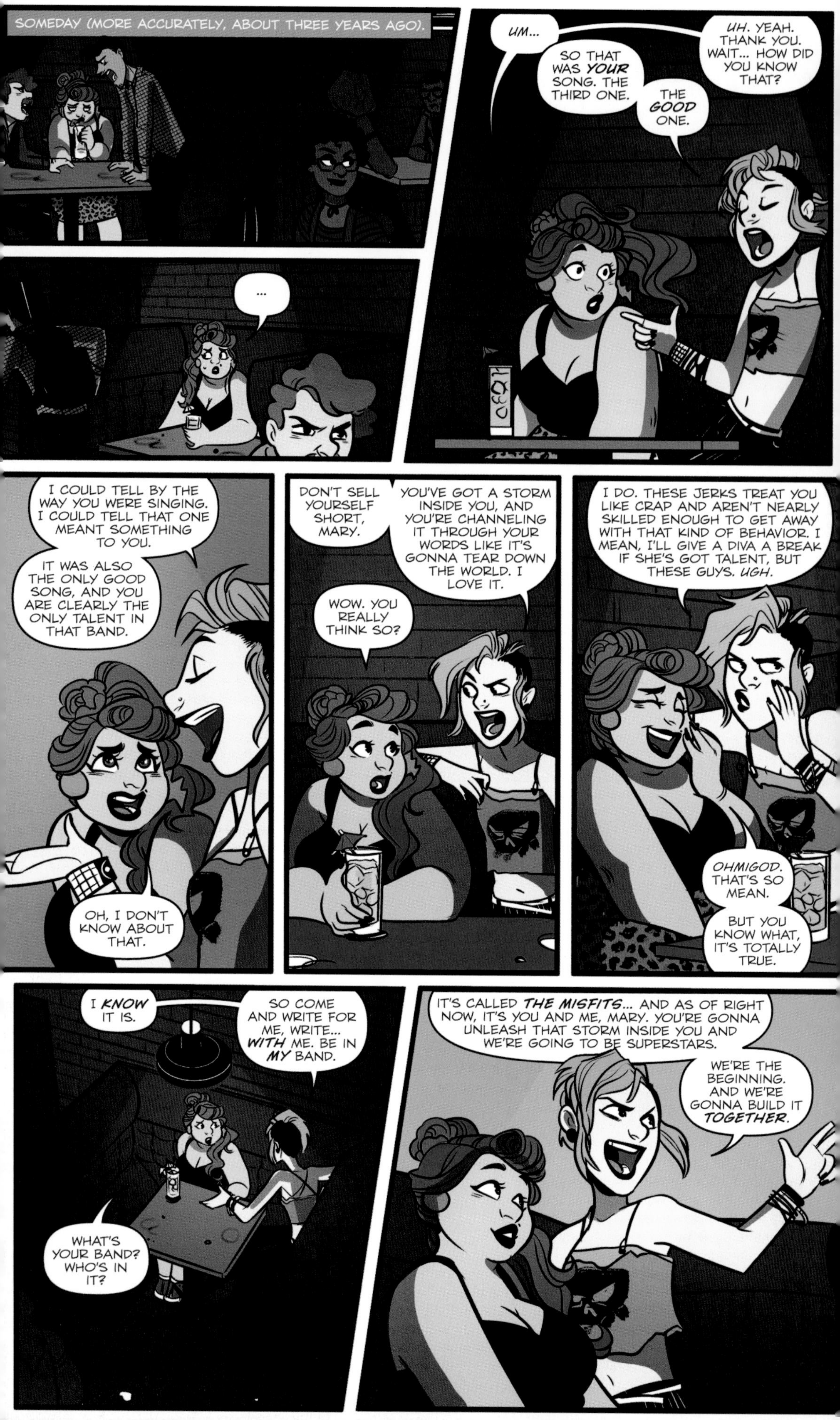
SOMEDAY (MORE ACCURATELY, ABOUT THREE YEARS AGO).
...
UM...
SO THAT WAS *YOUR* SONG. THE THIRD ONE.
THE *GOOD* ONE.
UH. YEAH. THANK YOU. WAIT... HOW DID YOU KNOW THAT?
I COULD TELL BY THE WAY YOU WERE SINGING. I COULD TELL THAT ONE MEANT SOMETHING TO YOU.
IT WAS ALSO THE ONLY GOOD SONG, AND YOU ARE CLEARLY THE ONLY TALENT IN THAT BAND.
OH, I DON'T KNOW ABOUT THAT.
DON'T SELL YOURSELF SHORT, MARY.
YOU'VE GOT A STORM INSIDE YOU, AND YOU'RE CHANNELING IT THROUGH YOUR WORDS LIKE IT'S GONNA TEAR DOWN THE WORLD. I LOVE IT.
WOW. YOU REALLY THINK SO?
I DO. THESE JERKS TREAT YOU LIKE CRAP AND AREN'T NEARLY SKILLED ENOUGH TO GET AWAY WITH THAT KIND OF BEHAVIOR. I MEAN, I'LL GIVE A DIVA A BREAK IF SHE'S GOT TALENT, BUT THESE GUYS. *UGH*.
OHMIGOD. THAT'S SO MEAN.
BUT YOU KNOW WHAT, IT'S TOTALLY TRUE.
I *KNOW* IT IS.
SO COME AND WRITE FOR ME, WRITE... *WITH* ME. BE IN *MY* BAND.
WHAT'S YOUR BAND? WHO'S IN IT?
IT'S CALLED ***THE MISFITS***... AND AS OF RIGHT NOW, IT'S YOU AND ME, MARY. YOU'RE GONNA UNLEASH THAT STORM INSIDE YOU AND WE'RE GOING TO BE SUPERSTARS.
WE'RE THE BEGINNING. AND WE'RE GONNA BUILD IT ***TOGETHER***.

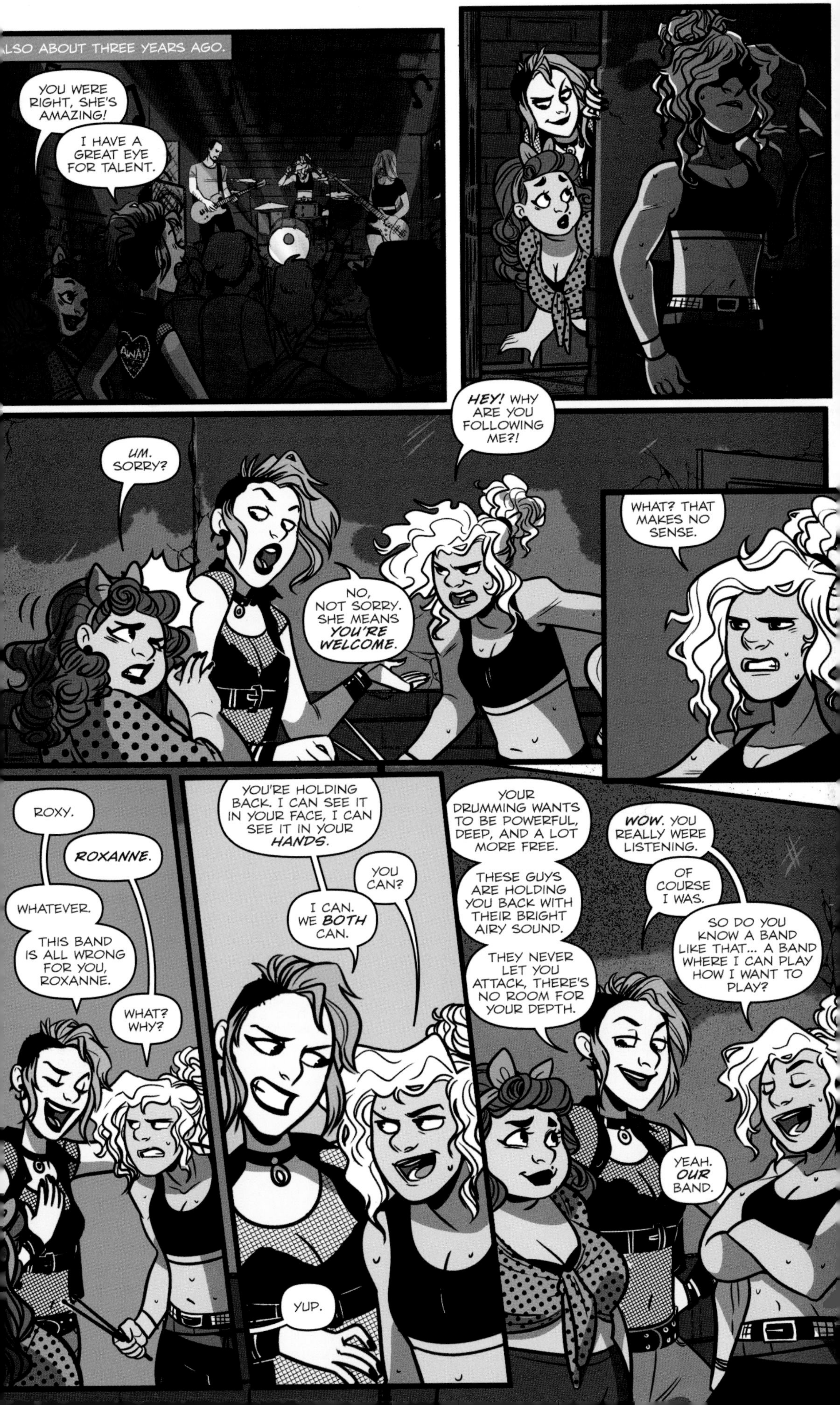

ALSO ABOUT THREE YEARS AGO.
YOU WERE RIGHT, SHE'S AMAZING!
I HAVE A GREAT EYE FOR TALENT.
HEY! WHY ARE YOU FOLLOWING ME?!
UM. SORRY?
NO, NOT SORRY. SHE MEANS YOU'RE WELCOME.
WHAT? THAT MAKES NO SENSE.
ROXY.
ROXANNE.
WHATEVER.
THIS BAND IS ALL WRONG FOR YOU, ROXANNE.
WHAT? WHY?
YOU'RE HOLDING BACK. I CAN SEE IT IN YOUR FACE, I CAN SEE IT IN YOUR HANDS.
YOU CAN?
I CAN. WE BOTH CAN.
YUP.
YOUR DRUMMING WANTS TO BE POWERFUL, DEEP, AND A LOT MORE FREE.
THESE GUYS ARE HOLDING YOU BACK WITH THEIR BRIGHT AIRY SOUND.
THEY NEVER LET YOU ATTACK, THERE'S NO ROOM FOR YOUR DEPTH.
WOW. YOU REALLY WERE LISTENING.
OF COURSE I WAS.
SO DO YOU KNOW A BAND LIKE THAT... A BAND WHERE I CAN PLAY HOW I WANT TO PLAY?
YEAH. OUR BAND.

JUST UNDER THREE YEARS AGO.

I'M TELLING YOU, SHE'S REALLY GOOD. SHE'S *EXACTLY* WHAT WE NEED. YOU LISTENED TO THE TAPE, RIGHT?

YEAH, ROX, THAT'S WHY WE'RE HERE. THE TAPE WAS GREAT, IF IT WASN'T WE WOULDN'T BE IN THE MIDDLE OF NOWHERE STUMBLING AROUND IN THE DARK.

BANG!

AHHHHH! LEMME GO!

OHMIGOD. THAT'S HER!

SAY IT AGAIN Y... DAFT BUG... I *DARE* Y...

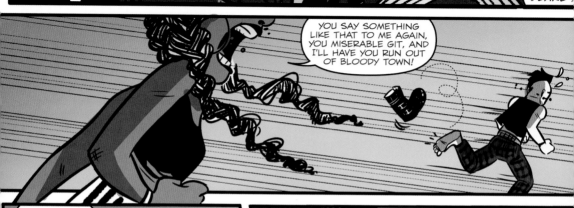

YOU SAY SOMETHING LIKE THAT TO ME AGAIN, YOU MISERABLE GIT, AND I'LL HAVE YOU RUN OUT OF BLOODY TOWN!

WELL, I CAN SEE WHY ROXY LIKES HER.

HEH. YEAH.

WHO WAS THAT GUY?

HE *WAS* MY BANDMATE. WHAT'S IT TO YOU?

HEH. WELL, I GUESS YOU'RE OUT OF *THAT* BAND.

AND JUST WHO THE HELL ARE *YOU?*

WE'RE THE MISFITS.

WANNA BE ONE?

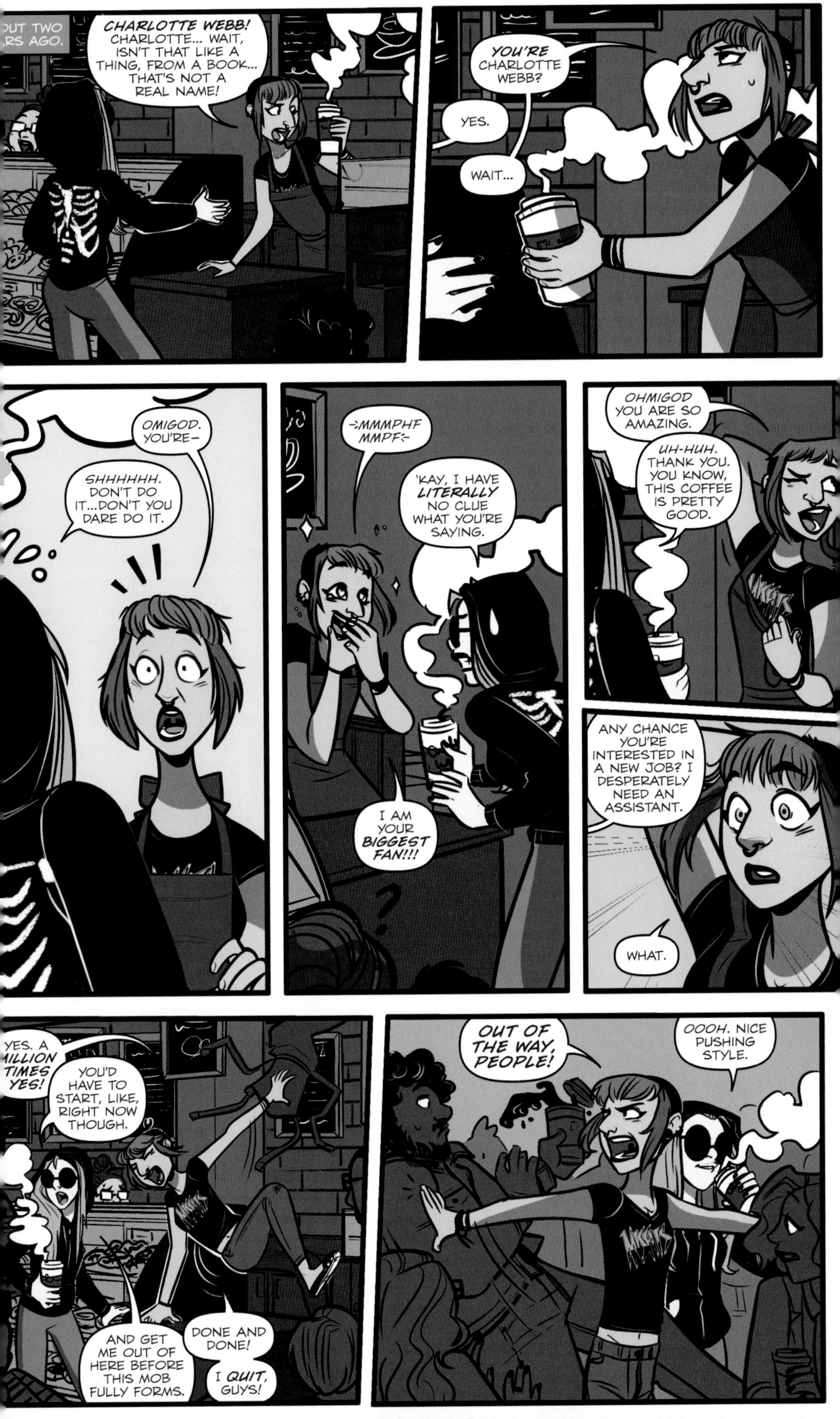
OUT TWO
RS AGO.
CHARLOTTE WEBB! CHARLOTTE... WAIT, ISN'T THAT LIKE A THING, FROM A BOOK... THAT'S NOT A REAL NAME!
YOU'RE CHARLOTTE WEBB?
YES.
WAIT...
OMIGOD. YOU'RE—
SHHHHHH. DON'T DO IT...DON'T YOU DARE DO IT.
MMMPHF MMPF
'KAY, I HAVE LITERALLY NO CLUE WHAT YOU'RE SAYING.
I AM YOUR BIGGEST FAN!!!
OHMIGOD YOU ARE SO AMAZING.
UH-HUH. THANK YOU. YOU KNOW, THIS COFFEE IS PRETTY GOOD.
ANY CHANCE YOU'RE INTERESTED IN A NEW JOB? I DESPERATELY NEED AN ASSISTANT.
WHAT.
YES. A MILLION TIMES YES!
YOU'D HAVE TO START, LIKE, RIGHT NOW THOUGH.
AND GET ME OUT OF HERE BEFORE THIS MOB FULLY FORMS.
DONE AND DONE!
I QUIT, GUYS!
OUT OF THE WAY, PEOPLE!
OOOH. NICE PUSHING STYLE.

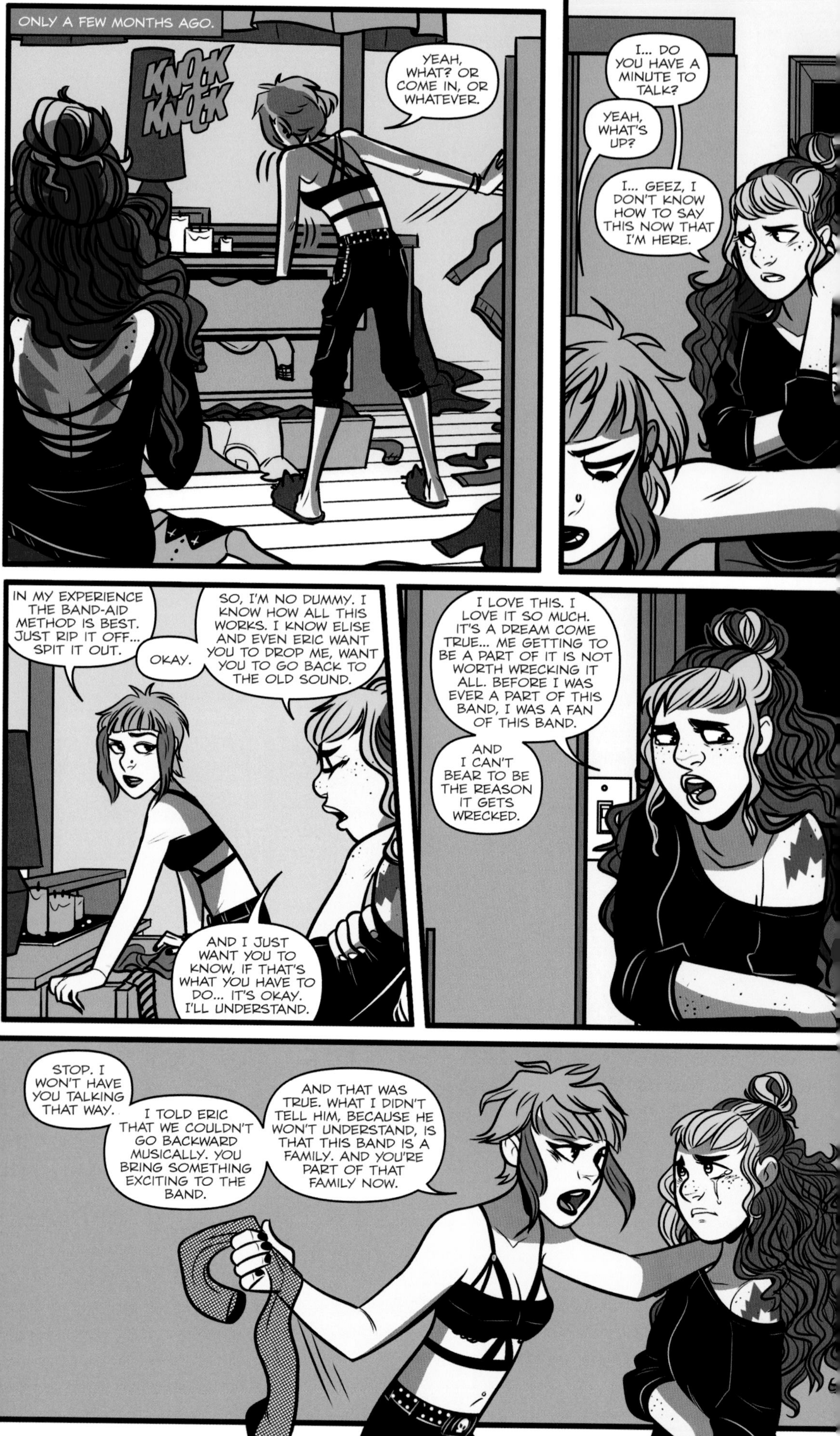
ONLY A FEW MONTHS AGO.
KNOCK KNOCK
YEAH, WHAT? OR COME IN, OR WHATEVER.
I... DO YOU HAVE A MINUTE TO TALK?
YEAH, WHAT'S UP?
I... GEEZ, I DON'T KNOW HOW TO SAY THIS NOW THAT I'M HERE.
IN MY EXPERIENCE THE BAND-AID METHOD IS BEST. JUST RIP IT OFF... SPIT IT OUT.
OKAY.
SO, I'M NO DUMMY. I KNOW HOW ALL THIS WORKS. I KNOW ELISE AND EVEN ERIC WANT YOU TO DROP ME, WANT YOU TO GO BACK TO THE OLD SOUND.
AND I JUST WANT YOU TO KNOW, IF THAT'S WHAT YOU HAVE TO DO... IT'S OKAY. I'LL UNDERSTAND.
I LOVE THIS. I LOVE IT SO MUCH. IT'S A DREAM COME TRUE... ME GETTING TO BE A PART OF IT IS NOT WORTH WRECKING IT ALL. BEFORE I WAS EVER A PART OF THIS BAND, I WAS A FAN OF THIS BAND.
AND I CAN'T BEAR TO BE THE REASON IT GETS WRECKED.
STOP. I WON'T HAVE YOU TALKING THAT WAY.
I TOLD ERIC THAT WE COULDN'T GO BACKWARD MUSICALLY. YOU BRING SOMETHING EXCITING TO THE BAND.
AND THAT WAS TRUE. WHAT I DIDN'T TELL HIM, BECAUSE HE WON'T UNDERSTAND, IS THAT THIS BAND IS A FAMILY. AND YOU'RE PART OF THAT FAMILY NOW.

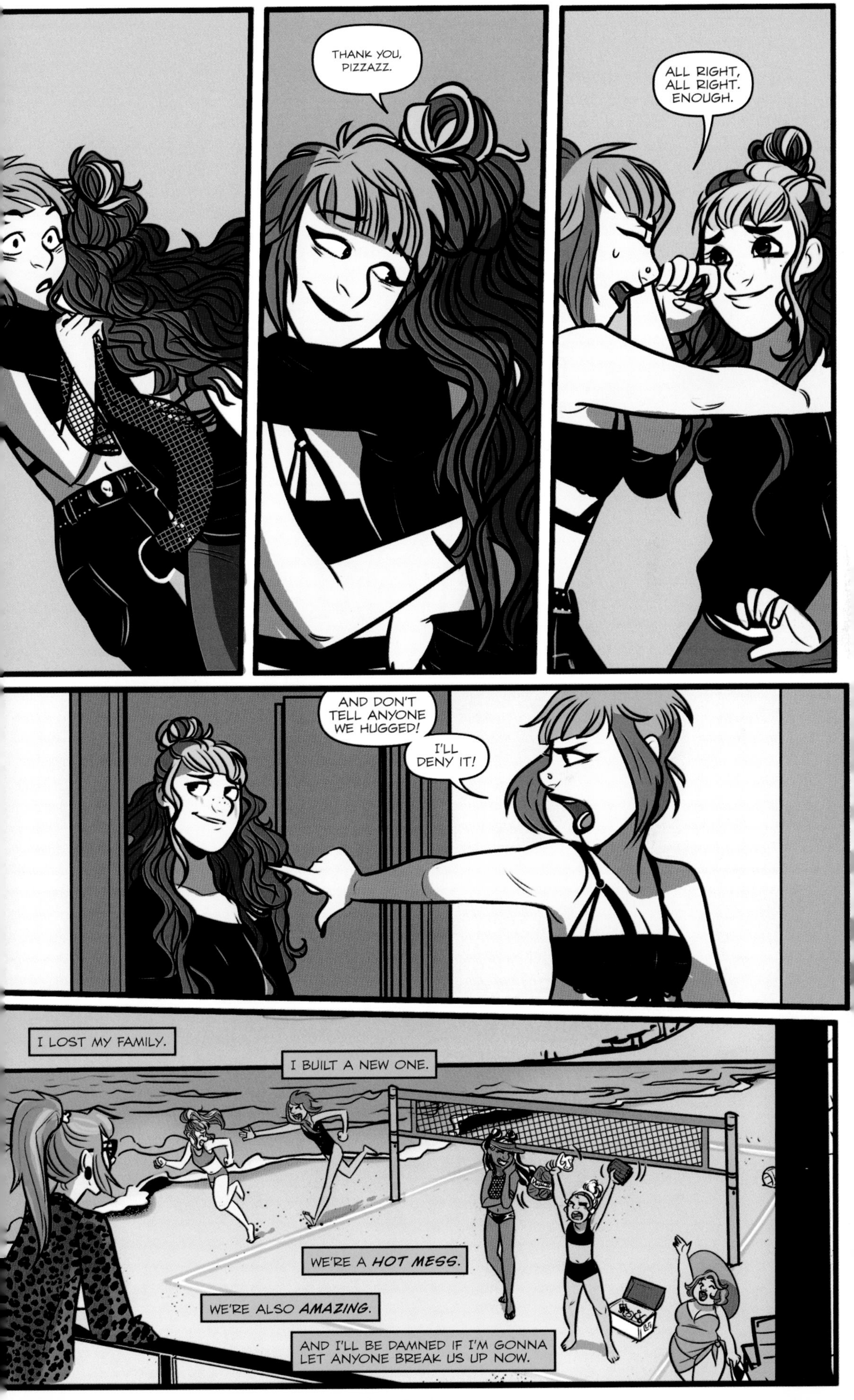
THANK YOU, PIZZAZZ.
ALL RIGHT, ALL RIGHT. ENOUGH.
AND DON'T TELL ANYONE WE HUGGED!
I'LL DENY IT!
I LOST MY FAMILY.
I BUILT A NEW ONE.
WE'RE A HOT MESS.
WE'RE ALSO AMAZING.
AND I'LL BE DAMNED IF I'M GONNA LET ANYONE BREAK US UP NOW.

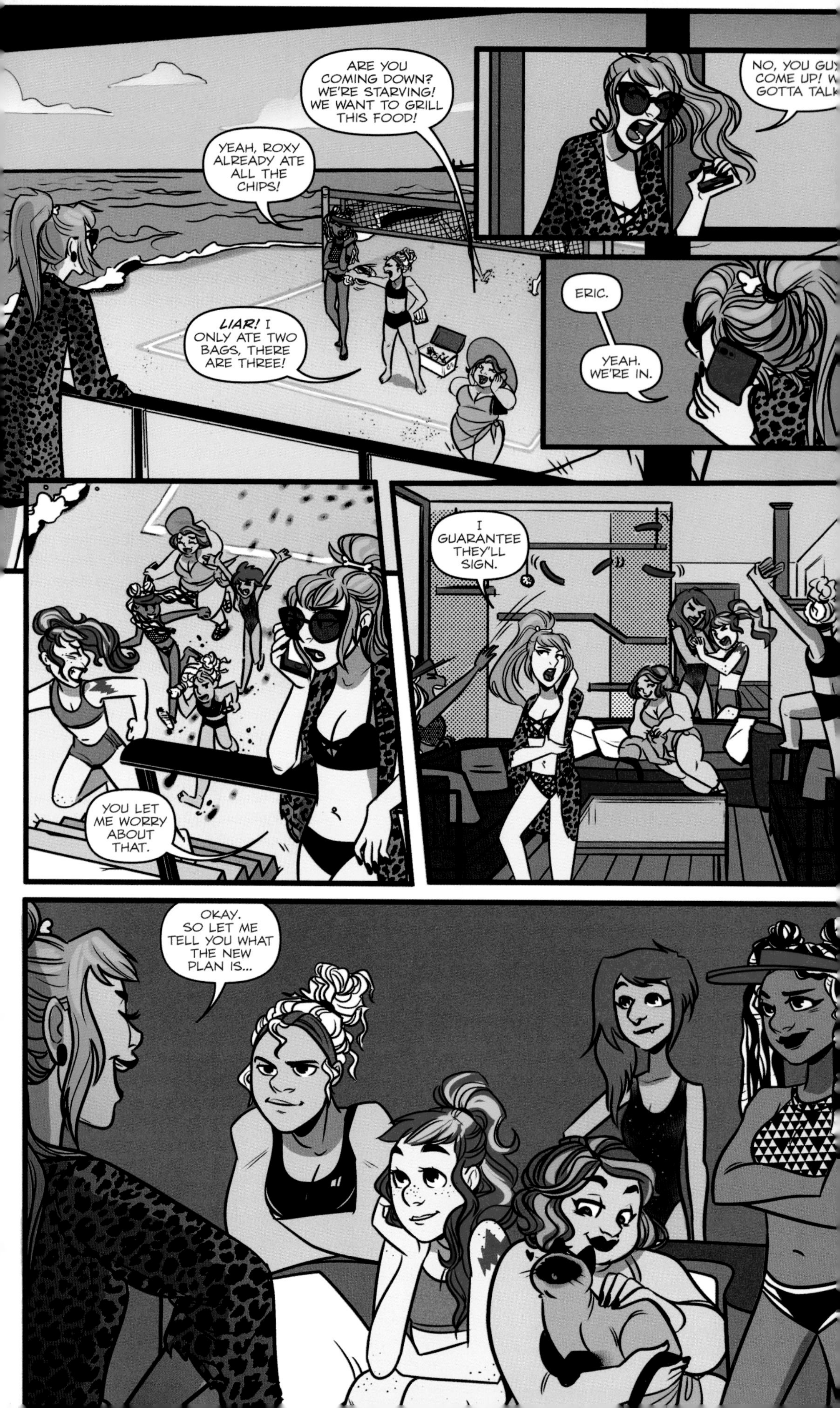
YEAH, ROXY ALREADY ATE ALL THE CHIPS!
ARE YOU COMING DOWN? WE'RE STARVING! WE WANT TO GRILL THIS FOOD!
LIAR! I ONLY ATE TWO BAGS, THERE ARE THREE!
NO, YOU GU COME UP! W GOTTA TALK
ERIC.
YEAH. WE'RE IN.
YOU LET ME WORRY ABOUT THAT.
I GUARANTEE THEY'LL SIGN.
OKAY. SO LET ME TELL YOU WHAT THE NEW PLAN IS...

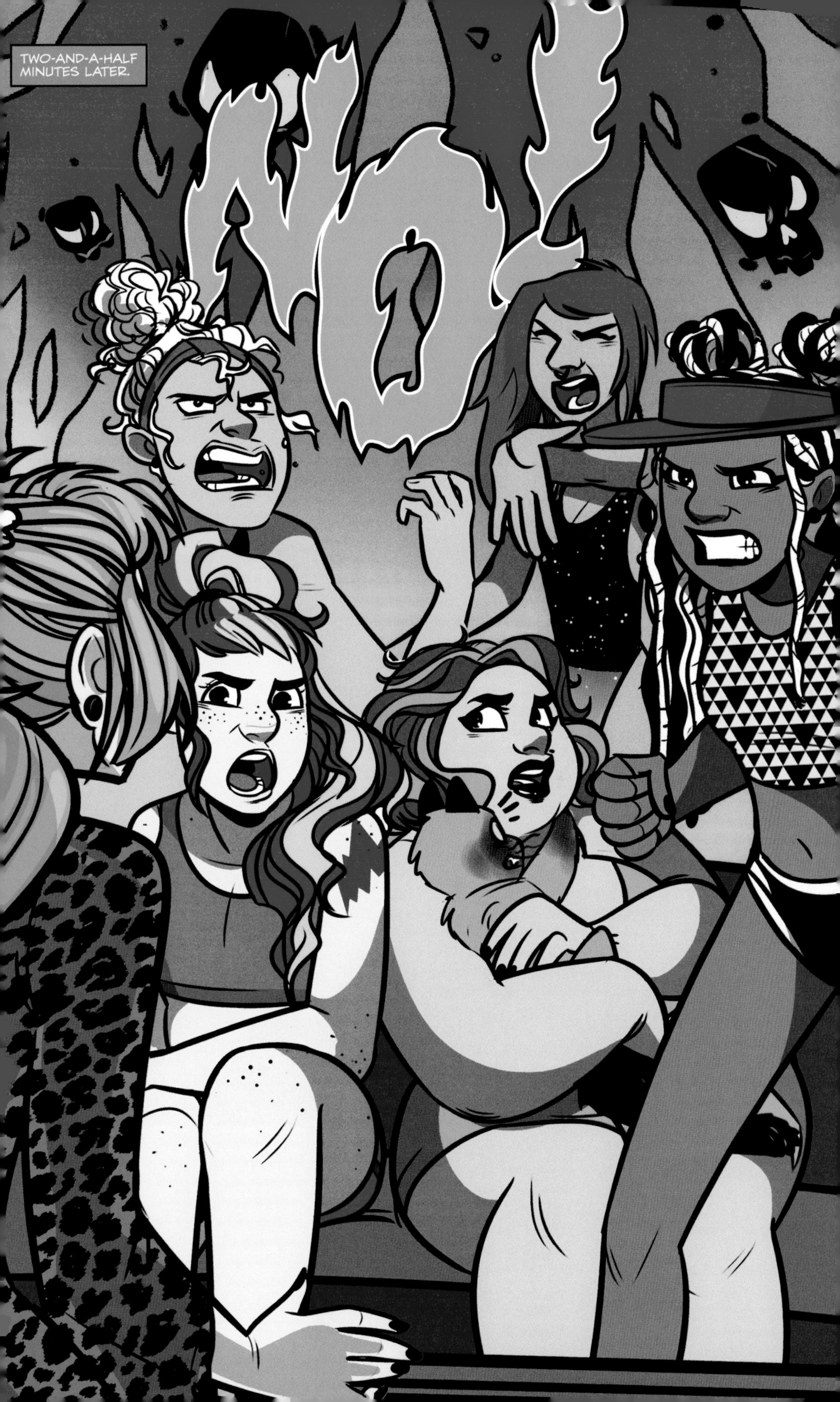
TWO-AND-A-HALF MINUTES LATER.
NO!

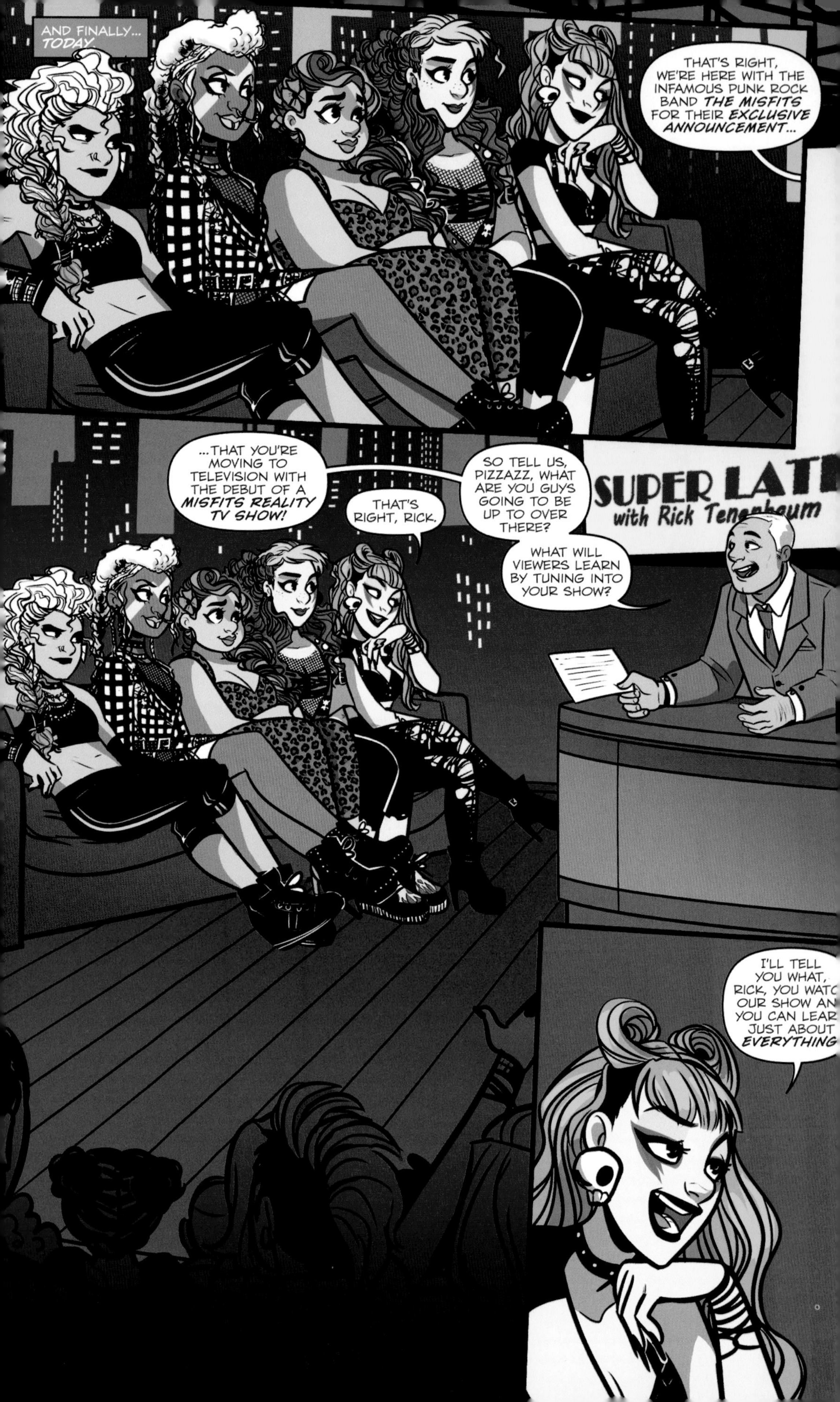
AND FINALLY... TODAY.
THAT'S RIGHT, WE'RE HERE WITH THE INFAMOUS PUNK ROCK BAND THE MISFITS FOR THEIR EXCLUSIVE ANNOUNCEMENT...
...THAT YOU'RE MOVING TO TELEVISION WITH THE DEBUT OF A MISFITS REALITY TV SHOW!
THAT'S RIGHT, RICK.
SO TELL US, PIZZAZZ, WHAT ARE YOU GUYS GOING TO BE UP TO OVER THERE?
WHAT WILL VIEWERS LEARN BY TUNING INTO YOUR SHOW?
SUPER LAT
with Rick Tene
I'LL TELL YOU WHAT, RICK, YOU WATC OUR SHOW AN YOU CAN LEAR JUST ABOUT EVERYTHING

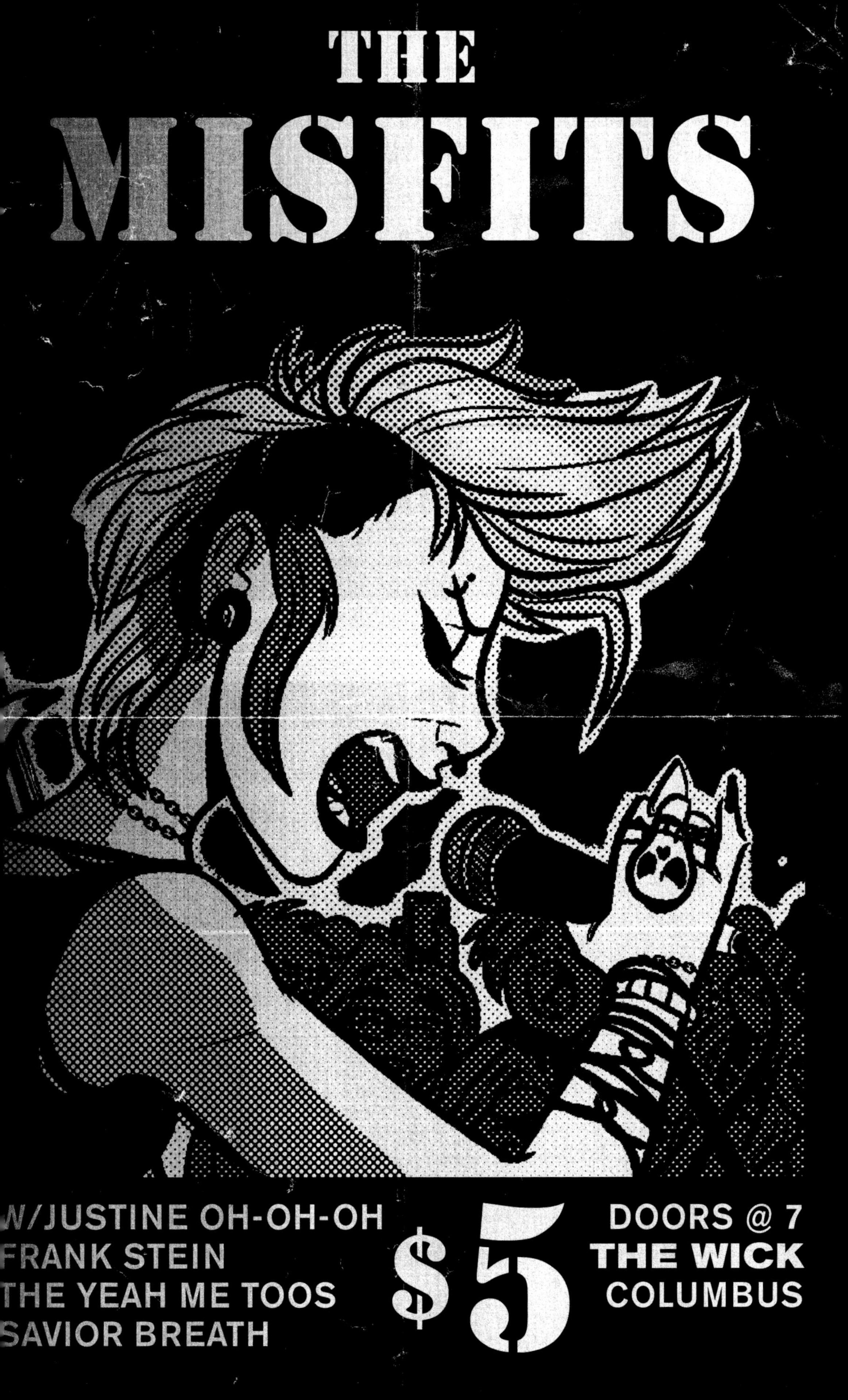

THE
MISFITS
W/JUSTINE OH-OH-OH
FRANK STEIN
THE YEAH ME TOOS
SAVIOR BREATH
$5
DOORS @ 7
THE WICK
COLUMBUS

ART M. VICTORIA ROBADO

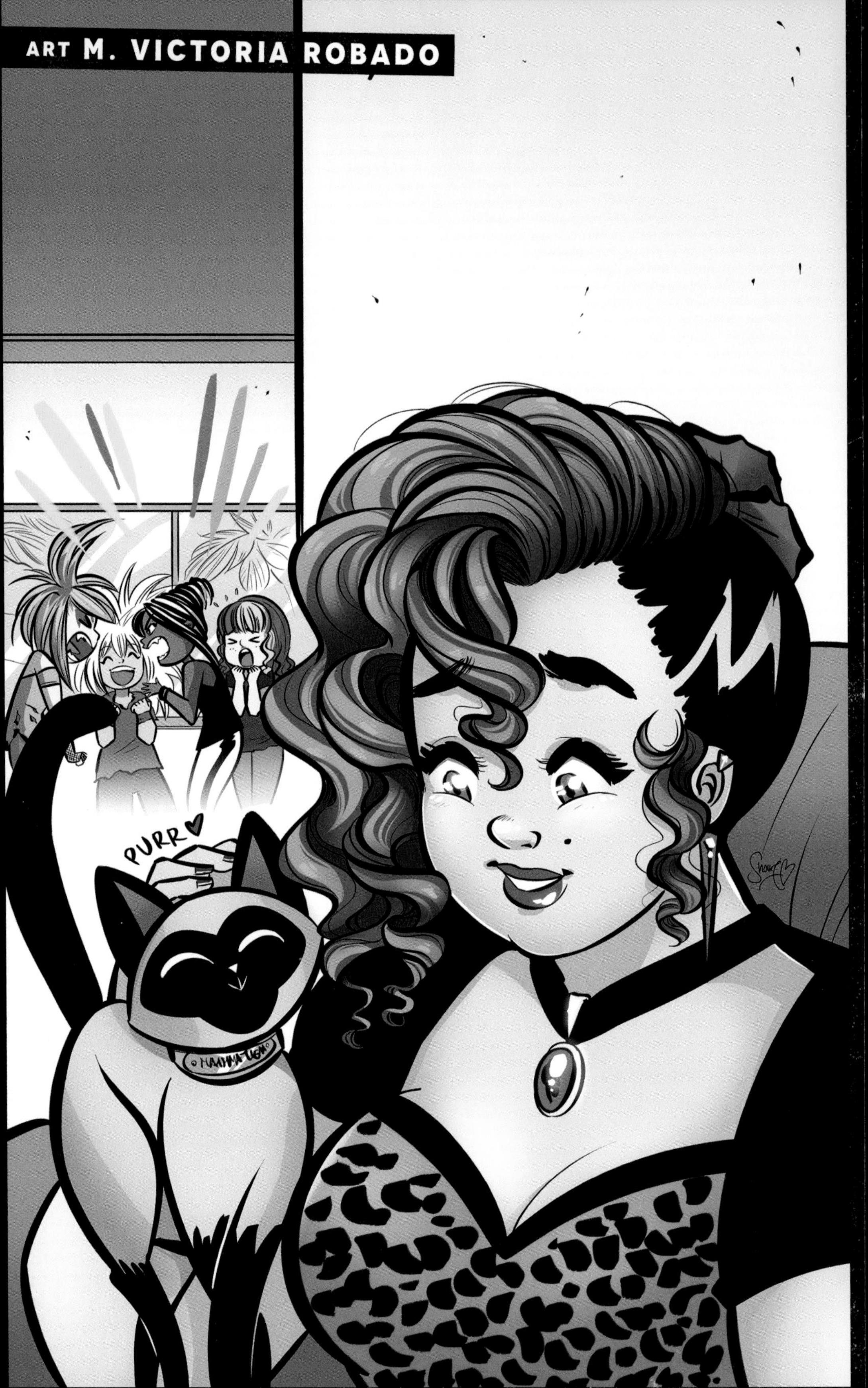
PURR

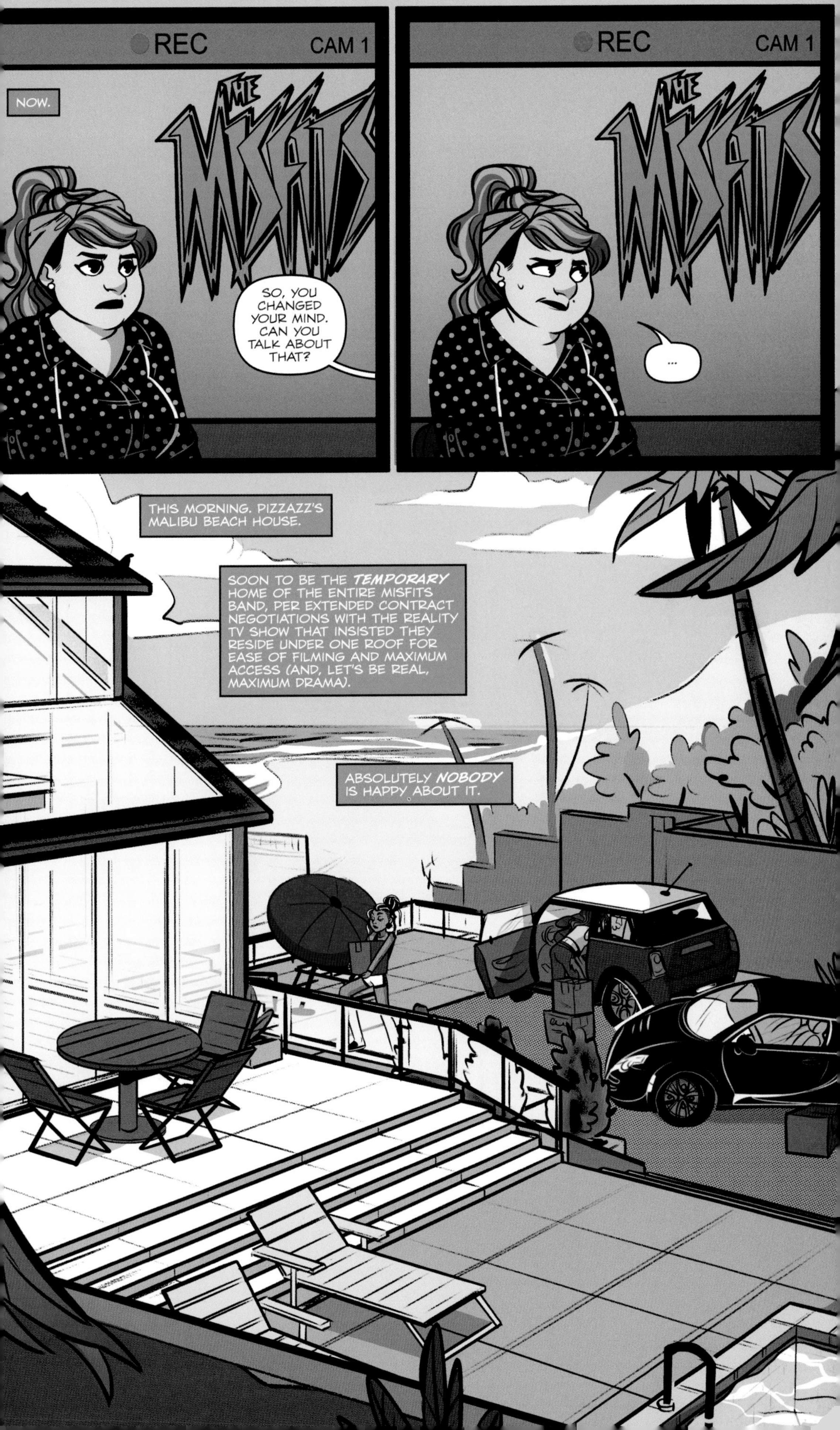
REC
CAM 1
NOW.
THE MISFITS
SO, YOU CHANGED YOUR MIND. CAN YOU TALK ABOUT THAT?
REC
CAM 1
THE MISFITS
...
THIS MORNING. PIZZAZZ'S MALIBU BEACH HOUSE.
SOON TO BE THE TEMPORARY HOME OF THE ENTIRE MISFITS BAND, PER EXTENDED CONTRACT NEGOTIATIONS WITH THE REALITY TV SHOW THAT INSISTED THEY RESIDE UNDER ONE ROOF FOR EASE OF FILMING AND MAXIMUM ACCESS (AND, LET'S BE REAL, MAXIMUM DRAMA).
ABSOLUTELY NOBODY IS HAPPY ABOUT IT.

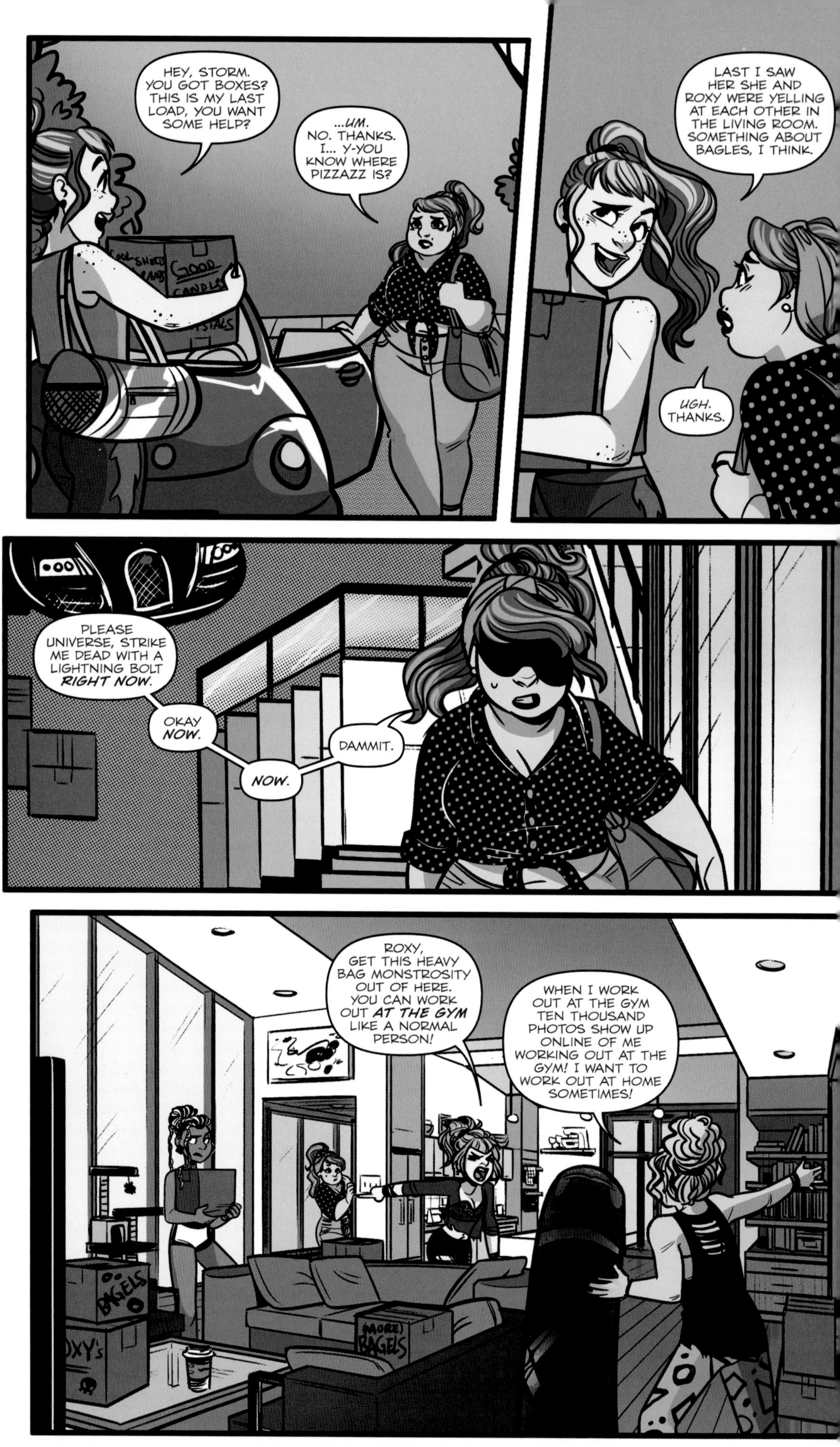
HEY, STORM. YOU GOT BOXES? THIS IS MY LAST LOAD, YOU WANT SOME HELP?
...UM. NO. THANKS. I... Y-YOU KNOW WHERE PIZZAZZ IS?
GOOD CANDLES
LAST I SAW HER SHE AND ROXY WERE YELLING AT EACH OTHER IN THE LIVING ROOM. SOMETHING ABOUT BAGELS, I THINK.
UGH. THANKS.
PLEASE UNIVERSE, STRIKE ME DEAD WITH A LIGHTNING BOLT RIGHT NOW.
OKAY NOW.
NOW.
DAMMIT.
ROXY, GET THIS HEAVY BAG MONSTROSITY OUT OF HERE. YOU CAN WORK OUT AT THE GYM LIKE A NORMAL PERSON!
WHEN I WORK OUT AT THE GYM TEN THOUSAND PHOTOS SHOW UP ONLINE OF ME WORKING OUT AT THE GYM! I WANT TO WORK OUT AT HOME SOMETIMES!
BAGELS
ROXY'S
(MORE) BAGELS

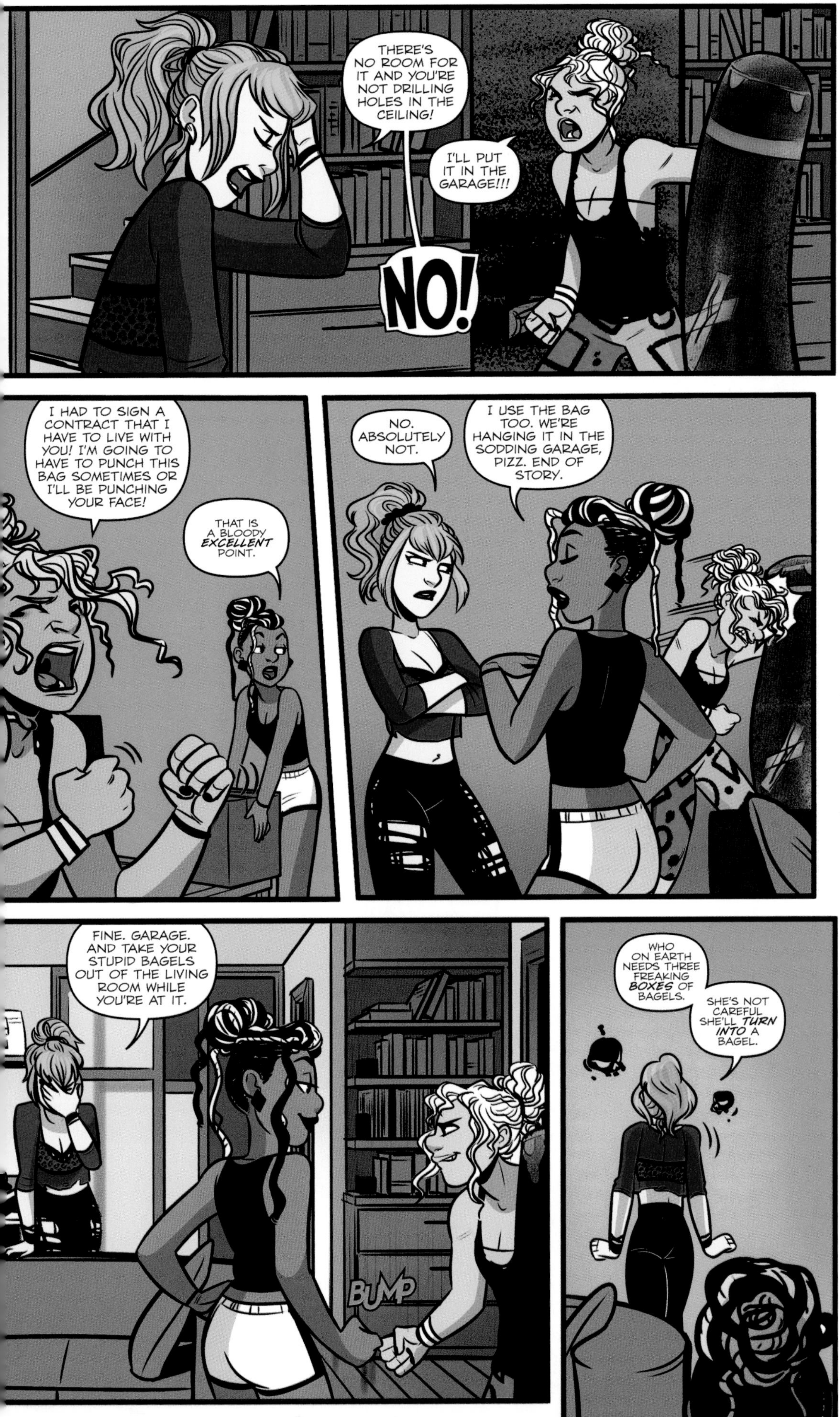
THERE'S NO ROOM FOR IT AND YOU'RE NOT DRILLING HOLES IN THE CEILING!
I'LL PUT IT IN THE GARAGE!!!
NO!
I HAD TO SIGN A CONTRACT THAT I HAVE TO LIVE WITH YOU! I'M GOING TO HAVE TO PUNCH THIS BAG SOMETIMES OR I'LL BE PUNCHING YOUR FACE!
THAT IS A BLOODY EXCELLENT POINT.
NO. ABSOLUTELY NOT.
I USE THE BAG TOO. WE'RE HANGING IT IN THE SODDING GARAGE, PIZZ. END OF STORY.
FINE. GARAGE. AND TAKE YOUR STUPID BAGELS OUT OF THE LIVING ROOM WHILE YOU'RE AT IT.
BUMP
WHO ON EARTH NEEDS THREE FREAKING BOXES OF BAGELS.
SHE'S NOT CAREFUL SHE'LL TURN INTO A BAGEL.

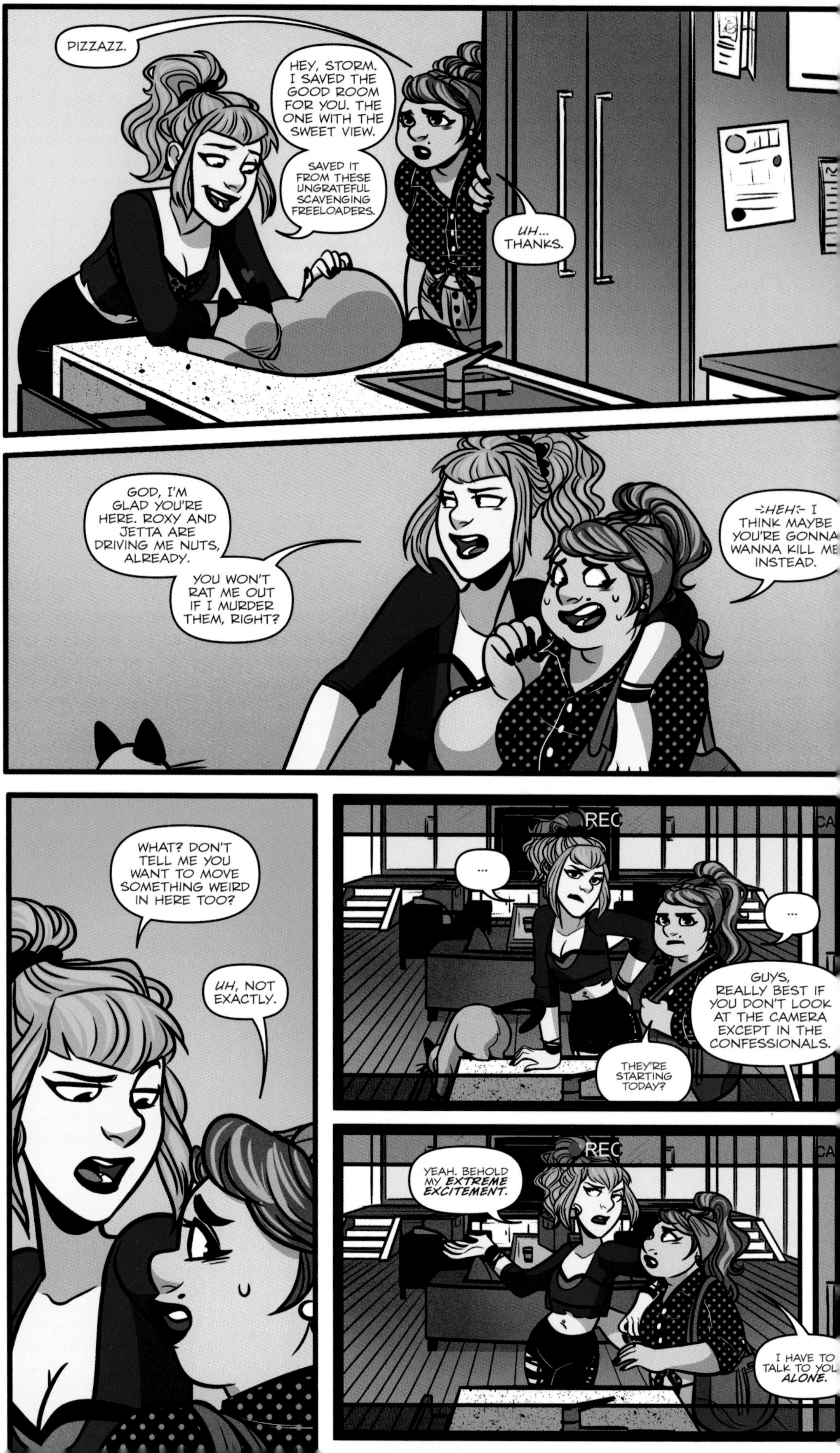
PIZZAZZ.
HEY, STORM. I SAVED THE GOOD ROOM FOR YOU. THE ONE WITH THE SWEET VIEW.
SAVED IT FROM THESE UNGRATEFUL SCAVENGING FREELOADERS.
UH... THANKS.
GOD, I'M GLAD YOU'RE HERE. ROXY AND JETTA ARE DRIVING ME NUTS, ALREADY.
YOU WON'T RAT ME OUT IF I MURDER THEM, RIGHT?
-HEH- I THINK MAYBE YOU'RE GONNA WANNA KILL ME INSTEAD.
WHAT? DON'T TELL ME YOU WANT TO MOVE SOMETHING WEIRD IN HERE TOO?
UH, NOT EXACTLY.
REC
...
...
GUYS, REALLY BEST IF YOU DON'T LOOK AT THE CAMERA EXCEPT IN THE CONFESSIONALS.
THEY'RE STARTING TODAY?
REC
YEAH. BEHOLD MY EXTREME EXCITEMENT.
I HAVE TO TALK TO YOU ALONE.

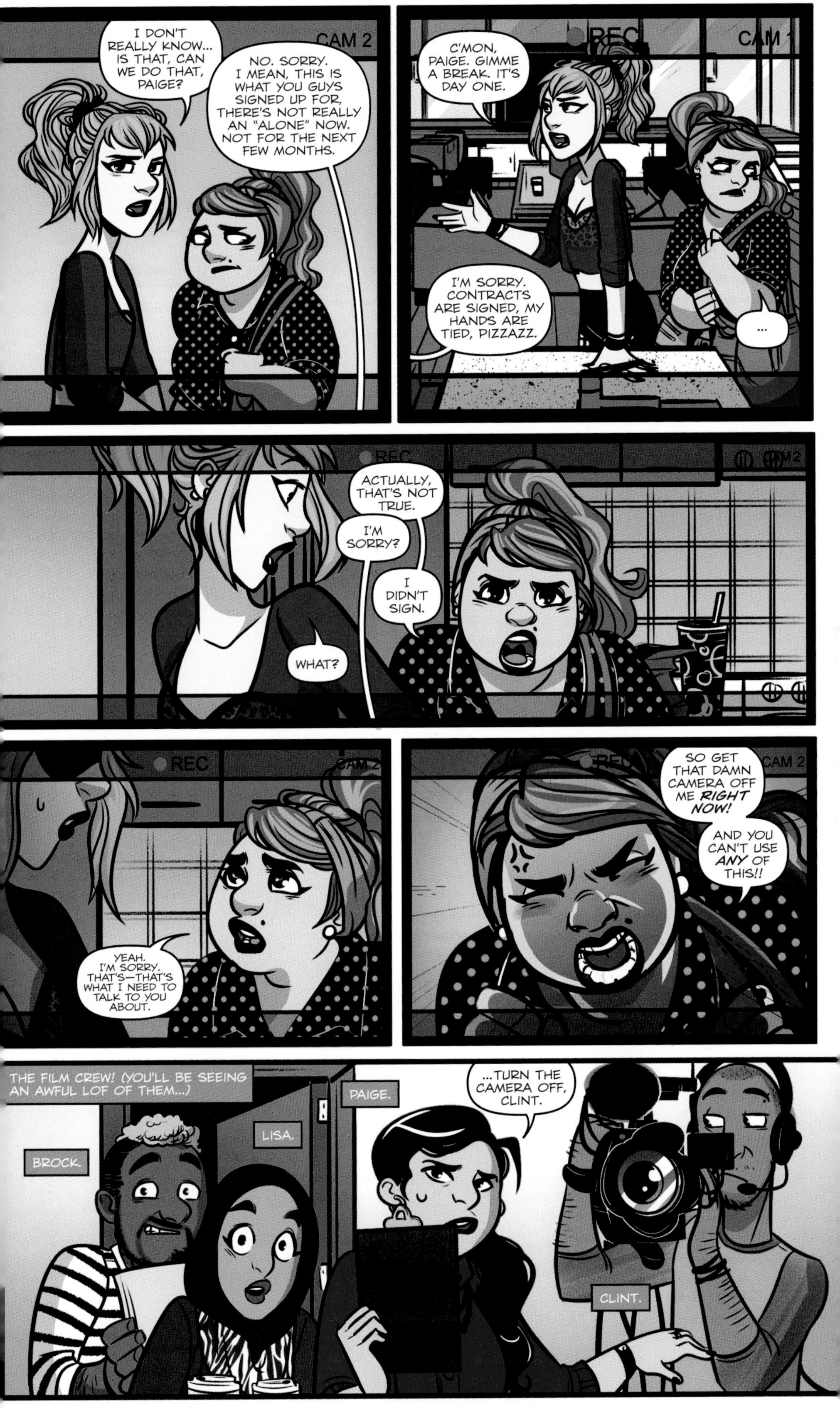

CAM 2
I DON'T REALLY KNOW... IS THAT, CAN WE DO THAT, PAIGE?
NO. SORRY. I MEAN, THIS IS WHAT YOU GUYS SIGNED UP FOR, THERE'S NOT REALLY AN "ALONE" NOW. NOT FOR THE NEXT FEW MONTHS.
REC
CAM 1
C'MON, PAIGE. GIMME A BREAK. IT'S DAY ONE.
I'M SORRY. CONTRACTS ARE SIGNED, MY HANDS ARE TIED, PIZZAZZ.
...
REC
ACTUALLY, THAT'S NOT TRUE.
I'M SORRY?
I DIDN'T SIGN.
WHAT?
REC
YEAH. I'M SORRY. THAT'S—THAT'S WHAT I NEED TO TALK TO YOU ABOUT.
CAM 2
SO GET THAT DAMN CAMERA OFF ME *RIGHT NOW!*
AND YOU CAN'T USE *ANY* OF THIS!!
THE FILM CREW! (YOU'LL BE SEEING AN AWFUL LOT OF THEM...)
PAIGE.
LISA.
BROCK.
...TURN THE CAMERA OFF, CLINT.
CLINT.

GET YOUR BUTT IN HERE.

I GOTTA CALL THE NETWORK.

YUP.

WHAT'S HAPPENING? WHY DIDN'T YOU SIGN THE CONTRACTS?

I... I TOLD YOU I HAD RESERVATIONS.

AND I UNDERSTAND THAT, I HAVE THEM TOO. BUT THIS IS OUR ONLY WAY OUT, STORM. AND I NEED YOU WITH ME.

SURE. BUT MY RESERVATIONS ARE... *DIFFERENT* THAN YOURS. THEY ALWAYS HAVE BEEN.

I DON'T...?

I-I GUESS YOU JUST THOUGHT IT WENT AWAY?

I MEAN, I KNOW I DID MY PART IN HIDING IT FROM YOU, SHIELDING YOU FROM IT... BUT YOU ACTUALLY REALLY THINK IT ALL JUST WENT AWAY? ARE YOU THAT BLIND?

STORM, I DON'T KNOW WHAT WE'RE TALKING ABOUT?

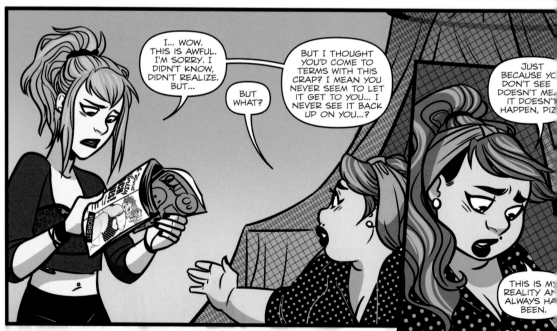

I... WOW. THIS IS AWFUL. I'M SORRY. I DIDN'T KNOW, DIDN'T REALIZE. BUT...

BUT WHAT?

BUT I THOUGHT YOU'D COME TO TERMS WITH THIS CRAP? I MEAN YOU NEVER SEEM TO LET IT GET TO YOU... I NEVER SEE IT BACK UP ON YOU...?

JUST BECAUSE YO DON'T SEE DOESN'T ME. IT DOESN'T HAPPEN, PIZ

THIS IS MY REALITY AN ALWAYS HA BEEN.

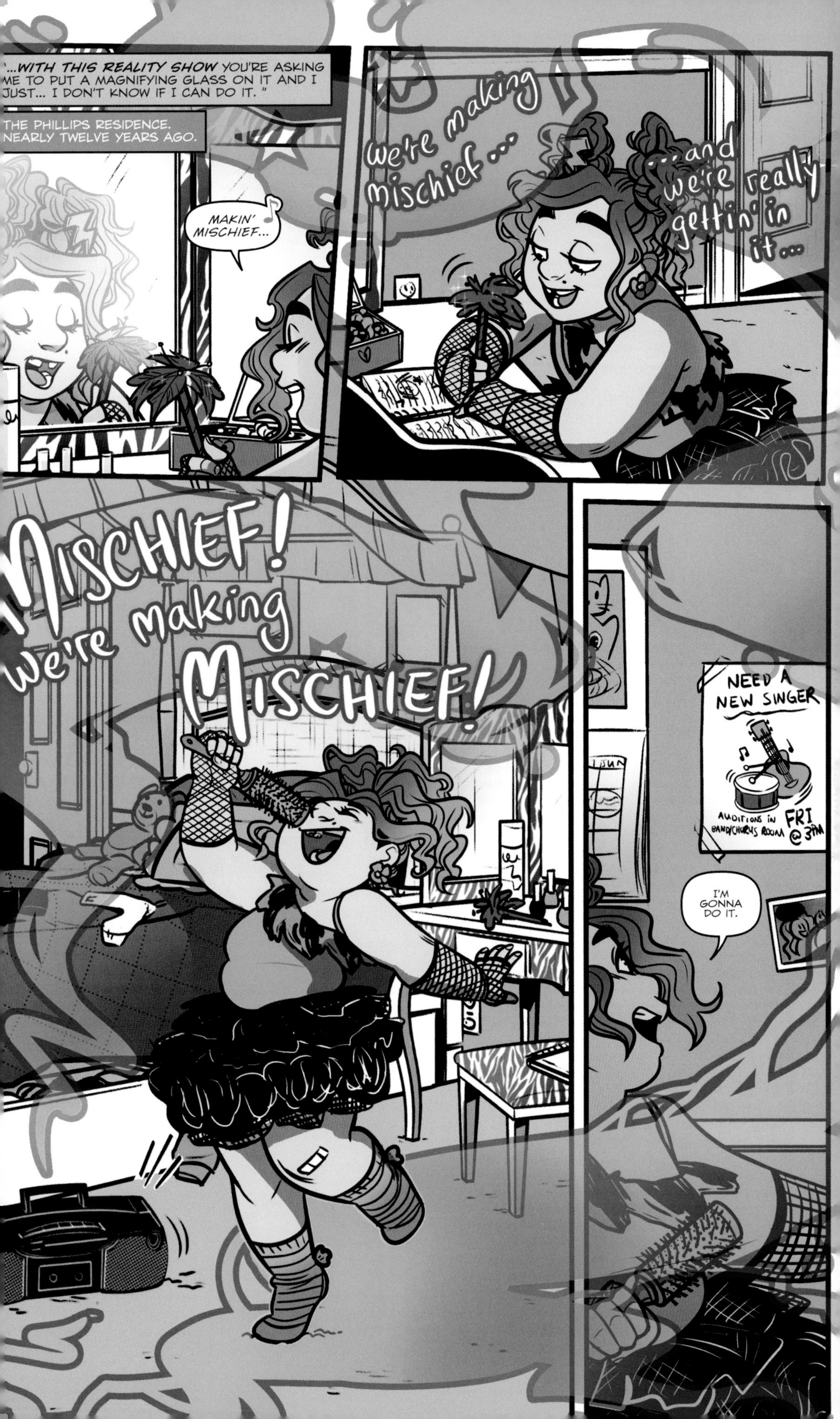
"...WITH THIS REALITY SHOW YOU'RE ASKING ME TO PUT A MAGNIFYING GLASS ON IT AND I JUST... I DON'T KNOW IF I CAN DO IT."
THE PHILLIPS RESIDENCE. NEARLY TWELVE YEARS AGO.
MAKIN' MISCHIEF...
We're making mischief...
...and we're really gettin' in it...
MISCHIEF! We're making MISCHIEF!
NEED A NEW SINGER
AUDITIONS IN BAND/CHORUS ROOM FRI @ 3PM
I'M GONNA DO IT.

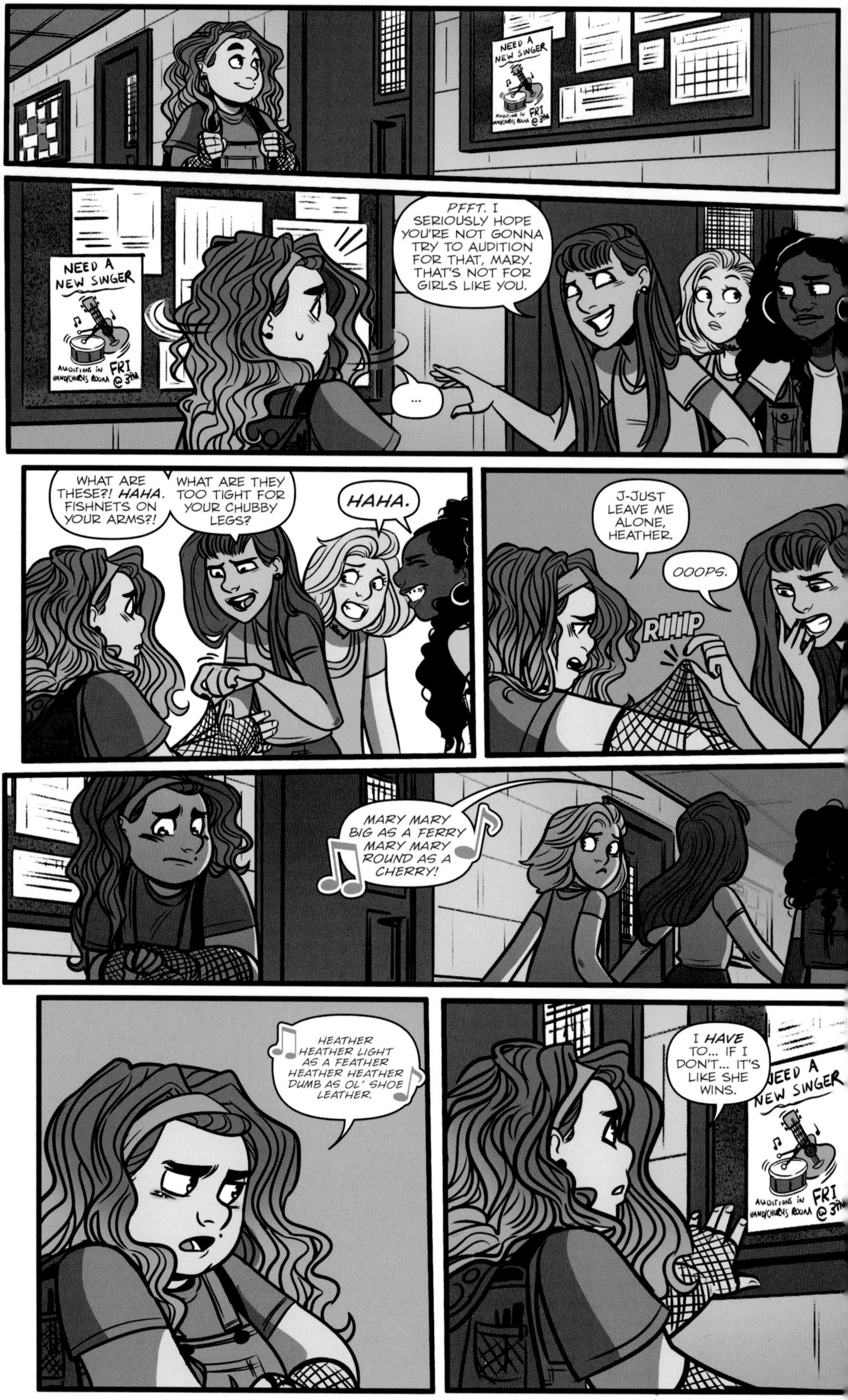
NEED A NEW SINGER
AUDITIONS IN BAND/CHORUS ROOM FRI @ 3PM
PFFT. I SERIOUSLY HOPE YOU'RE NOT GONNA TRY TO AUDITION FOR THAT, MARY. THAT'S NOT FOR GIRLS LIKE YOU.
...
WHAT ARE THESE?! HAHA. FISHNETS ON YOUR ARMS?!
WHAT ARE THEY TOO TIGHT FOR YOUR CHUBBY LEGS?
HAHA.
J-JUST LEAVE ME ALONE, HEATHER.
OOOPS.
RIIIP
MARY MARY BIG AS A FERRY MARY MARY ROUND AS A CHERRY!
HEATHER HEATHER LIGHT AS A FEATHER HEATHER HEATHER DUMB AS OL' SHOE LEATHER.
I HAVE TO... IF I DON'T... IT'S LIKE SHE WINS.

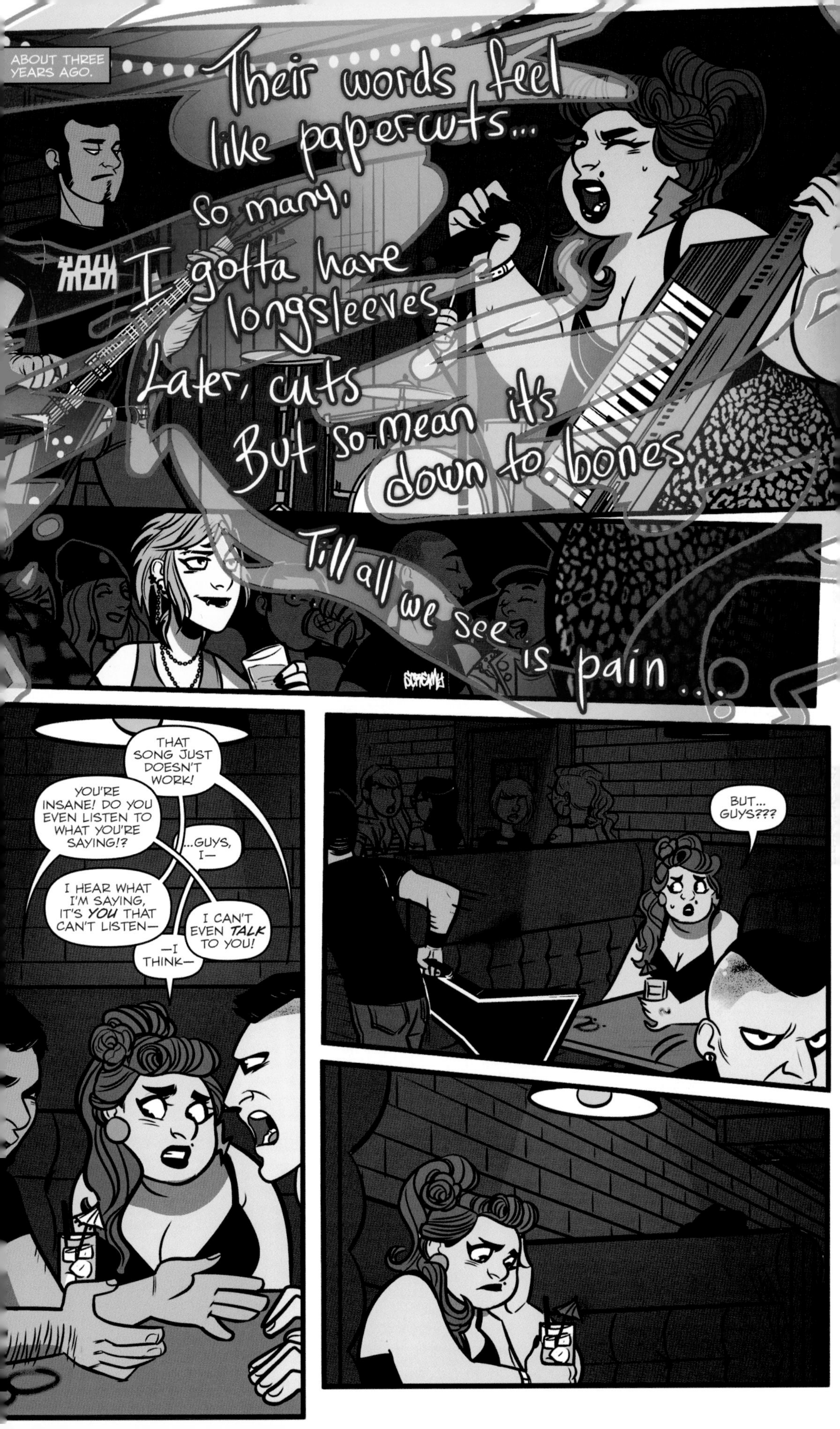
ABOUT THREE YEARS AGO.
Their words feel like papercuts...
So many,
I gotta have longsleeves
Later, cuts
But so mean it's down to bones
Till all we see is pain...
THAT SONG JUST DOESN'T WORK!
YOU'RE INSANE! DO YOU EVEN LISTEN TO WHAT YOU'RE SAYING!?
...GUYS, I—
I HEAR WHAT I'M SAYING, IT'S YOU THAT CAN'T LISTEN—
I CAN'T EVEN TALK TO YOU!
—I THINK—
BUT... GUYS???

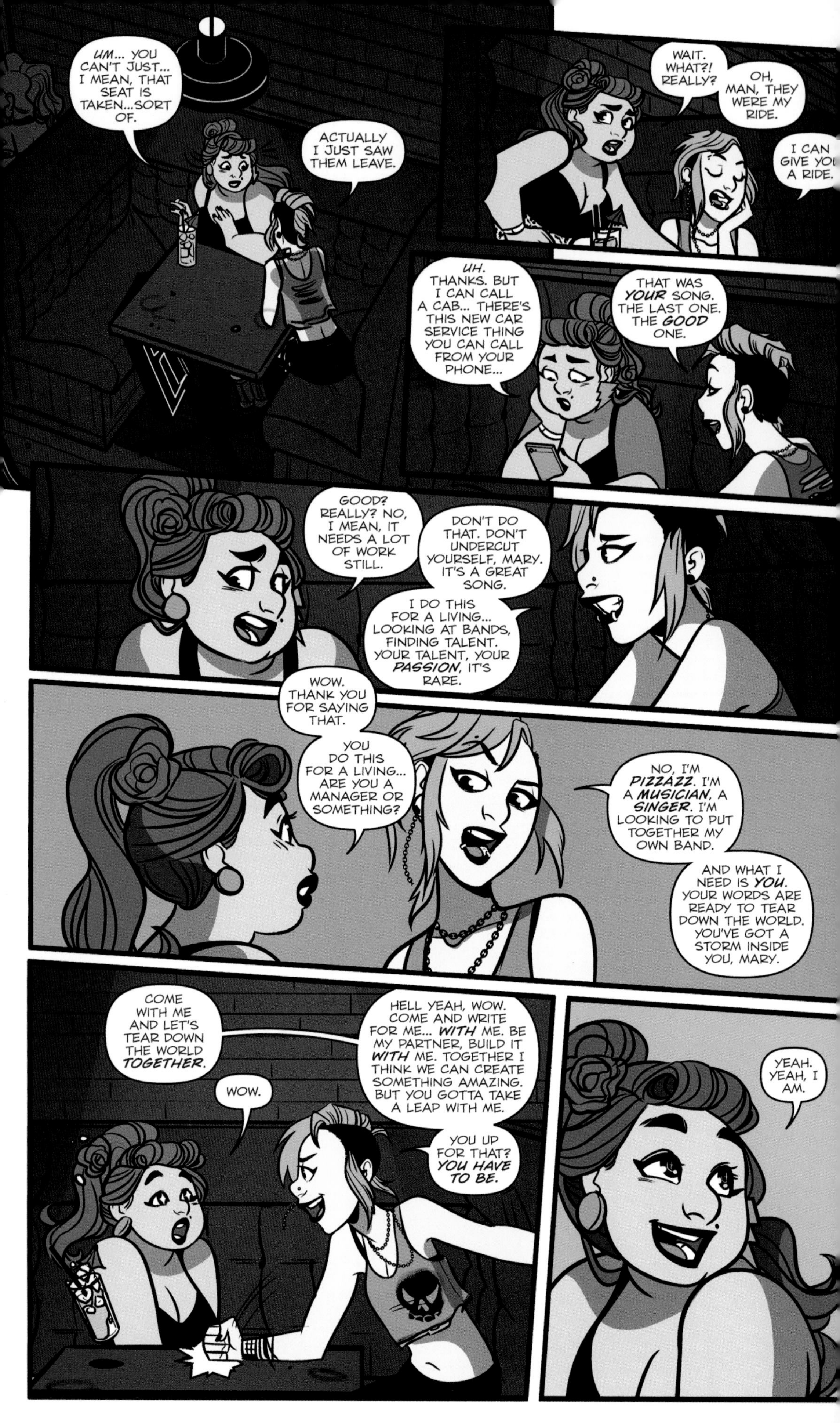
UM... YOU CAN'T JUST... I MEAN, THAT SEAT IS TAKEN...SORT OF.
ACTUALLY I JUST SAW THEM LEAVE.
WAIT. WHAT?! REALLY?
OH, MAN, THEY WERE MY RIDE.
I CAN GIVE YOU A RIDE.
UH. THANKS. BUT I CAN CALL A CAB... THERE'S THIS NEW CAR SERVICE THING YOU CAN CALL FROM YOUR PHONE...
THAT WAS YOUR SONG. THE LAST ONE. THE GOOD ONE.
GOOD? REALLY? NO, I MEAN, IT NEEDS A LOT OF WORK STILL.
DON'T DO THAT. DON'T UNDERCUT YOURSELF, MARY. IT'S A GREAT SONG.
I DO THIS FOR A LIVING... LOOKING AT BANDS, FINDING TALENT. YOUR TALENT, YOUR PASSION, IT'S RARE.
WOW. THANK YOU FOR SAYING THAT.
YOU DO THIS FOR A LIVING... ARE YOU A MANAGER OR SOMETHING?
NO, I'M PIZZAZZ. I'M A MUSICIAN, A SINGER. I'M LOOKING TO PUT TOGETHER MY OWN BAND.
AND WHAT I NEED IS YOU. YOUR WORDS ARE READY TO TEAR DOWN THE WORLD. YOU'VE GOT A STORM INSIDE YOU, MARY.
HELL YEAH, WOW. COME AND WRITE FOR ME... WITH ME. BE MY PARTNER, BUILD IT WITH ME. TOGETHER I THINK WE CAN CREATE SOMETHING AMAZING. BUT YOU GOTTA TAKE A LEAP WITH ME.
COME WITH ME AND LET'S TEAR DOWN THE WORLD TOGETHER.
WOW.
YOU UP FOR THAT? YOU HAVE TO BE.
YEAH. YEAH, I AM.

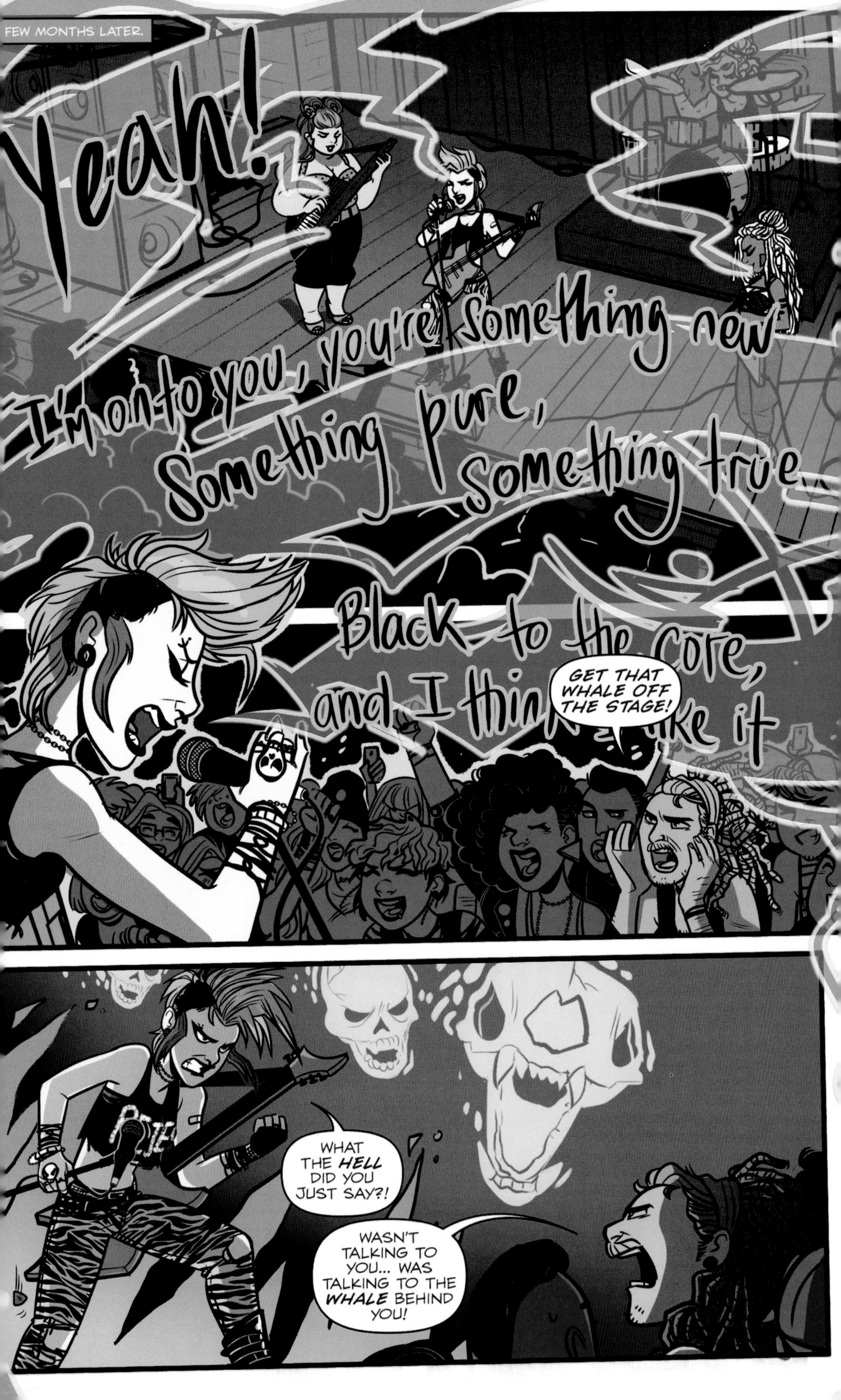

FEW MONTHS LATER.
Yeah!
I'm onto you, you're something new
Something pure, something true
Black to the core,
and I thin ike it
GET THAT WHALE OFF THE STAGE!
WHAT THE *HELL* DID YOU JUST SAY?!
WASN'T TALKING TO YOU... WAS TALKING TO THE *WHALE* BEHIND YOU!

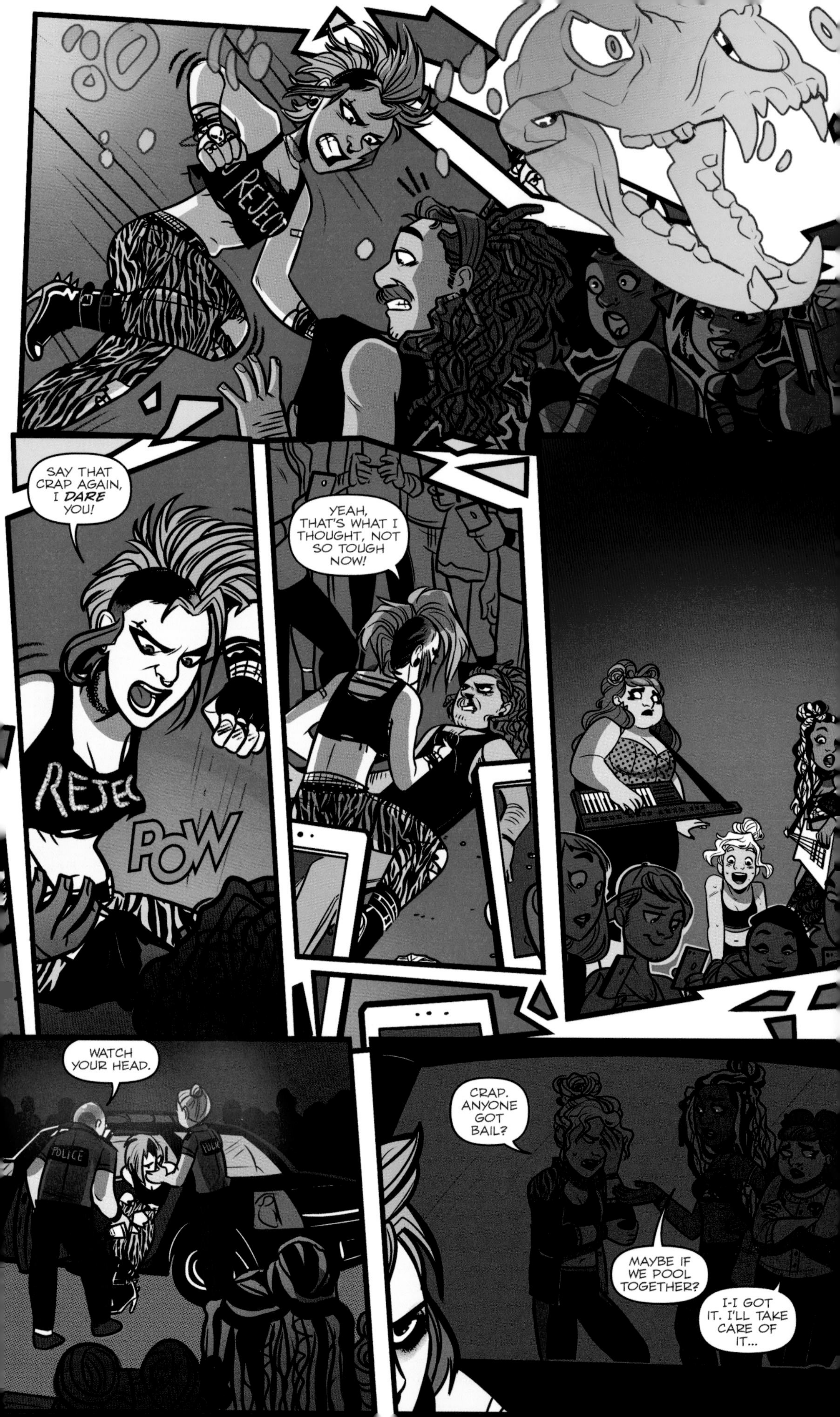
REJEC
SAY THAT CRAP AGAIN, I ***DARE*** YOU!
REJEC
POW
YEAH, THAT'S WHAT I THOUGHT, NOT SO TOUGH NOW!
WATCH YOUR HEAD.
POLICE
POLICE
CRAP. ANYONE GOT BAIL?
MAYBE IF WE POOL TOGETHER?
I-I GOT IT. I'LL TAKE CARE OF IT...

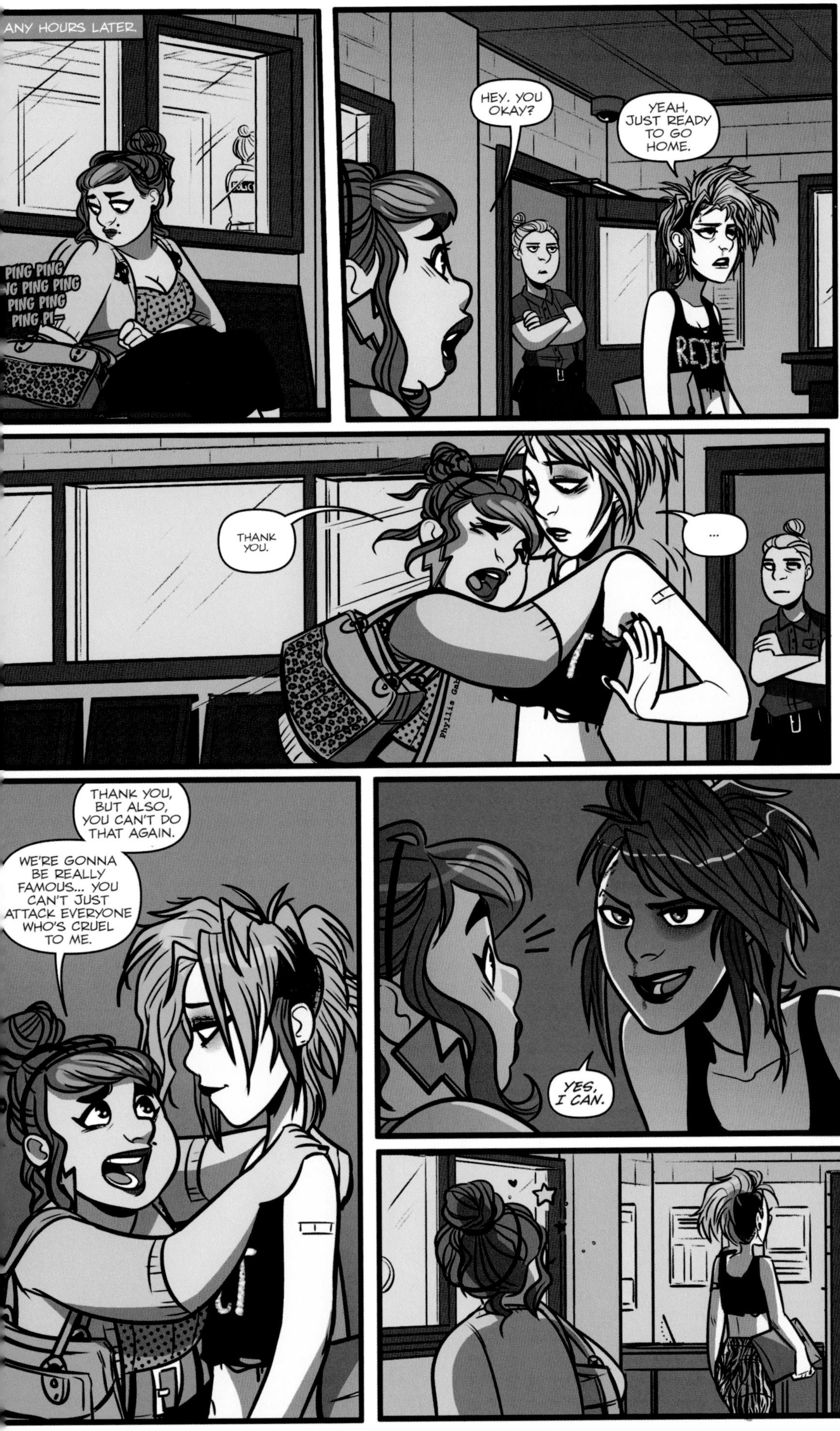
ANY HOURS LATER.
PING PING
NG PING PING
PING PING
PING PI
HEY. YOU OKAY?
YEAH, JUST READY TO GO HOME.
THANK YOU.
...
THANK YOU, BUT ALSO, YOU CAN'T DO THAT AGAIN.
WE'RE GONNA BE REALLY FAMOUS... YOU CAN'T JUST ATTACK EVERYONE WHO'S CRUEL TO ME.
YES, I CAN.

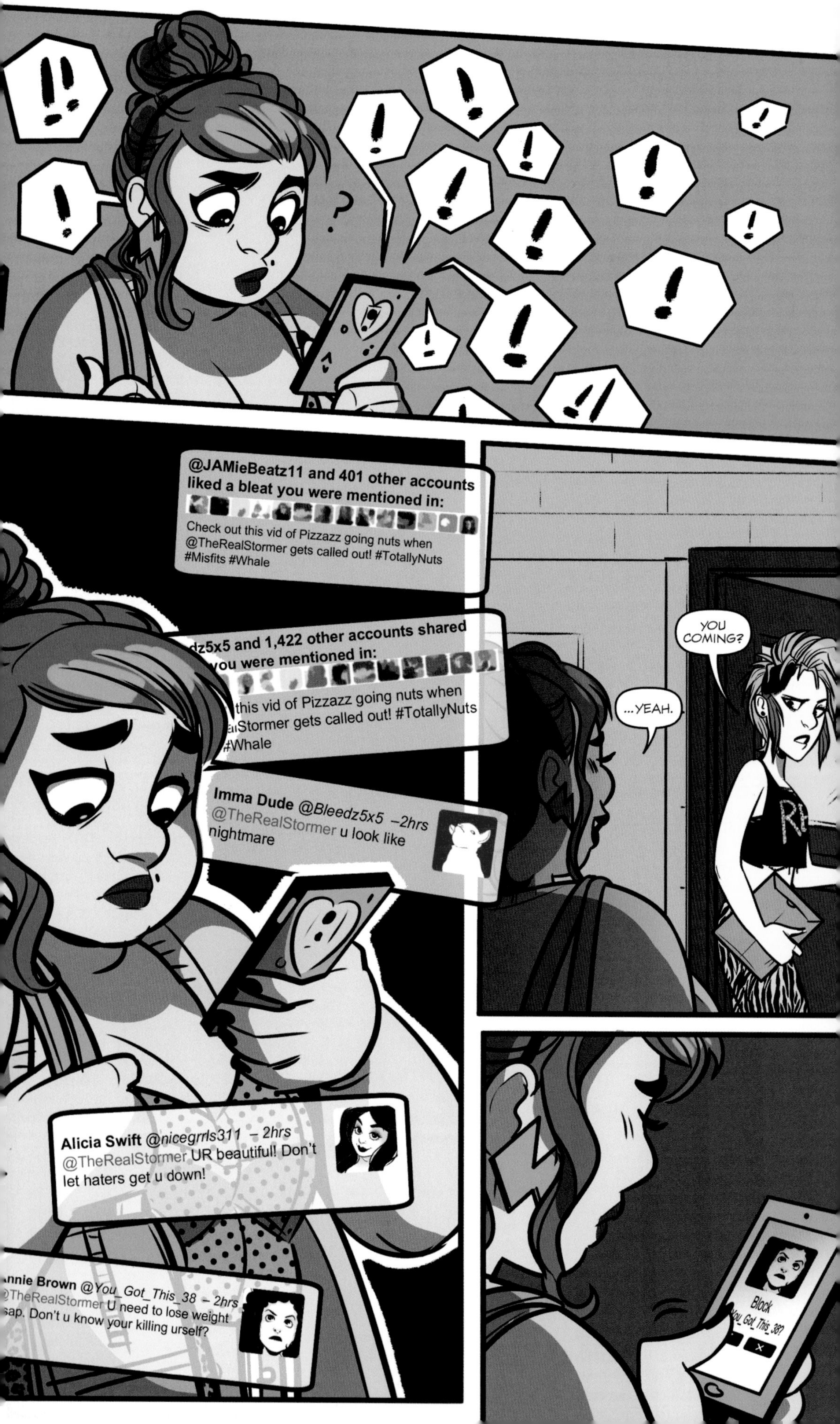
?
@JAMieBeatz11 and 401 other accounts liked a bleat you were mentioned in:
Check out this vid of Pizzazz going nuts when @TheRealStormer gets called out! #TotallyNuts #Misfits #Whale
dz5x5 and 1,422 other accounts shared you were mentioned in:
this vid of Pizzazz going nuts when Stormer gets called out! #TotallyNuts #Whale
Imma Dude @Bleedz5x5 –2hrs
@TheRealStormer u look like nightmare
Alicia Swift @nicegrrls311 – 2hrs
@TheRealStormer UR beautiful! Don't let haters get u down!
nnie Brown @You_Got_This_38 – 2hrs
@TheRealStormer U need to lose weight sap. Don't u know your killing urself?
YOU COMING?
...YEAH.
Block
You_Got_This_38?

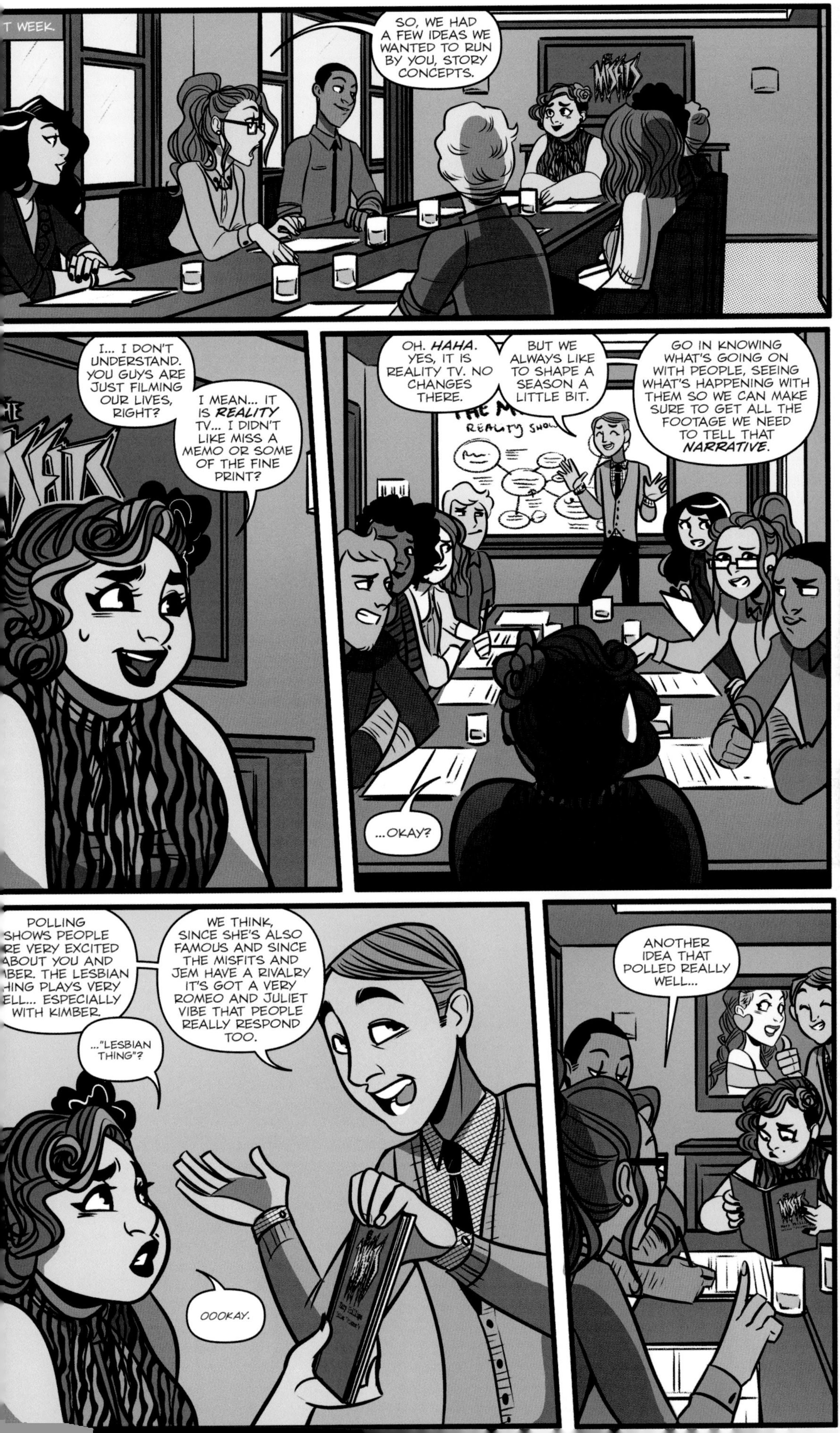
T WEEK.
SO, WE HAD A FEW IDEAS WE WANTED TO RUN BY YOU, STORY CONCEPTS.
I... I DON'T UNDERSTAND. YOU GUYS ARE JUST FILMING OUR LIVES, RIGHT?
I MEAN... IT IS REALITY TV... I DIDN'T LIKE MISS A MEMO OR SOME OF THE FINE PRINT?
OH. HAHA. YES, IT IS REALITY TV. NO CHANGES THERE.
BUT WE ALWAYS LIKE TO SHAPE A SEASON A LITTLE BIT.
GO IN KNOWING WHAT'S GOING ON WITH PEOPLE, SEEING WHAT'S HAPPENING WITH THEM SO WE CAN MAKE SURE TO GET ALL THE FOOTAGE WE NEED TO TELL THAT NARRATIVE.
...OKAY?
POLLING SHOWS PEOPLE RE VERY EXCITED ABOUT YOU AND IBER. THE LESBIAN HING PLAYS VERY ELL... ESPECIALLY WITH KIMBER.
WE THINK, SINCE SHE'S ALSO FAMOUS AND SINCE THE MISFITS AND JEM HAVE A RIVALRY IT'S GOT A VERY ROMEO AND JULIET VIBE THAT PEOPLE REALLY RESPOND TOO.
..."LESBIAN THING"?
OOOKAY.
ANOTHER IDEA THAT POLLED REALLY WELL...

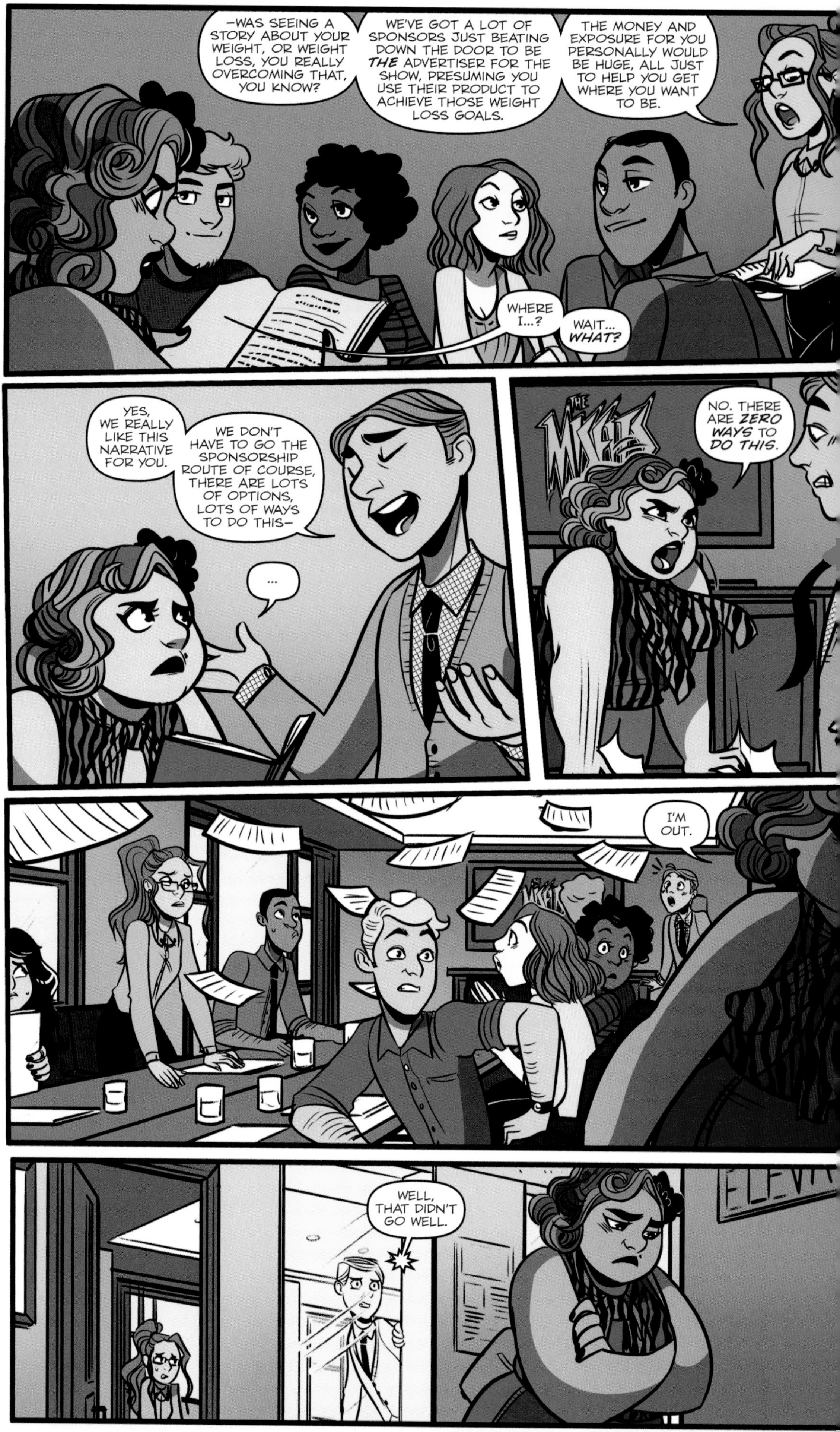
–WAS SEEING A STORY ABOUT YOUR WEIGHT, OR WEIGHT LOSS, YOU REALLY OVERCOMING THAT, YOU KNOW?
WE'VE GOT A LOT OF SPONSORS JUST BEATING DOWN THE DOOR TO BE *THE* ADVERTISER FOR THE SHOW, PRESUMING YOU USE THEIR PRODUCT TO ACHIEVE THOSE WEIGHT LOSS GOALS.
THE MONEY AND EXPOSURE FOR YOU PERSONALLY WOULD BE HUGE, ALL JUST TO HELP YOU GET WHERE YOU WANT TO BE.
WHERE I...?
WAIT... *WHAT?*
YES, WE REALLY LIKE THIS NARRATIVE FOR YOU.
WE DON'T HAVE TO GO THE SPONSORSHIP ROUTE OF COURSE, THERE ARE LOTS OF OPTIONS, LOTS OF WAYS TO DO THIS–
...
NO. THERE ARE *ZERO WAYS* TO *DO THIS.*
I'M OUT.
WELL, THAT DIDN'T GO WELL.

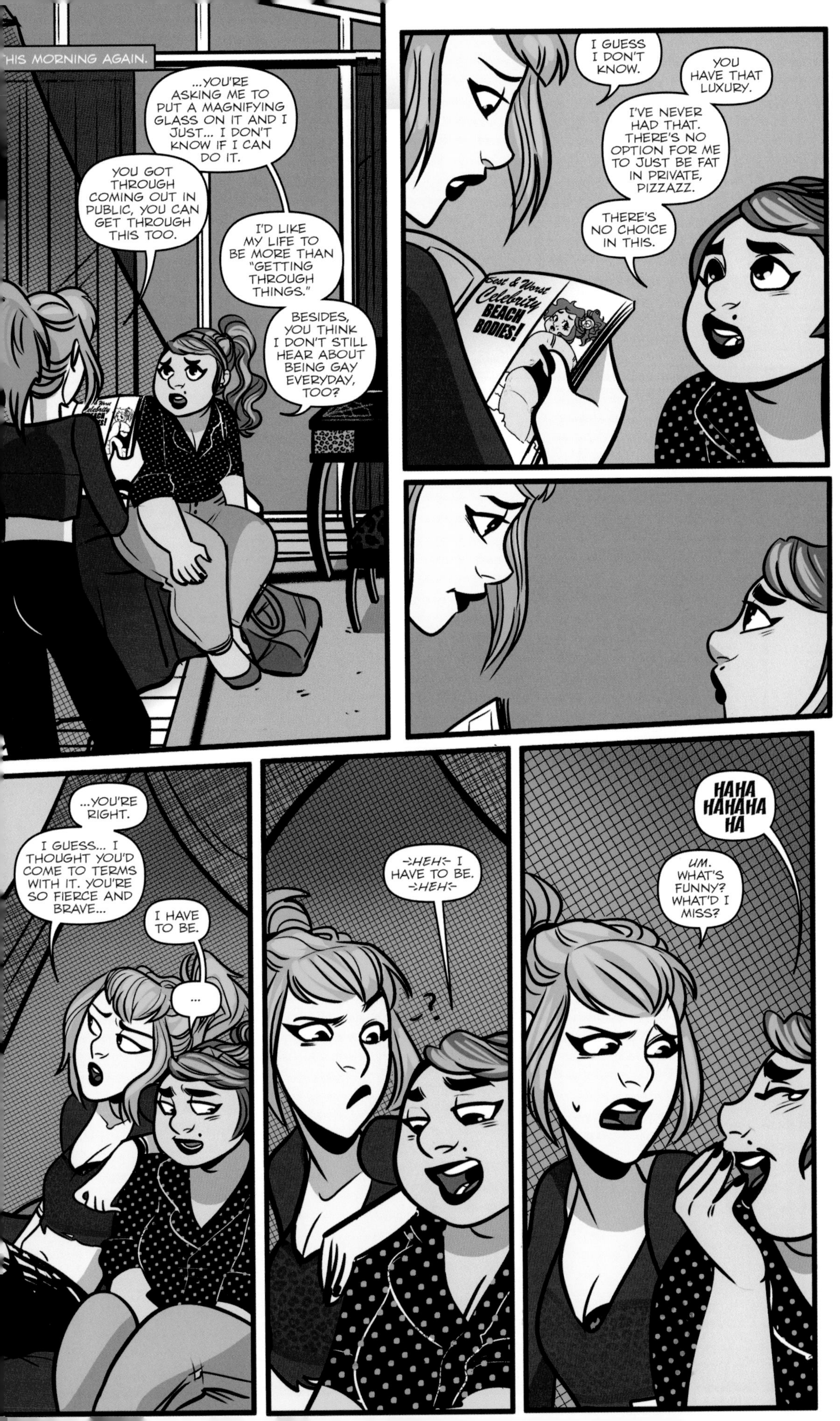
THIS MORNING AGAIN.
...YOU'RE ASKING ME TO PUT A MAGNIFYING GLASS ON IT AND I JUST... I DON'T KNOW IF I CAN DO IT.
YOU GOT THROUGH COMING OUT IN PUBLIC, YOU CAN GET THROUGH THIS TOO.
I'D LIKE MY LIFE TO BE MORE THAN "GETTING THROUGH THINGS."
BESIDES, YOU THINK I DON'T STILL HEAR ABOUT BEING GAY EVERYDAY, TOO?
I GUESS I DON'T KNOW.
YOU HAVE THAT LUXURY.
I'VE NEVER HAD THAT. THERE'S NO OPTION FOR ME TO JUST BE FAT IN PRIVATE, PIZZAZZ.
THERE'S NO CHOICE IN THIS.
Best & Worst Celebrity BEACH BODIES!
...YOU'RE RIGHT.
I GUESS... I THOUGHT YOU'D COME TO TERMS WITH IT. YOU'RE SO FIERCE AND BRAVE...
I HAVE TO BE.
...
HEH I HAVE TO BE. HEH
?
HAHA HAHAHA HA
UM. WHAT'S FUNNY? WHAT'D I MISS?

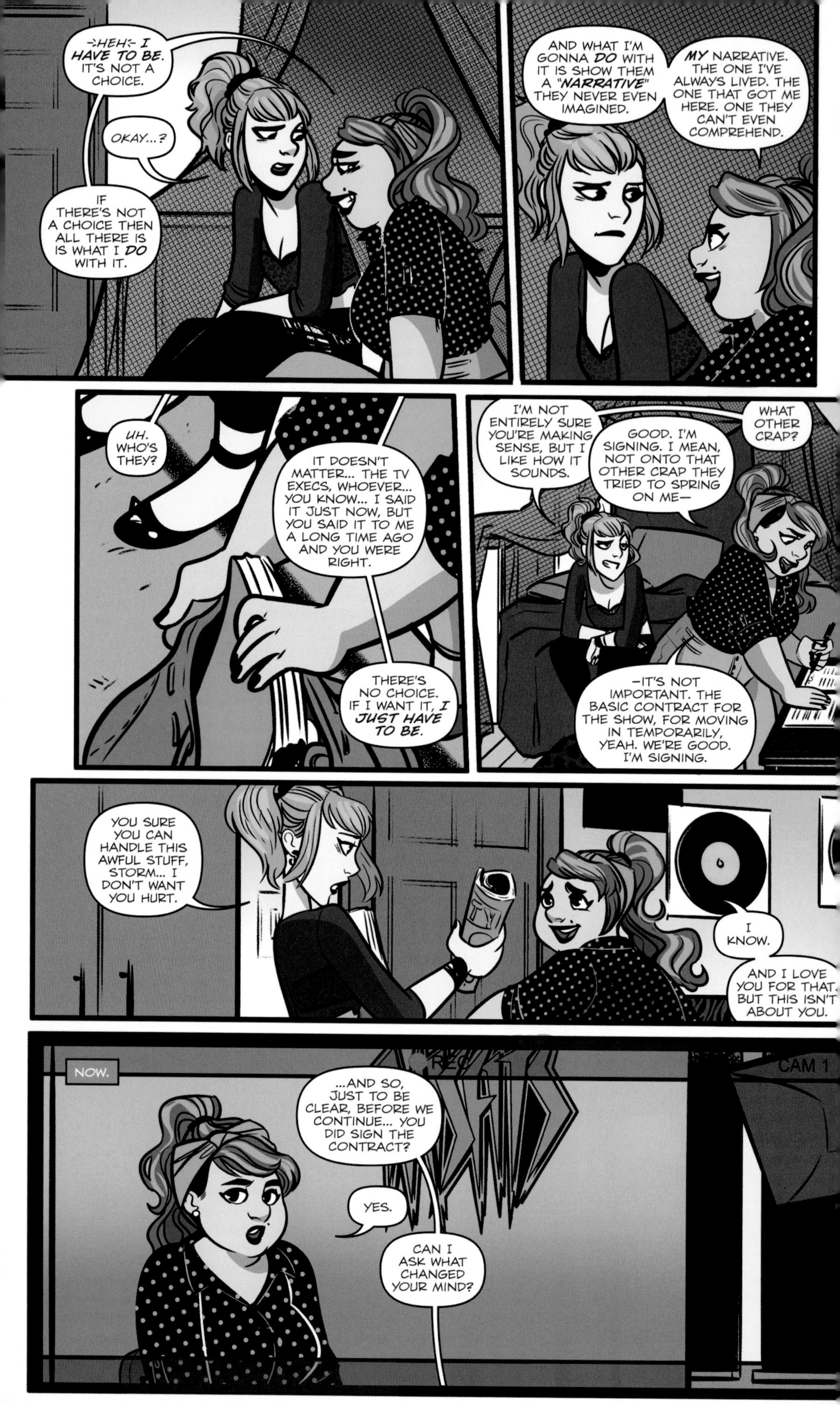

-HEH- I HAVE TO BE. IT'S NOT A CHOICE.
OKAY...?
IF THERE'S NOT A CHOICE THEN ALL THERE IS IS WHAT I DO WITH IT.
AND WHAT I'M GONNA DO WITH IT IS SHOW THEM A "NARRATIVE" THEY NEVER EVEN IMAGINED.
MY NARRATIVE. THE ONE I'VE ALWAYS LIVED. THE ONE THAT GOT ME HERE. ONE THEY CAN'T EVEN COMPREHEND.
UH. WHO'S THEY?
IT DOESN'T MATTER... THE TV EXECS, WHOEVER... YOU KNOW... I SAID IT JUST NOW, BUT YOU SAID IT TO ME A LONG TIME AGO AND YOU WERE RIGHT.
THERE'S NO CHOICE. IF I WANT IT, I JUST HAVE TO BE.
I'M NOT ENTIRELY SURE YOU'RE MAKING SENSE, BUT I LIKE HOW IT SOUNDS.
GOOD. I'M SIGNING. I MEAN, NOT ONTO THAT OTHER CRAP THEY TRIED TO SPRING ON ME—
WHAT OTHER CRAP?
—IT'S NOT IMPORTANT. THE BASIC CONTRACT FOR THE SHOW, FOR MOVING IN TEMPORARILY, YEAH. WE'RE GOOD. I'M SIGNING.
YOU SURE YOU CAN HANDLE THIS AWFUL STUFF, STORM... I DON'T WANT YOU HURT.
I KNOW.
AND I LOVE YOU FOR THAT. BUT THIS ISN'T ABOUT YOU.
NOW.
REC
CAM 1
...AND SO, JUST TO BE CLEAR, BEFORE WE CONTINUE... YOU DID SIGN THE CONTRACT?
YES.
CAN I ASK WHAT CHANGED YOUR MIND?

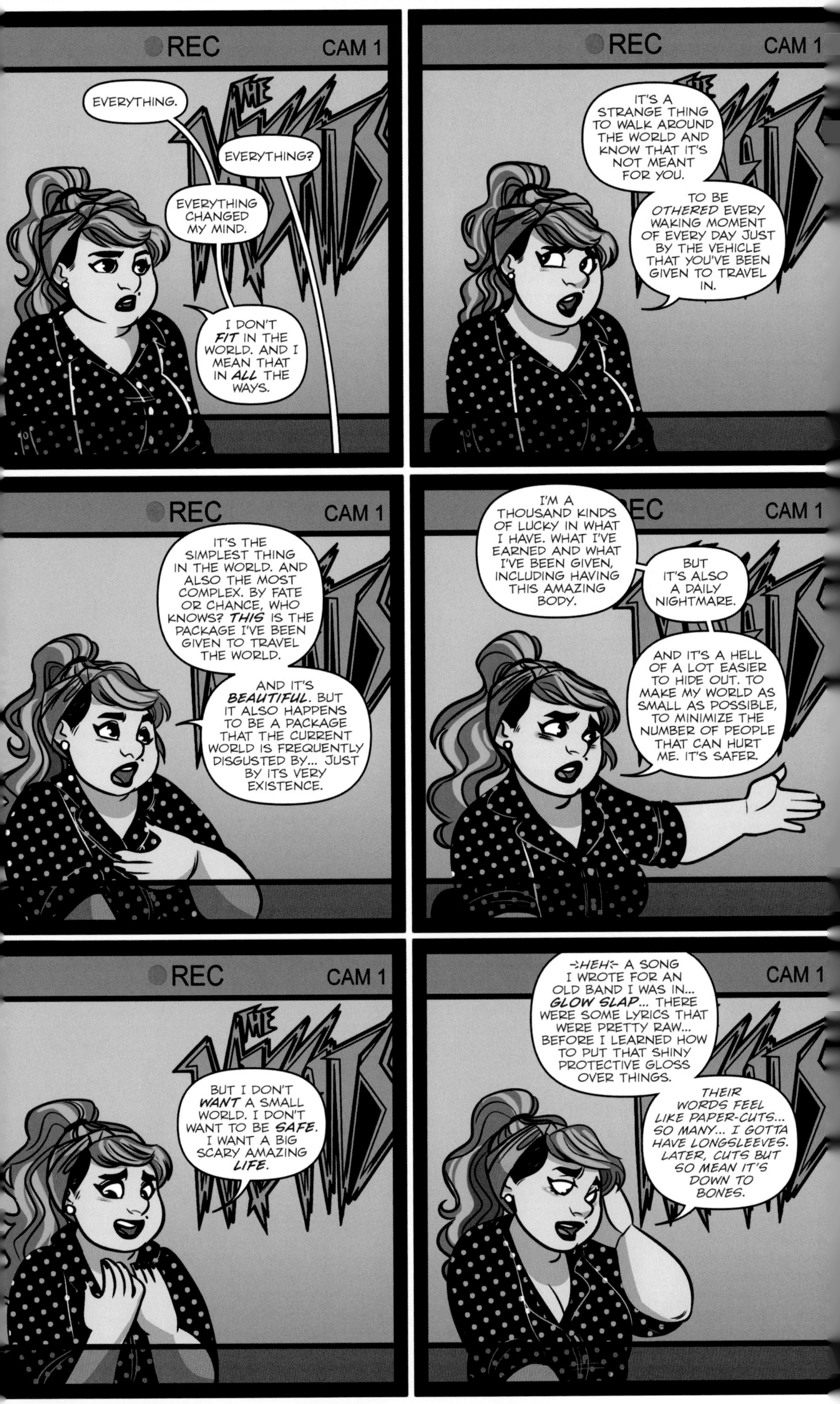
REC
CAM 1
EVERYTHING.
EVERYTHING?
EVERYTHING CHANGED MY MIND.
I DON'T *FIT* IN THE WORLD. AND I MEAN THAT IN *ALL* THE WAYS.
REC
CAM 1
IT'S A STRANGE THING TO WALK AROUND THE WORLD AND KNOW THAT IT'S NOT MEANT FOR YOU.
TO BE *OTHERED* EVERY WAKING MOMENT OF EVERY DAY JUST BY THE VEHICLE THAT YOU'VE BEEN GIVEN TO TRAVEL IN.
REC
CAM 1
IT'S THE SIMPLEST THING IN THE WORLD. AND ALSO THE MOST COMPLEX. BY FATE OR CHANCE, WHO KNOWS? *THIS* IS THE PACKAGE I'VE BEEN GIVEN TO TRAVEL THE WORLD.
AND IT'S *BEAUTIFUL*. BUT IT ALSO HAPPENS TO BE A PACKAGE THAT THE CURRENT WORLD IS FREQUENTLY DISGUSTED BY... JUST BY ITS VERY EXISTENCE.
CAM 1
I'M A THOUSAND KINDS OF LUCKY IN WHAT I HAVE. WHAT I'VE EARNED AND WHAT I'VE BEEN GIVEN, INCLUDING HAVING THIS AMAZING BODY.
BUT IT'S ALSO A DAILY NIGHTMARE.
AND IT'S A HELL OF A LOT EASIER TO HIDE OUT. TO MAKE MY WORLD AS SMALL AS POSSIBLE, TO MINIMIZE THE NUMBER OF PEOPLE THAT CAN HURT ME. IT'S SAFER.
REC
CAM 1
BUT I DON'T *WANT* A SMALL WORLD. I DON'T WANT TO BE *SAFE*. I WANT A BIG SCARY AMAZING *LIFE*.
CAM 1
HEH A SONG I WROTE FOR AN OLD BAND I WAS IN... *GLOW SLAP*... THERE WERE SOME LYRICS THAT WERE PRETTY RAW... BEFORE I LEARNED HOW TO PUT THAT SHINY PROTECTIVE GLOSS OVER THINGS.
THEIR WORDS FEEL LIKE PAPER-CUTS... SO MANY... I GOTTA HAVE LONGSLEEVES. LATER, CUTS BUT SO MEAN IT'S DOWN TO BONES.

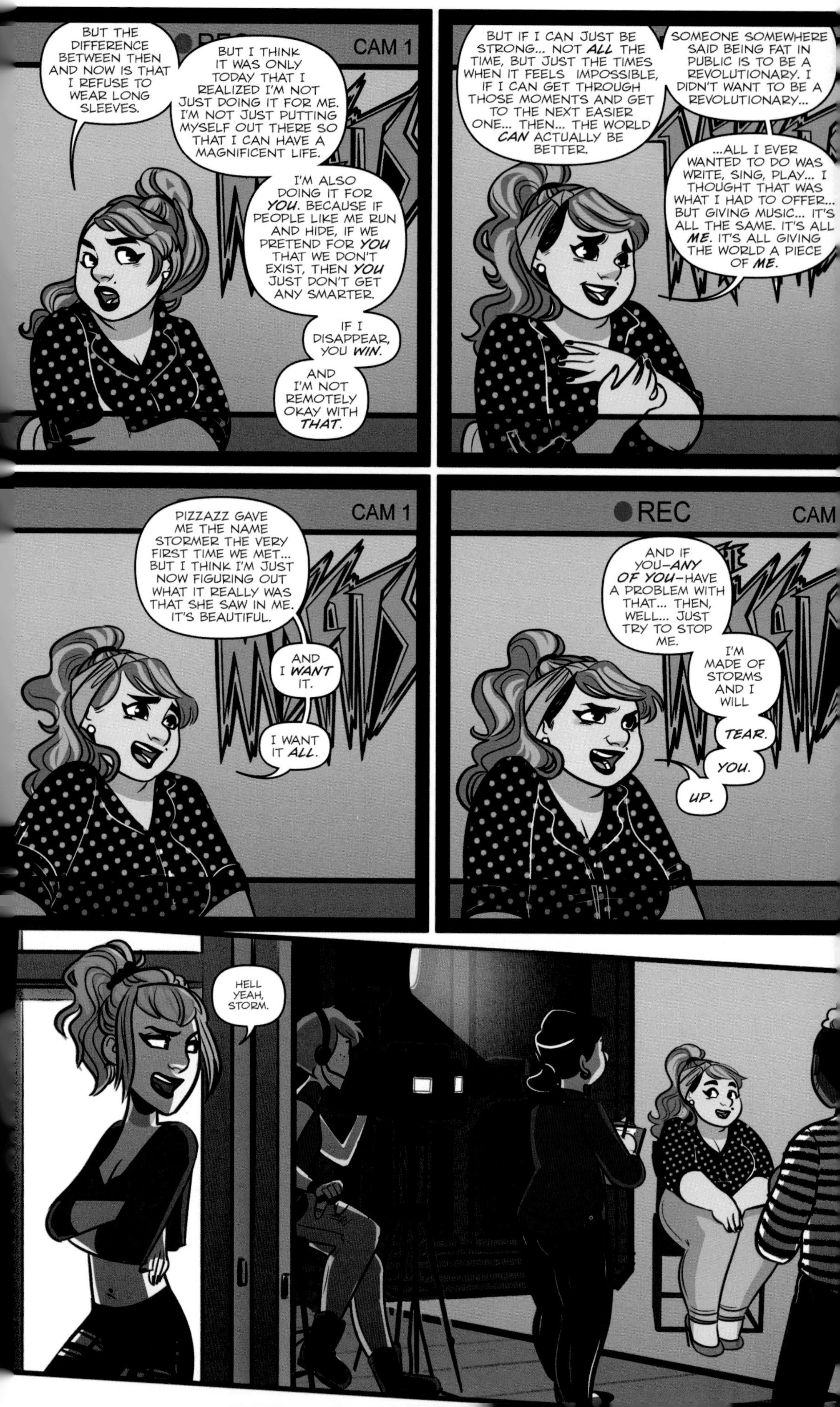
CAM 1
BUT THE DIFFERENCE BETWEEN THEN AND NOW IS THAT I REFUSE TO WEAR LONG SLEEVES.
BUT I THINK IT WAS ONLY TODAY THAT I REALIZED I'M NOT JUST DOING IT FOR ME. I'M NOT JUST PUTTING MYSELF OUT THERE SO THAT I CAN HAVE A MAGNIFICENT LIFE.
I'M ALSO DOING IT FOR YOU. BECAUSE IF PEOPLE LIKE ME RUN AND HIDE, IF WE PRETEND FOR YOU THAT WE DON'T EXIST, THEN YOU JUST DON'T GET ANY SMARTER.
IF I DISAPPEAR, YOU WIN.
AND I'M NOT REMOTELY OKAY WITH THAT.
BUT IF I CAN JUST BE STRONG... NOT ALL THE TIME, BUT JUST THE TIMES WHEN IT FEELS IMPOSSIBLE, IF I CAN GET THROUGH THOSE MOMENTS AND GET TO THE NEXT EASIER ONE... THEN... THE WORLD CAN ACTUALLY BE BETTER.
SOMEONE SOMEWHERE SAID BEING FAT IN PUBLIC IS TO BE A REVOLUTIONARY. I DIDN'T WANT TO BE A REVOLUTIONARY...
...ALL I EVER WANTED TO DO WAS WRITE, SING, PLAY... I THOUGHT THAT WAS WHAT I HAD TO OFFER... BUT GIVING MUSIC... IT'S ALL THE SAME. IT'S ALL ME. IT'S ALL GIVING THE WORLD A PIECE OF ME.
CAM 1
PIZZAZZ GAVE ME THE NAME STORMER THE VERY FIRST TIME WE MET... BUT I THINK I'M JUST NOW FIGURING OUT WHAT IT REALLY WAS THAT SHE SAW IN ME. IT'S BEAUTIFUL.
AND I WANT IT.
I WANT IT ALL.
REC
CAM
AND IF YOU—ANY OF YOU—HAVE A PROBLEM WITH THAT... THEN, WELL... JUST TRY TO STOP ME.
I'M MADE OF STORMS AND I WILL
TEAR.
YOU.
UP.
HELL YEAH, STORM.

HALLOWEEN

WITH THE MISFITS

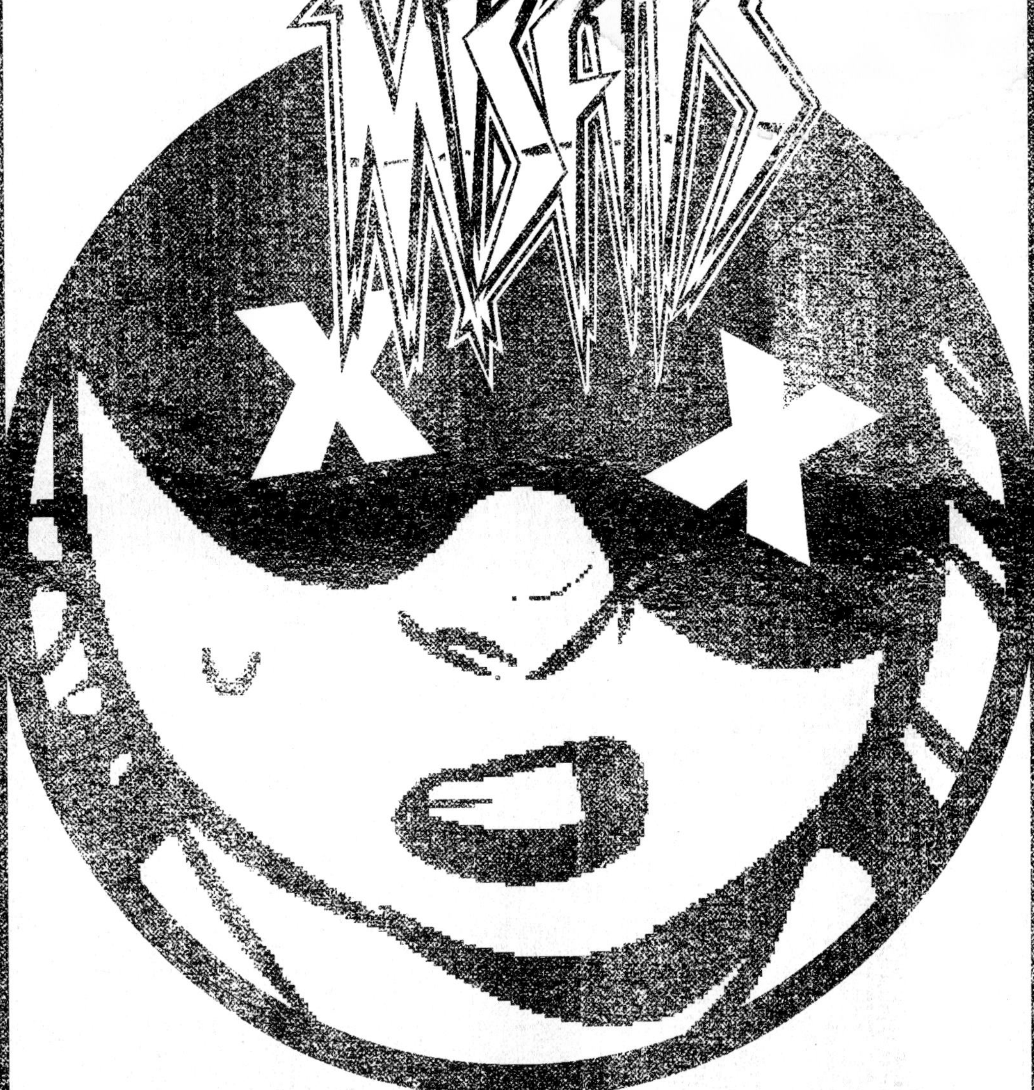

COSTUME CONTEST!

WIN A GOODIE BAG WITH A SHIRT, PINS, STICKERS, RECORDS, AND IF YOU'RE LUCKY, YOU'LL ESCAPE WITH YOUR LIFE! SEE YOU IN THE PIT!

THE BREAKROOM
SAN DIEGO

$10

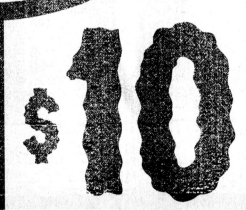

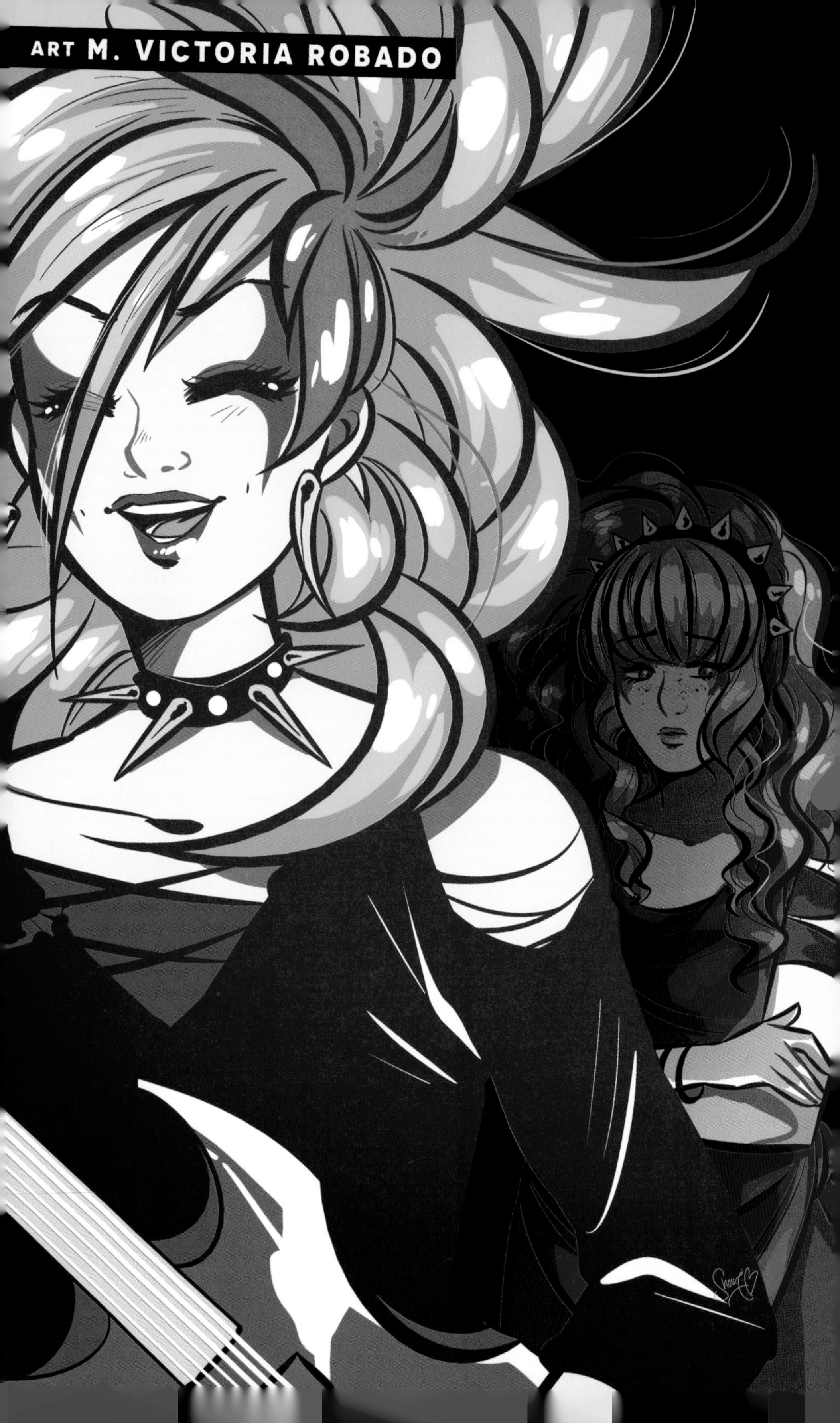
ART M. VICTORIA ROBADO

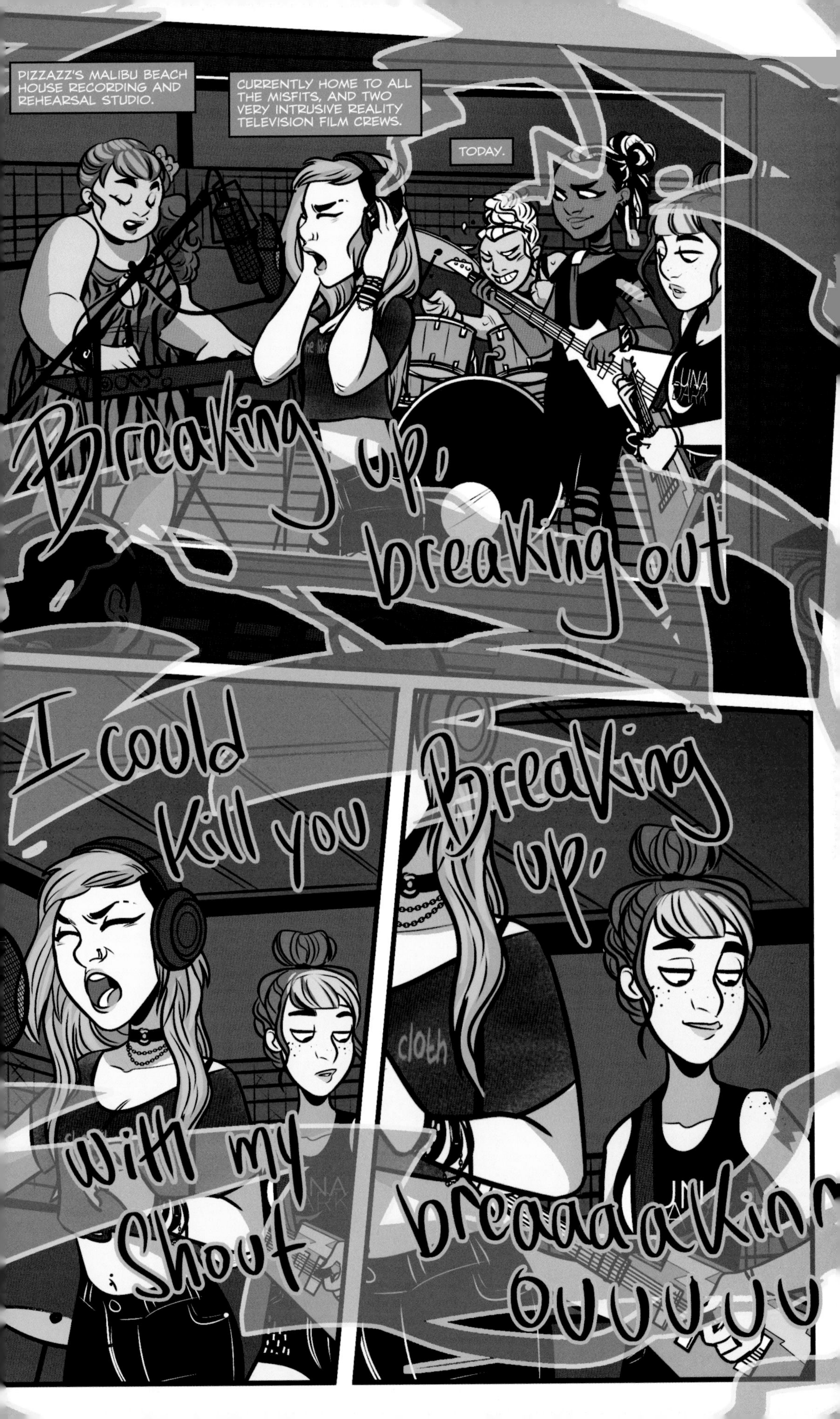
PIZZAZZ'S MALIBU BEACH HOUSE RECORDING AND REHEARSAL STUDIO.
CURRENTLY HOME TO ALL THE MISFITS, AND TWO VERY INTRUSIVE REALITY TELEVISION FILM CREWS.
TODAY.
Breaking up, breaking out
I could kill you with my shout
Breaking up, breaaaaakinn ouuuuuu

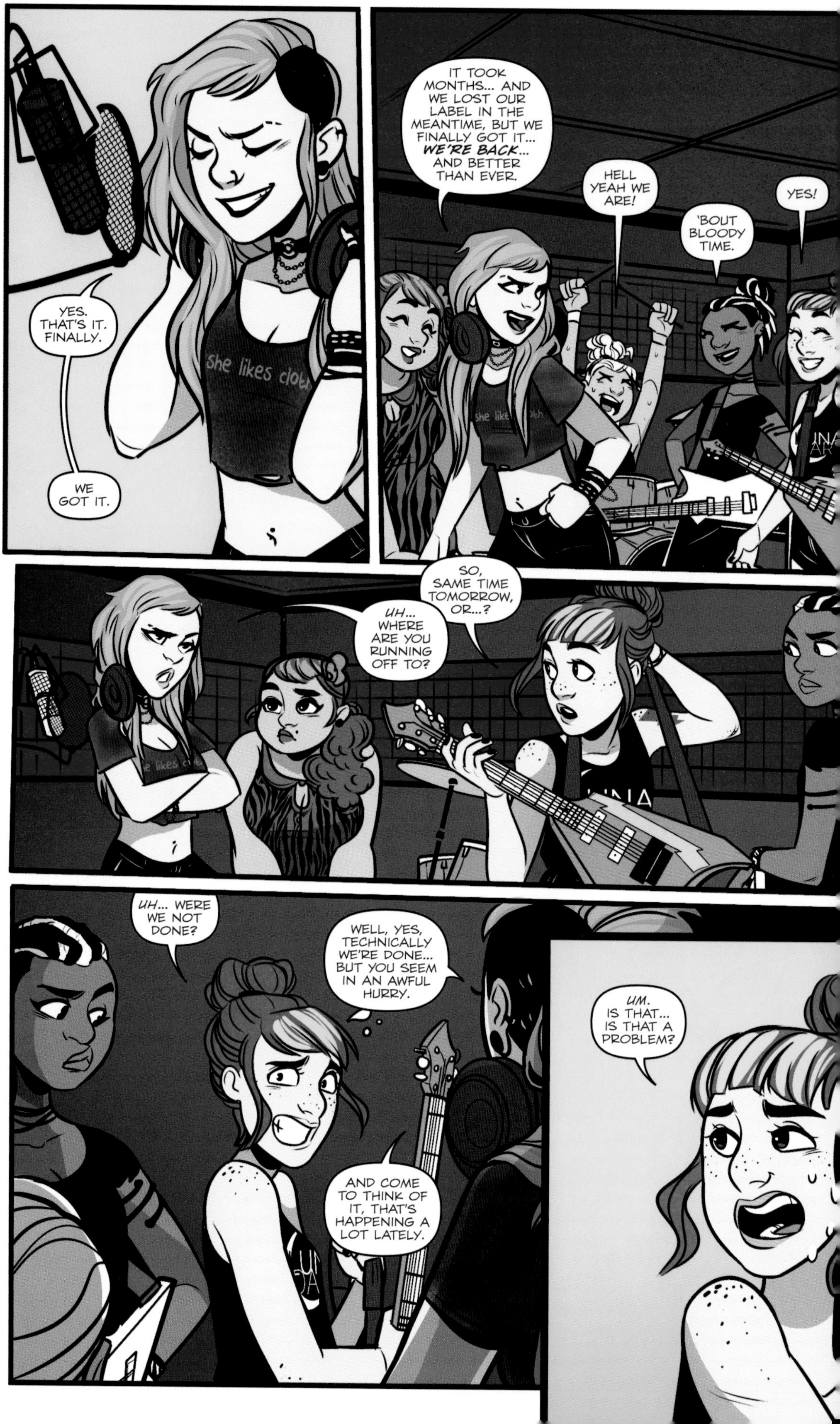
YES. THAT'S IT. FINALLY.
WE GOT IT.
she likes cloth
IT TOOK MONTHS... AND WE LOST OUR LABEL IN THE MEANTIME, BUT WE FINALLY GOT IT... *WE'RE BACK*... AND BETTER THAN EVER.
HELL YEAH WE ARE!
'BOUT BLOODY TIME.
YES!
SO, SAME TIME TOMORROW, OR...?
UH... WHERE ARE YOU RUNNING OFF TO?
UH... WERE WE NOT DONE?
WELL, YES, TECHNICALLY WE'RE DONE... BUT YOU SEEM IN AN AWFUL HURRY.
AND COME TO THINK OF IT, THAT'S HAPPENING A LOT LATELY.
UM. IS THAT... IS THAT A PROBLEM?

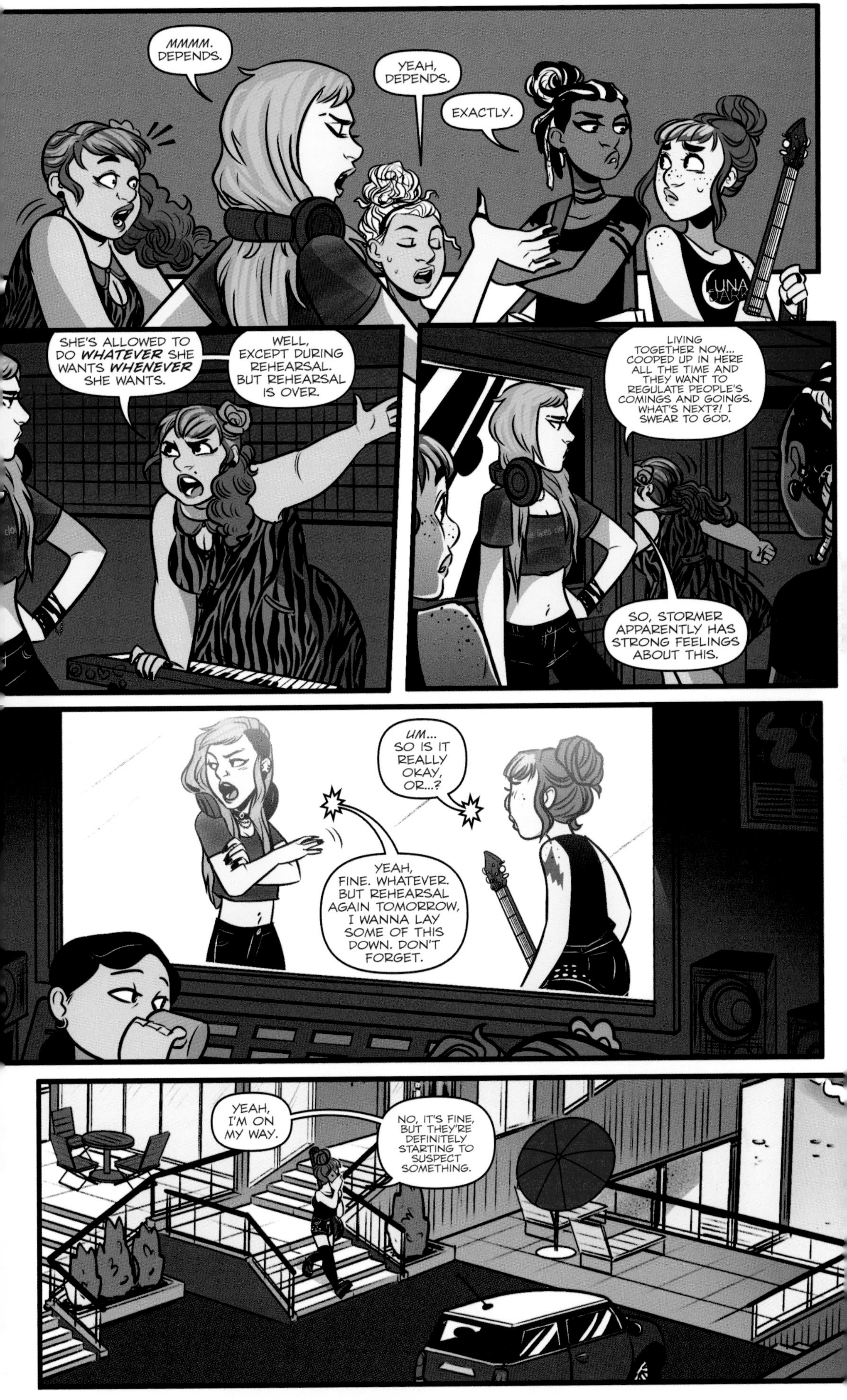
MMMM. DEPENDS.
YEAH, DEPENDS.
EXACTLY.
LUNA DARK
SHE'S ALLOWED TO DO **WHATEVER** SHE WANTS **WHENEVER** SHE WANTS.
WELL, EXCEPT DURING REHEARSAL. BUT REHEARSAL IS OVER.
LIVING TOGETHER NOW... COOPED UP IN HERE ALL THE TIME AND THEY WANT TO REGULATE PEOPLE'S COMINGS AND GOINGS. WHAT'S NEXT?! I SWEAR TO GOD.
SO, STORMER APPARENTLY HAS STRONG FEELINGS ABOUT THIS.
UM... SO IS IT REALLY OKAY, OR...?
YEAH, FINE. WHATEVER. BUT REHEARSAL AGAIN TOMORROW, I WANNA LAY SOME OF THIS DOWN. DON'T FORGET.
YEAH, I'M ON MY WAY.
NO, IT'S FINE, BUT THEY'RE DEFINITELY STARTING TO SUSPECT SOMETHING.

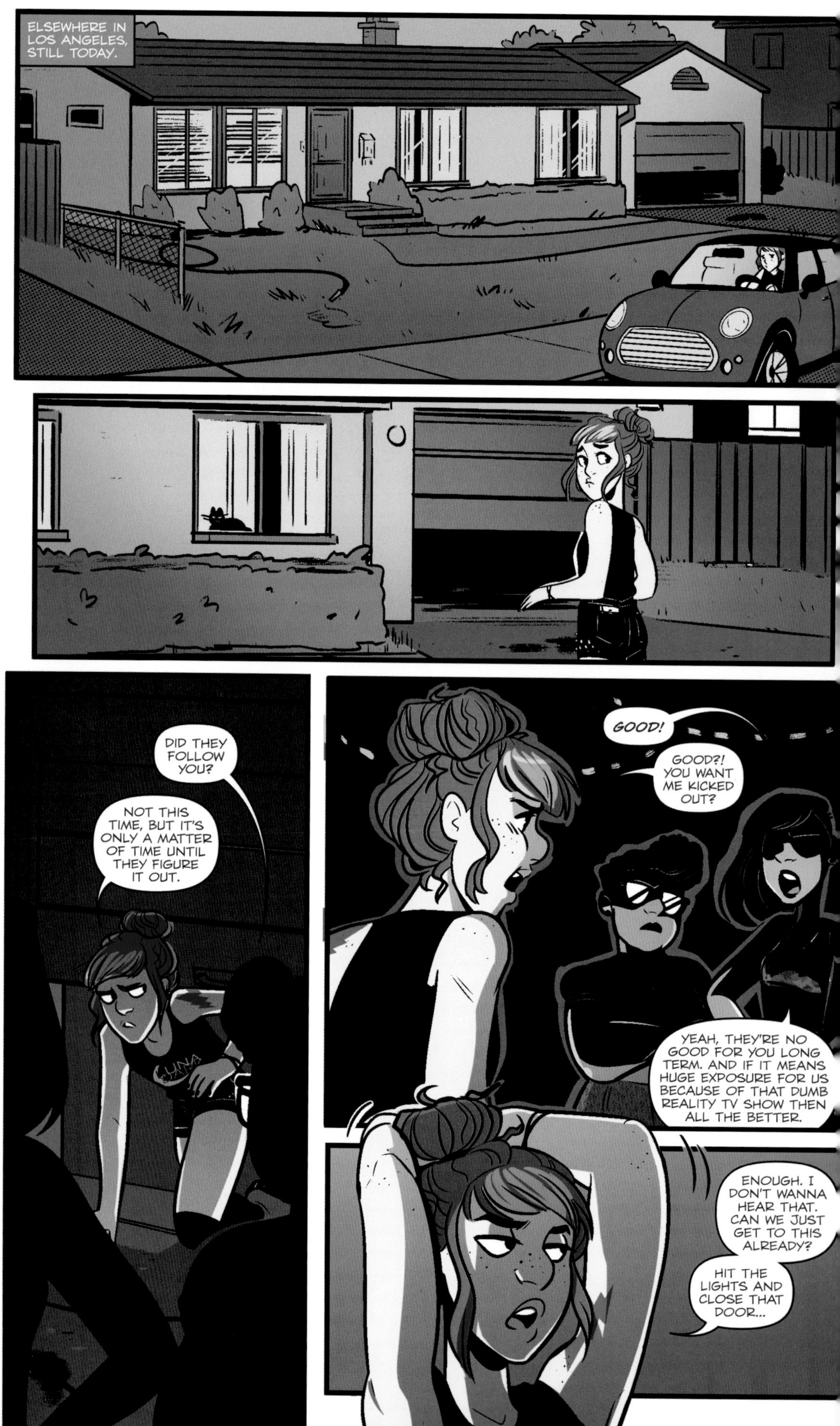
ELSEWHERE IN LOS ANGELES, STILL TODAY.
DID THEY FOLLOW YOU?
NOT THIS TIME, BUT IT'S ONLY A MATTER OF TIME UNTIL THEY FIGURE IT OUT.
GOOD!
GOOD?! YOU WANT ME KICKED OUT?
YEAH, THEY'RE NO GOOD FOR YOU LONG TERM. AND IF IT MEANS HUGE EXPOSURE FOR US BECAUSE OF THAT DUMB REALITY TV SHOW THEN ALL THE BETTER.
ENOUGH. I DON'T WANNA HEAR THAT. CAN WE JUST GET TO THIS ALREADY?
HIT THE LIGHTS AND CLOSE THAT DOOR...

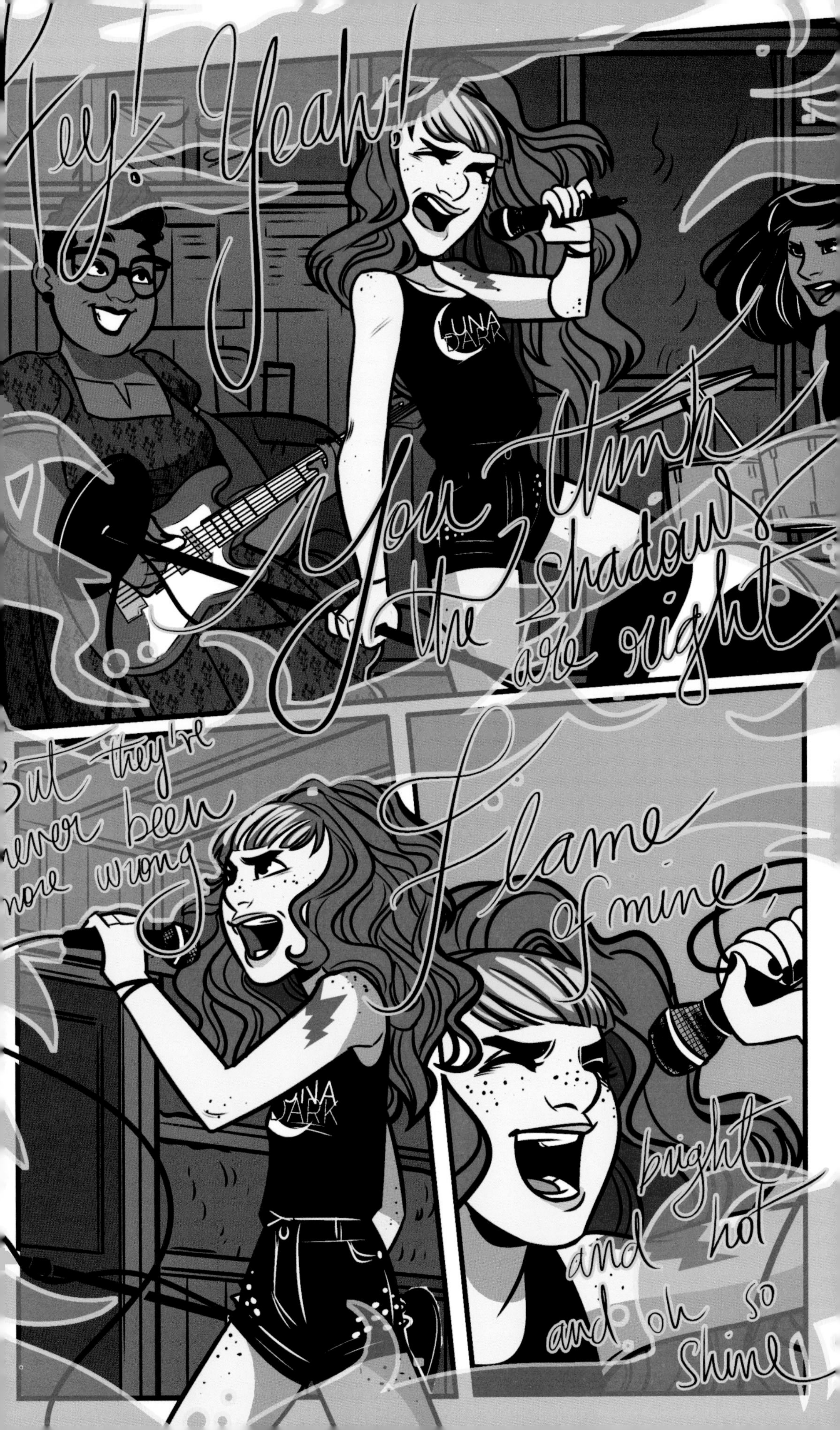
Hey! Yeah!
You think the shadows are right
LUNA DARK
But they've never been more wrong
LUNA DARK
Flame of mine,
bright and hot and oh so shine

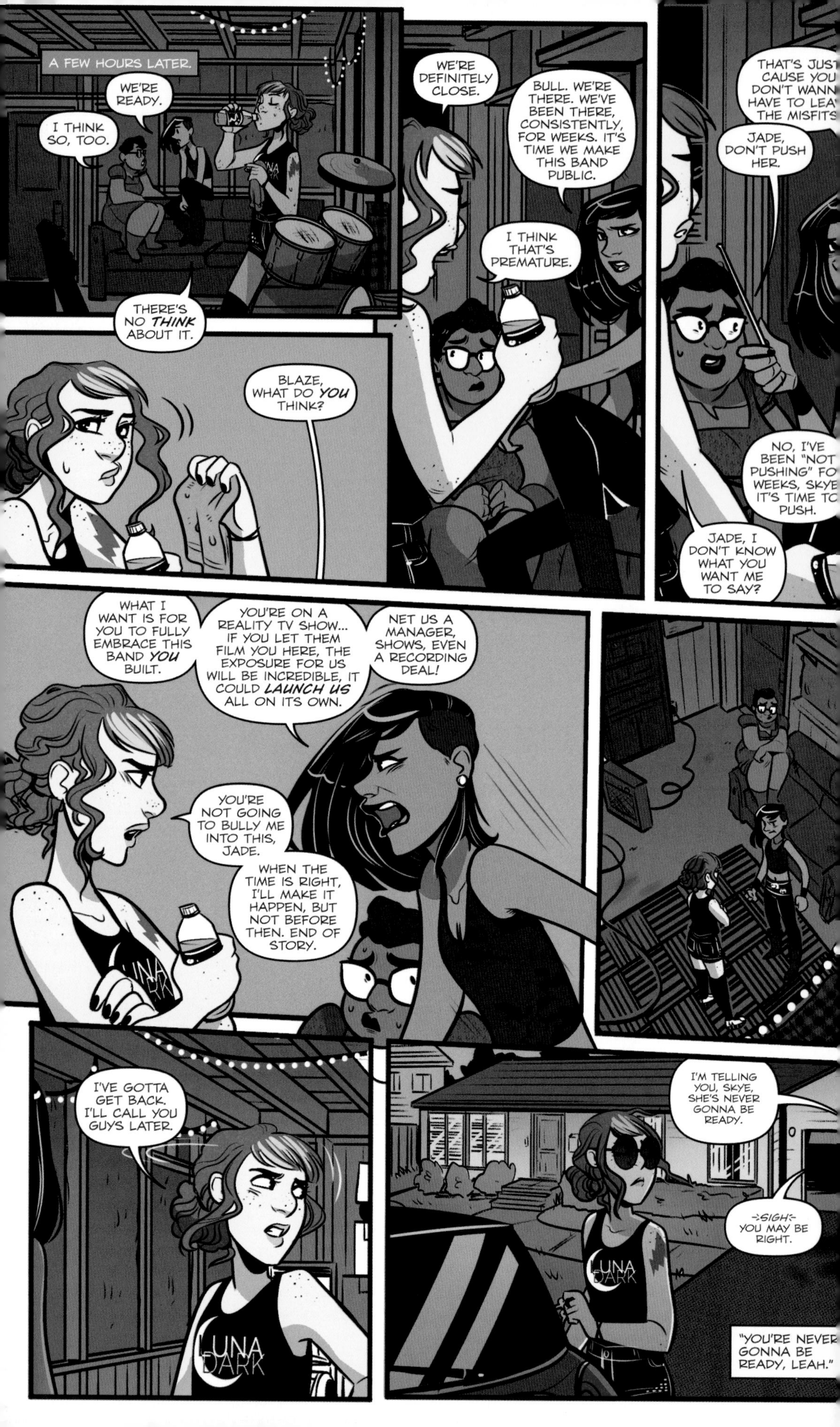

A FEW HOURS LATER.
WE'RE READY.
I THINK SO, TOO.
THERE'S NO ***THINK*** ABOUT IT.
WE'RE DEFINITELY CLOSE.
BULL. WE'RE THERE. WE'VE BEEN THERE, CONSISTENTLY, FOR WEEKS. IT'S TIME WE MAKE THIS BAND PUBLIC.
I THINK THAT'S PREMATURE.
THAT'S JUST CAUSE YOU DON'T WANN HAVE TO LEA THE MISFITS
JADE, DON'T PUSH HER.
BLAZE, WHAT DO ***YOU*** THINK?
NO, I'VE BEEN "NOT PUSHING" FO WEEKS, SKYE IT'S TIME TO PUSH.
JADE, I DON'T KNOW WHAT YOU WANT ME TO SAY?
WHAT I WANT IS FOR YOU TO FULLY EMBRACE THIS BAND ***YOU*** BUILT.
YOU'RE ON A REALITY TV SHOW... IF YOU LET THEM FILM YOU HERE, THE EXPOSURE FOR US WILL BE INCREDIBLE, IT COULD ***LAUNCH US*** ALL ON ITS OWN.
NET US A MANAGER, SHOWS, EVEN A RECORDING DEAL!
YOU'RE NOT GOING TO BULLY ME INTO THIS, JADE.
WHEN THE TIME IS RIGHT, I'LL MAKE IT HAPPEN, BUT NOT BEFORE THEN. END OF STORY.
I'VE GOTTA GET BACK. I'LL CALL YOU GUYS LATER.
LUNA DARK
I'M TELLING YOU, SKYE, SHE'S NEVER GONNA BE READY.
-SIGH- YOU MAY BE RIGHT.
"YOU'RE NEVER GONNA BE READY, LEAH."

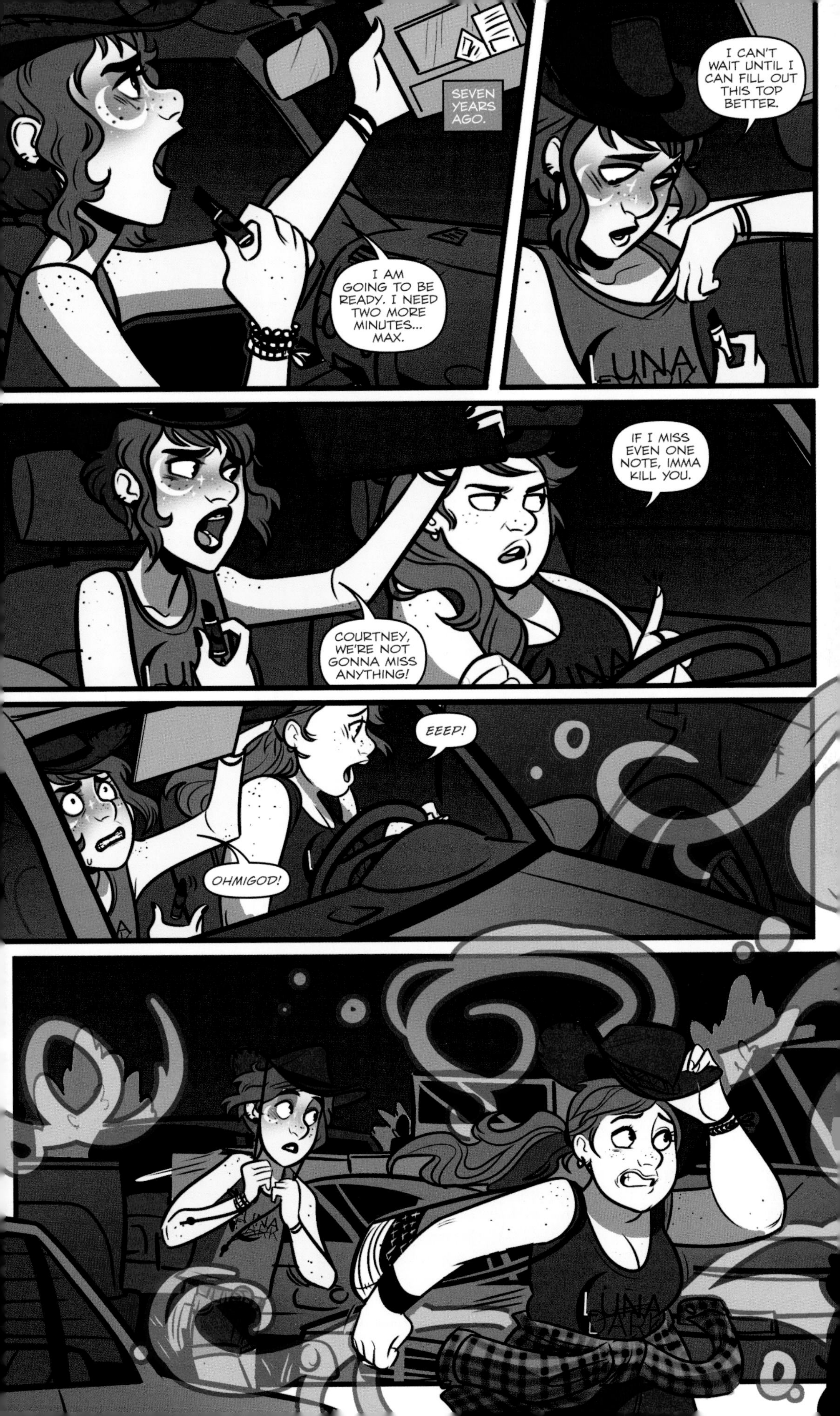
SEVEN YEARS AGO.
I AM GOING TO BE READY. I NEED TWO MORE MINUTES... MAX.
I CAN'T WAIT UNTIL I CAN FILL OUT THIS TOP BETTER.
LUNA
IF I MISS EVEN ONE NOTE, IMMA KILL YOU.
COURTNEY, WE'RE NOT GONNA MISS ANYTHING!
EEEP!
OHMIGOD!

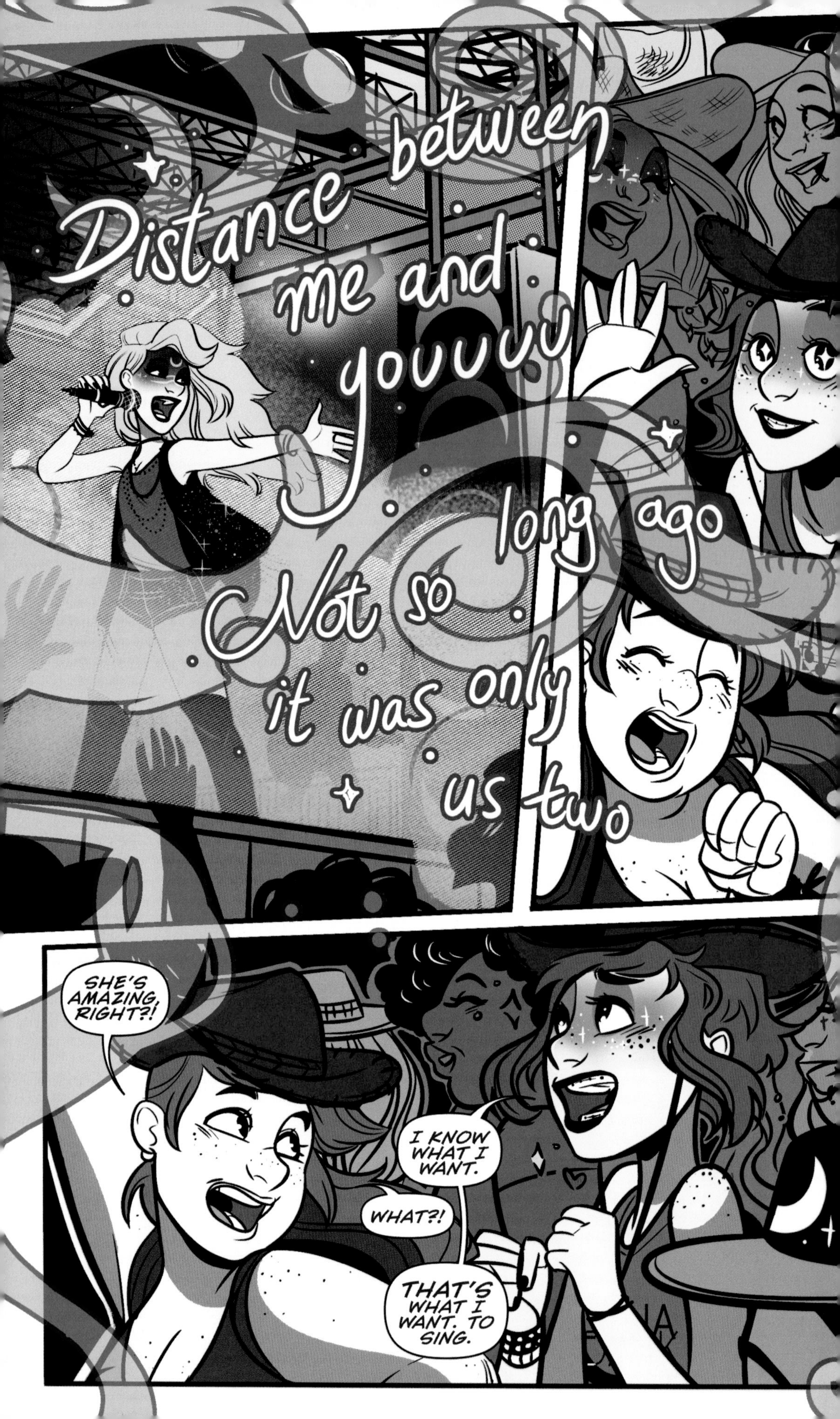
Distance between
me and
youuuu
Not so long ago
it was only
us two
SHE'S AMAZING, RIGHT?!
I KNOW WHAT I WANT.
WHAT?!
THAT'S WHAT I WANT. TO SING.

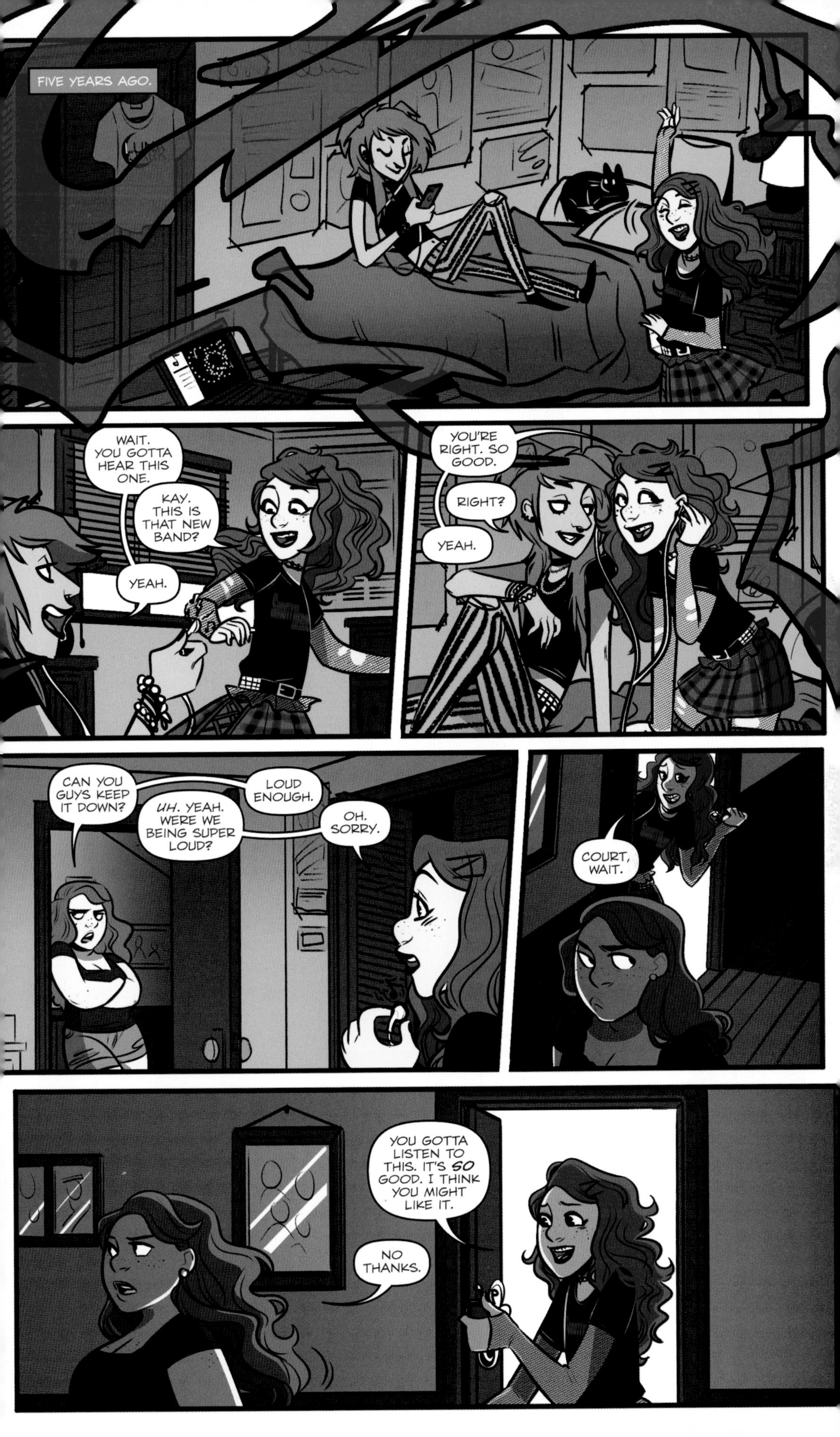
FIVE YEARS AGO.
WAIT. YOU GOTTA HEAR THIS ONE.
KAY. THIS IS THAT NEW BAND?
YEAH.
YOU'RE RIGHT. SO GOOD.
RIGHT?
YEAH.
CAN YOU GUYS KEEP IT DOWN?
UH. YEAH. WERE WE BEING SUPER LOUD?
LOUD ENOUGH.
OH. SORRY.
COURT, WAIT.
YOU GOTTA LISTEN TO THIS. IT'S SO GOOD. I THINK YOU MIGHT LIKE IT.
NO THANKS.

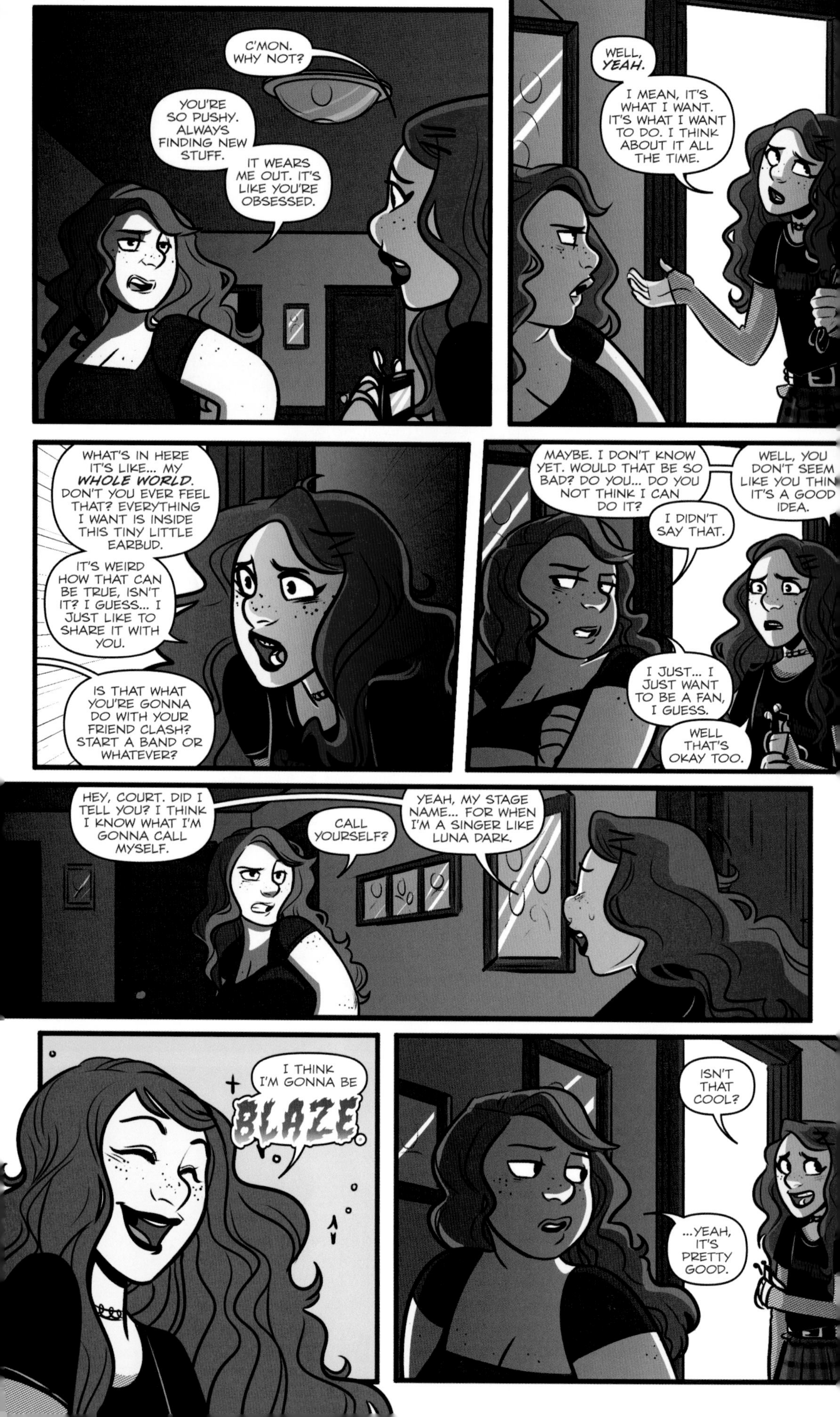
C'MON. WHY NOT?
YOU'RE SO PUSHY. ALWAYS FINDING NEW STUFF.
IT WEARS ME OUT. IT'S LIKE YOU'RE OBSESSED.
WELL, YEAH.
I MEAN, IT'S WHAT I WANT. IT'S WHAT I WANT TO DO. I THINK ABOUT IT ALL THE TIME.
WHAT'S IN HERE IT'S LIKE... MY WHOLE WORLD. DON'T YOU EVER FEEL THAT? EVERYTHING I WANT IS INSIDE THIS TINY LITTLE EARBUD.
IT'S WEIRD HOW THAT CAN BE TRUE, ISN'T IT? I GUESS... I JUST LIKE TO SHARE IT WITH YOU.
IS THAT WHAT YOU'RE GONNA DO WITH YOUR FRIEND CLASH? START A BAND OR WHATEVER?
MAYBE. I DON'T KNOW YET. WOULD THAT BE SO BAD? DO YOU... DO YOU NOT THINK I CAN DO IT?
WELL, YOU DON'T SEEM LIKE YOU THIN IT'S A GOOD IDEA.
I DIDN'T SAY THAT.
I JUST... I JUST WANT TO BE A FAN, I GUESS.
WELL THAT'S OKAY TOO.
HEY, COURT. DID I TELL YOU? I THINK I KNOW WHAT I'M GONNA CALL MYSELF.
CALL YOURSELF?
YEAH, MY STAGE NAME... FOR WHEN I'M A SINGER LIKE LUNA DARK.
I THINK I'M GONNA BE BLAZE.
ISN'T THAT COOL?
...YEAH, IT'S PRETTY GOOD.

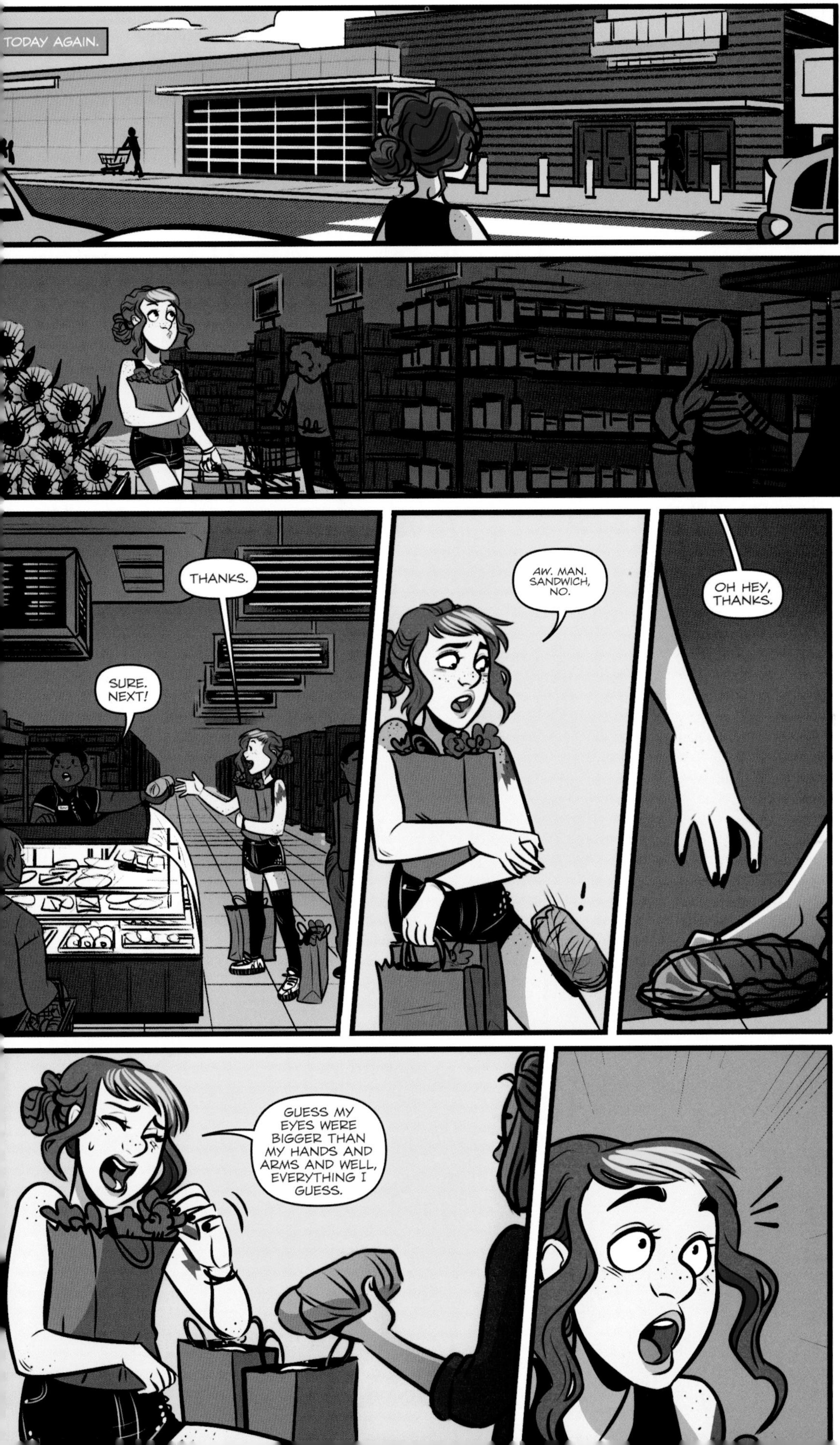
TODAY AGAIN.
THANKS.
SURE. NEXT!
AW. MAN. SANDWICH, NO.
!
OH HEY, THANKS.
GUESS MY EYES WERE BIGGER THAN MY HANDS AND ARMS AND WELL, EVERYTHING I GUESS.

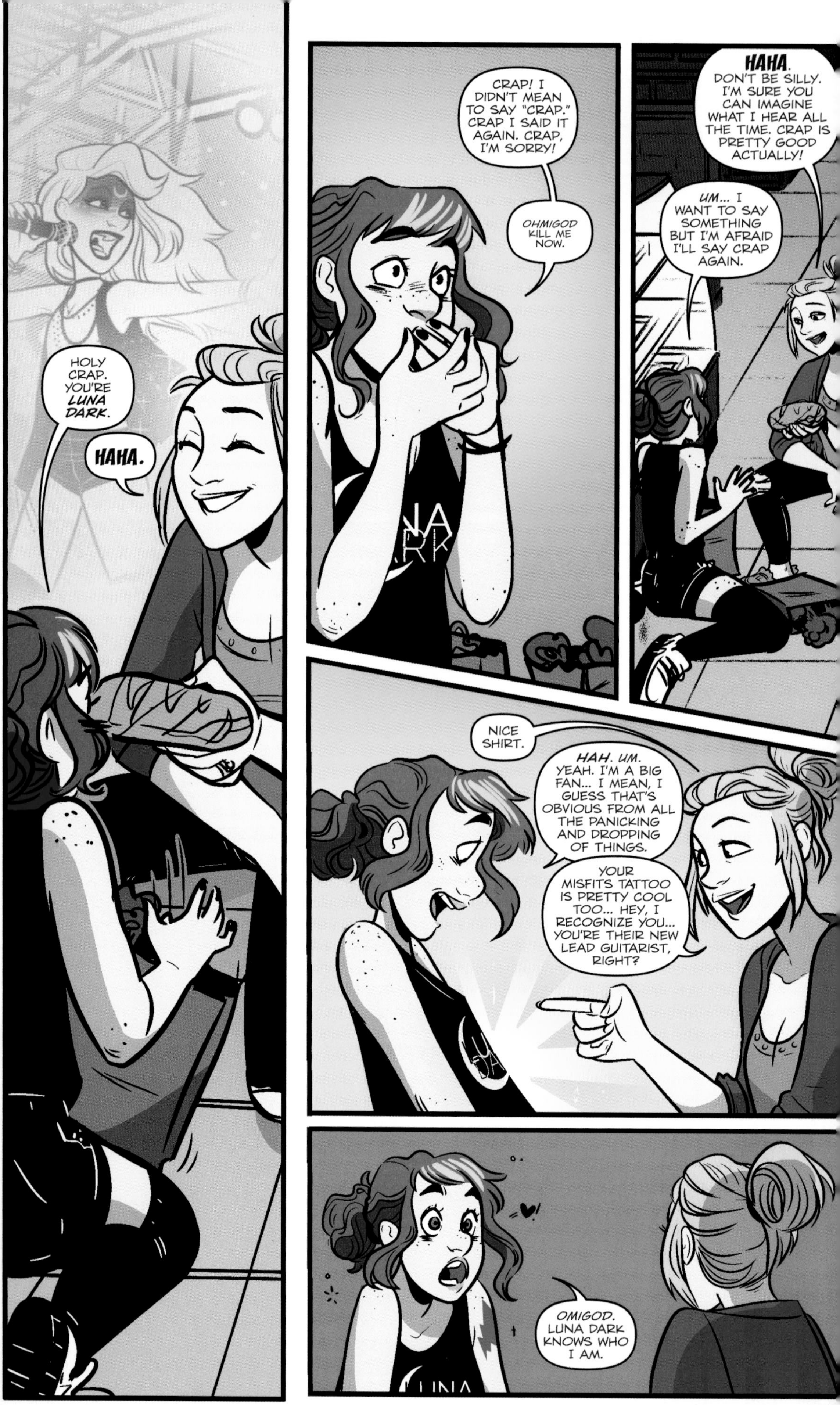
HOLY CRAP. YOU'RE LUNA DARK.
HAHA.
CRAP! I DIDN'T MEAN TO SAY "CRAP." CRAP I SAID IT AGAIN. CRAP, I'M SORRY!
OHMIGOD KILL ME NOW.
HAHA. DON'T BE SILLY. I'M SURE YOU CAN IMAGINE WHAT I HEAR ALL THE TIME. CRAP IS PRETTY GOOD ACTUALLY!
UM... I WANT TO SAY SOMETHING BUT I'M AFRAID I'LL SAY CRAP AGAIN.
NICE SHIRT.
HAH. UM. YEAH. I'M A BIG FAN... I MEAN, I GUESS THAT'S OBVIOUS FROM ALL THE PANICKING AND DROPPING OF THINGS.
YOUR MISFITS TATTOO IS PRETTY COOL TOO... HEY, I RECOGNIZE YOU... YOU'RE THEIR NEW LEAD GUITARIST, RIGHT?
OMIGOD. LUNA DARK KNOWS WHO I AM.

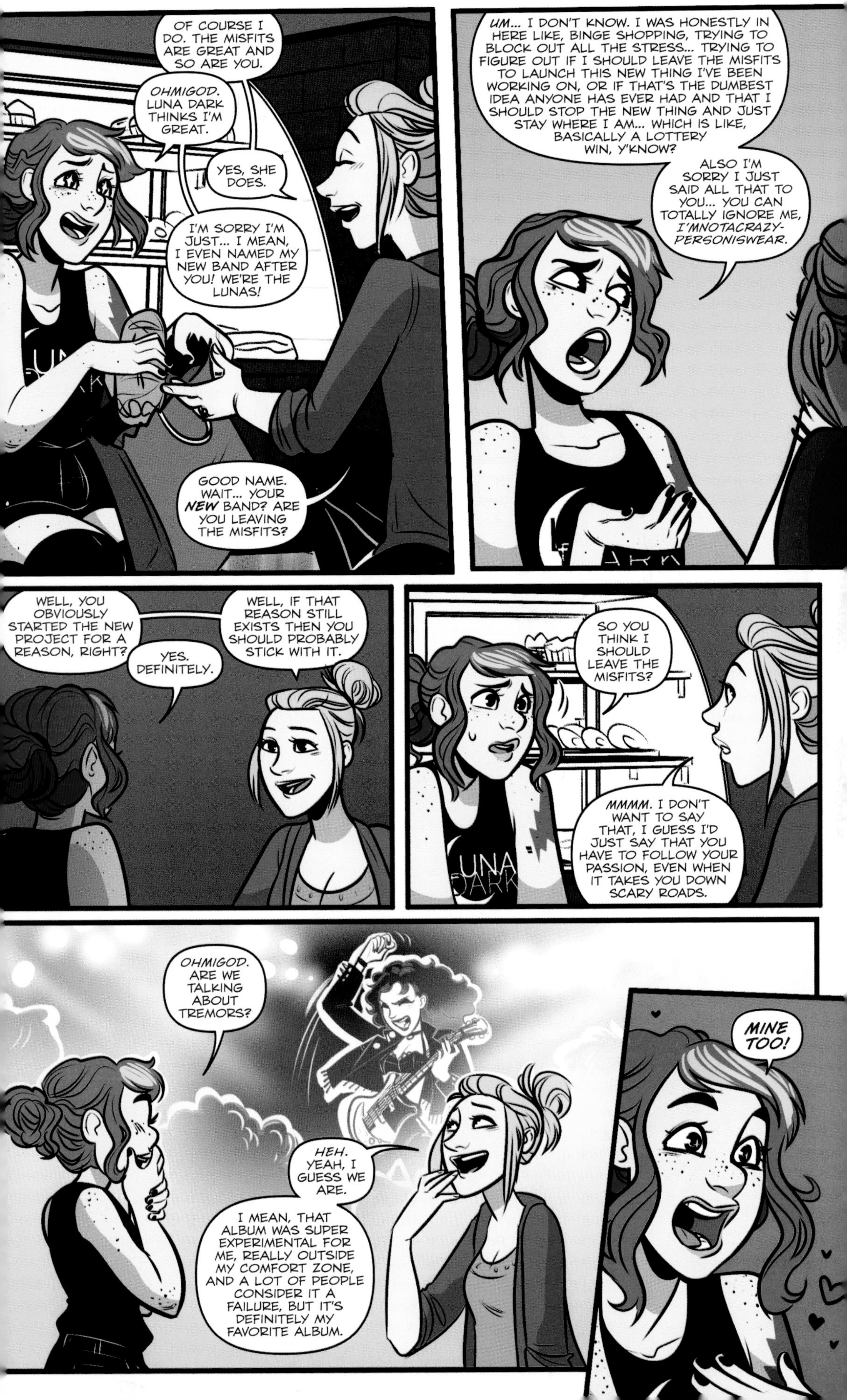

OF COURSE I DO. THE MISFITS ARE GREAT AND SO ARE YOU.
OHMIGOD. LUNA DARK THINKS I'M GREAT.
YES, SHE DOES.
I'M SORRY I'M JUST... I MEAN, I EVEN NAMED MY NEW BAND AFTER YOU! WE'RE THE LUNAS!
GOOD NAME. WAIT... YOUR NEW BAND? ARE YOU LEAVING THE MISFITS?
UM... I DON'T KNOW. I WAS HONESTLY IN HERE LIKE, BINGE SHOPPING, TRYING TO BLOCK OUT ALL THE STRESS... TRYING TO FIGURE OUT IF I SHOULD LEAVE THE MISFITS TO LAUNCH THIS NEW THING I'VE BEEN WORKING ON, OR IF THAT'S THE DUMBEST IDEA ANYONE HAS EVER HAD AND THAT I SHOULD STOP THE NEW THING AND JUST STAY WHERE I AM... WHICH IS LIKE, BASICALLY A LOTTERY WIN, Y'KNOW?
ALSO I'M SORRY I JUST SAID ALL THAT TO YOU... YOU CAN TOTALLY IGNORE ME, I'MNOTACRAZYPERSONISWEAR.
WELL, YOU OBVIOUSLY STARTED THE NEW PROJECT FOR A REASON, RIGHT?
YES. DEFINITELY.
WELL, IF THAT REASON STILL EXISTS THEN YOU SHOULD PROBABLY STICK WITH IT.
SO YOU THINK I SHOULD LEAVE THE MISFITS?
MMMM. I DON'T WANT TO SAY THAT, I GUESS I'D JUST SAY THAT YOU HAVE TO FOLLOW YOUR PASSION, EVEN WHEN IT TAKES YOU DOWN SCARY ROADS.
OHMIGOD. ARE WE TALKING ABOUT TREMORS?
HEH. YEAH, I GUESS WE ARE.
I MEAN, THAT ALBUM WAS SUPER EXPERIMENTAL FOR ME, REALLY OUTSIDE MY COMFORT ZONE, AND A LOT OF PEOPLE CONSIDER IT A FAILURE, BUT IT'S DEFINITELY MY FAVORITE ALBUM.
MINE TOO!

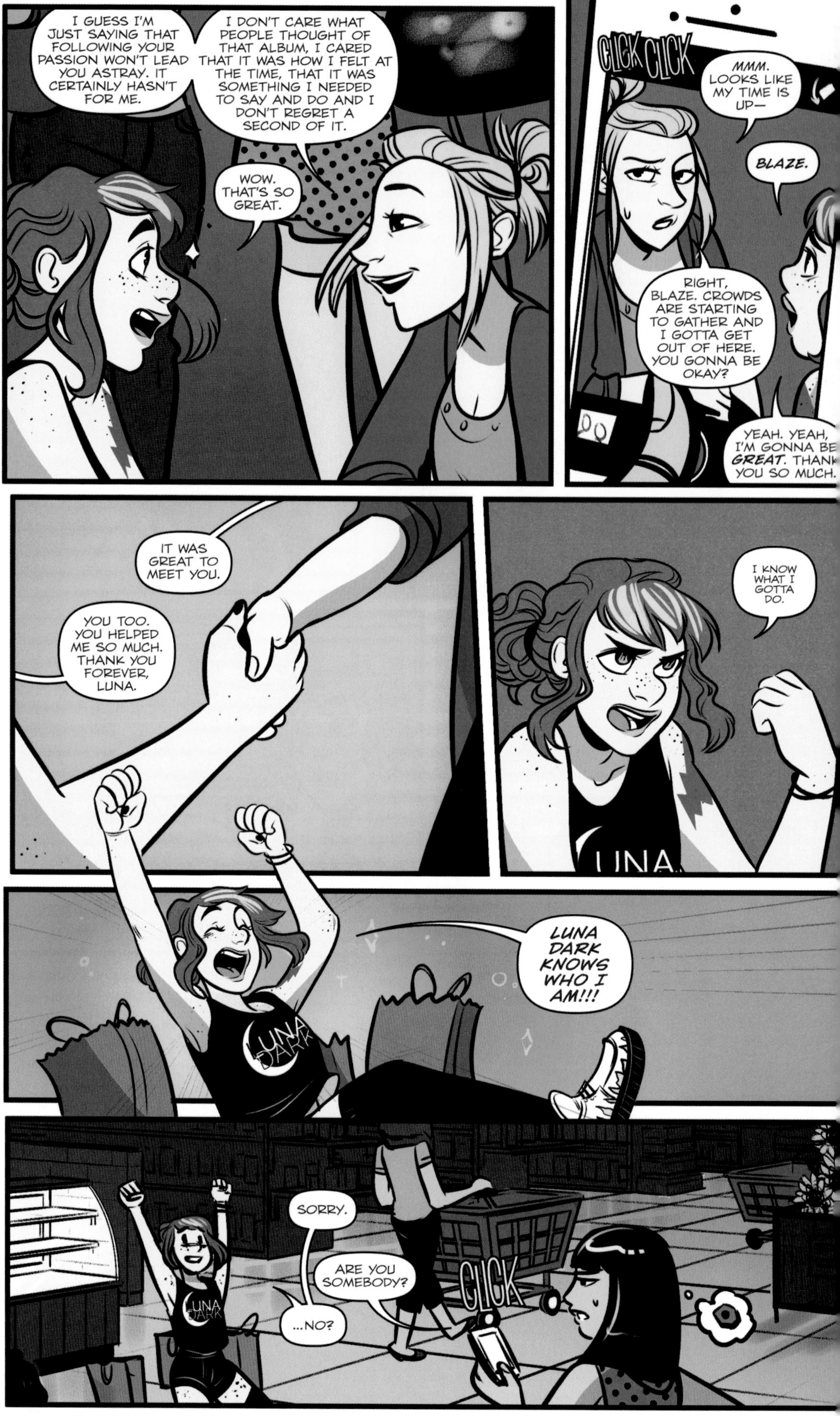

I GUESS I'M JUST SAYING THAT FOLLOWING YOUR PASSION WON'T LEAD YOU ASTRAY. IT CERTAINLY HASN'T FOR ME.
I DON'T CARE WHAT PEOPLE THOUGHT OF THAT ALBUM, I CARED THAT IT WAS HOW I FELT AT THE TIME, THAT IT WAS SOMETHING I NEEDED TO SAY AND DO AND I DON'T REGRET A SECOND OF IT.
WOW. THAT'S SO GREAT.
CLICK CLICK
MMM. LOOKS LIKE MY TIME IS UP—
BLAZE.
RIGHT, BLAZE. CROWDS ARE STARTING TO GATHER AND I GOTTA GET OUT OF HERE. YOU GONNA BE OKAY?
YEAH. YEAH, I'M GONNA BE GREAT. THANK YOU SO MUCH.
IT WAS GREAT TO MEET YOU.
YOU TOO. YOU HELPED ME SO MUCH. THANK YOU FOREVER, LUNA.
I KNOW WHAT I GOTTA DO.
LUNA
LUNA DARK KNOWS WHO I AM!!!
LUNA DARK
SORRY.
ARE YOU SOMEBODY?
...NO?
CLICK
LUNA DARK

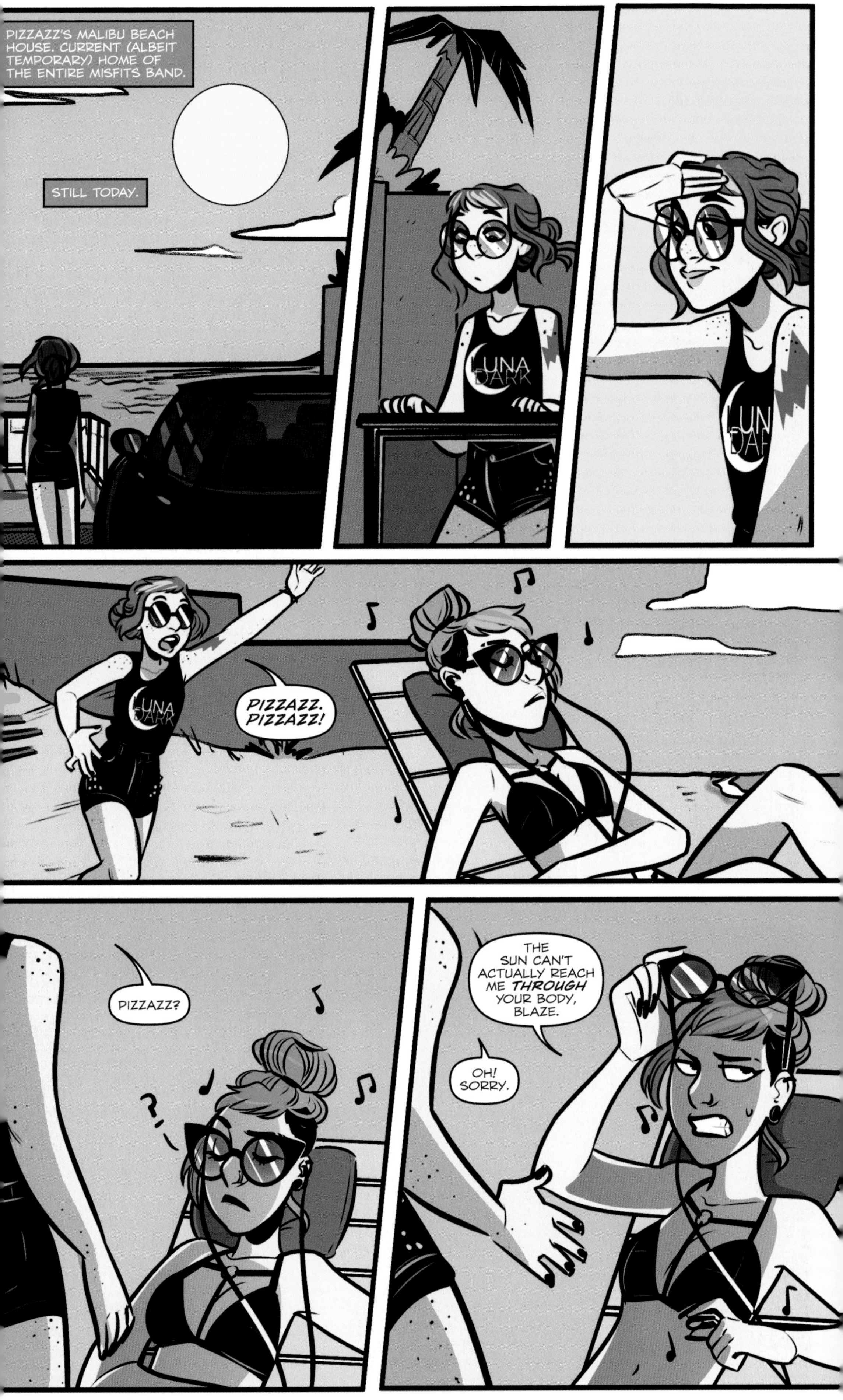
PIZZAZZ'S MALIBU BEACH HOUSE. CURRENT (ALBEIT TEMPORARY) HOME OF THE ENTIRE MISFITS BAND.
STILL TODAY.
LUNA DARK
PIZZAZZ. PIZZAZZ!
PIZZAZZ?
?
THE SUN CAN'T ACTUALLY REACH ME ***THROUGH*** YOUR BODY, BLAZE.
OH! SORRY.

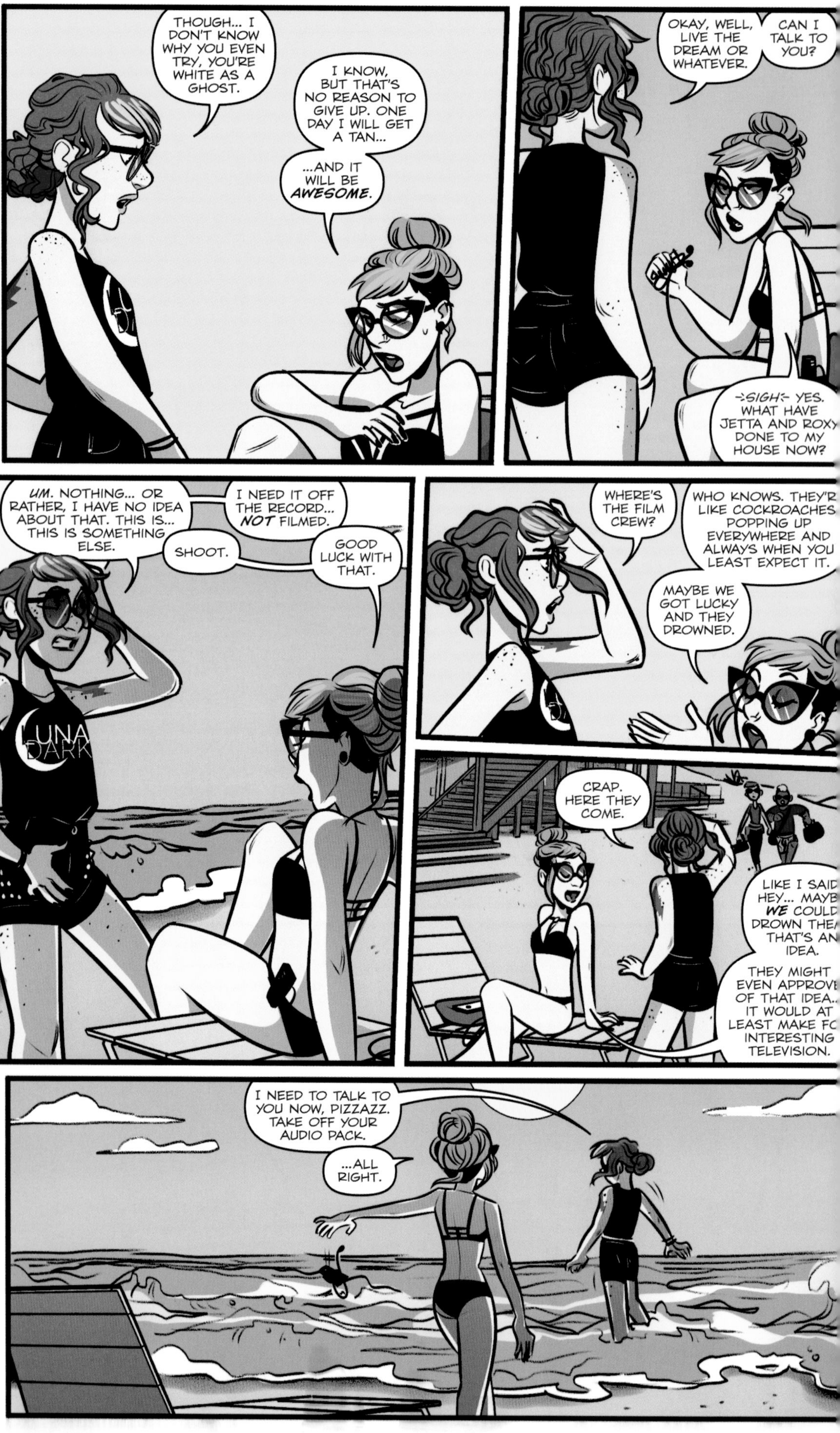
THOUGH... I DON'T KNOW WHY YOU EVEN TRY, YOU'RE WHITE AS A GHOST.
I KNOW, BUT THAT'S NO REASON TO GIVE UP. ONE DAY I WILL GET A TAN...
...AND IT WILL BE *AWESOME*.
OKAY, WELL, LIVE THE DREAM OR WHATEVER.
CAN I TALK TO YOU?
-SIGH- YES. WHAT HAVE JETTA AND ROXY DONE TO MY HOUSE NOW?
UM. NOTHING... OR RATHER, I HAVE NO IDEA ABOUT THAT. THIS IS... THIS IS SOMETHING ELSE.
I NEED IT OFF THE RECORD... *NOT* FILMED.
SHOOT.
GOOD LUCK WITH THAT.
LUNA DARK
WHERE'S THE FILM CREW?
WHO KNOWS. THEY'RE LIKE COCKROACHES POPPING UP EVERYWHERE AND ALWAYS WHEN YOU LEAST EXPECT IT.
MAYBE WE GOT LUCKY AND THEY DROWNED.
CRAP. HERE THEY COME.
LIKE I SAID HEY... MAYBE *WE* COULD DROWN THEM. THAT'S AN IDEA.
THEY MIGHT EVEN APPROVE OF THAT IDEA... IT WOULD AT LEAST MAKE FOR INTERESTING TELEVISION.
I NEED TO TALK TO YOU NOW, PIZZAZZ. TAKE OFF YOUR AUDIO PACK.
...ALL RIGHT.

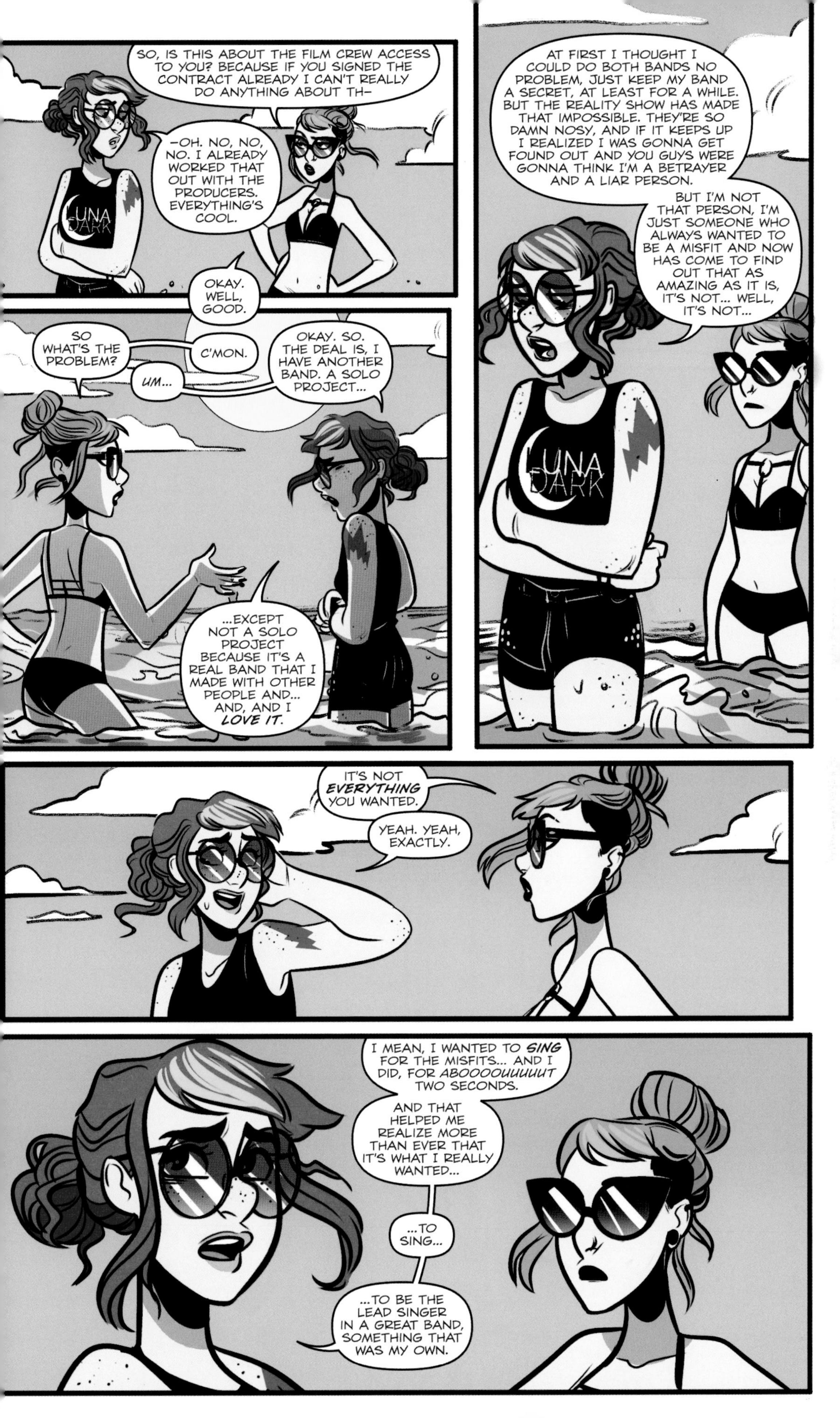
SO, IS THIS ABOUT THE FILM CREW ACCESS TO YOU? BECAUSE IF YOU SIGNED THE CONTRACT ALREADY I CAN'T REALLY DO ANYTHING ABOUT TH–
–OH. NO, NO, NO. I ALREADY WORKED THAT OUT WITH THE PRODUCERS. EVERYTHING'S COOL.
OKAY. WELL, GOOD.
SO WHAT'S THE PROBLEM?
C'MON.
UM...
OKAY. SO. THE DEAL IS, I HAVE ANOTHER BAND. A SOLO PROJECT...
...EXCEPT NOT A SOLO PROJECT BECAUSE IT'S A REAL BAND THAT I MADE WITH OTHER PEOPLE AND... AND, AND I *LOVE IT*.
LUNA DARK
AT FIRST I THOUGHT I COULD DO BOTH BANDS NO PROBLEM, JUST KEEP MY BAND A SECRET, AT LEAST FOR A WHILE. BUT THE REALITY SHOW HAS MADE THAT IMPOSSIBLE. THEY'RE SO DAMN NOSY, AND IF IT KEEPS UP I REALIZED I WAS GONNA GET FOUND OUT AND YOU GUYS WERE GONNA THINK I'M A BETRAYER AND A LIAR PERSON.
BUT I'M NOT THAT PERSON, I'M JUST SOMEONE WHO ALWAYS WANTED TO BE A MISFIT AND NOW HAS COME TO FIND OUT THAT AS AMAZING AS IT IS, IT'S NOT... WELL, IT'S NOT...
IT'S NOT *EVERYTHING* YOU WANTED.
YEAH. YEAH, EXACTLY.
I MEAN, I WANTED TO *SING* FOR THE MISFITS... AND I DID, FOR *ABOOOOUUUUUT* TWO SECONDS.
AND THAT HELPED ME REALIZE MORE THAN EVER THAT IT'S WHAT I REALLY WANTED...
...TO SING...
...TO BE THE LEAD SINGER IN A GREAT BAND, SOMETHING THAT WAS MY OWN.

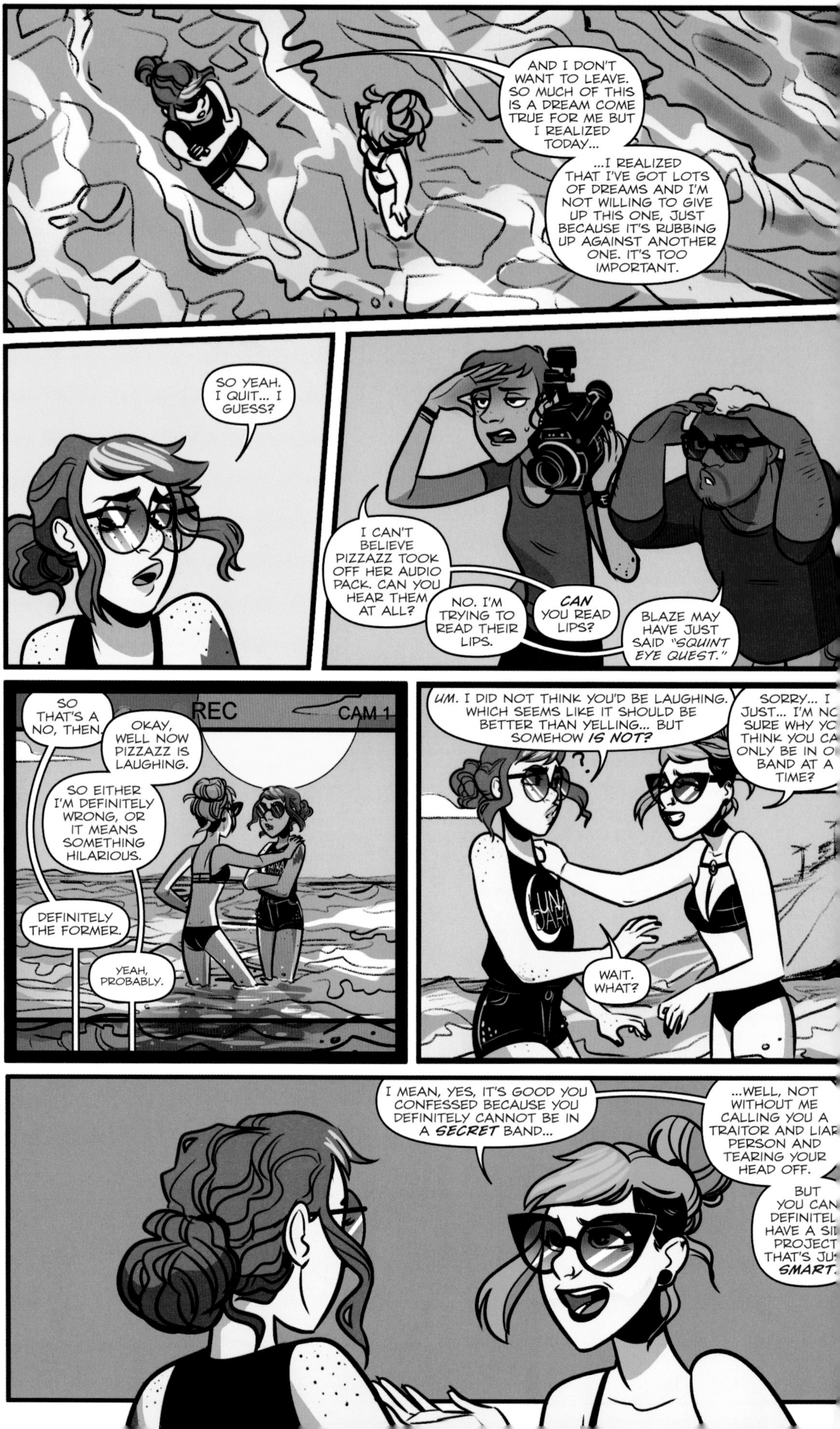
AND I DON'T WANT TO LEAVE. SO MUCH OF THIS IS A DREAM COME TRUE FOR ME BUT I REALIZED TODAY...
...I REALIZED THAT I'VE GOT LOTS OF DREAMS AND I'M NOT WILLING TO GIVE UP THIS ONE, JUST BECAUSE IT'S RUBBING UP AGAINST ANOTHER ONE. IT'S TOO IMPORTANT.
SO YEAH. I QUIT... I GUESS?
I CAN'T BELIEVE PIZZAZZ TOOK OFF HER AUDIO PACK. CAN YOU HEAR THEM AT ALL?
NO. I'M TRYING TO READ THEIR LIPS.
CAN YOU READ LIPS?
BLAZE MAY HAVE JUST SAID *"SQUINT EYE QUEST."*
REC
CAM 1
SO THAT'S A NO, THEN.
OKAY, WELL NOW PIZZAZZ IS LAUGHING.
SO EITHER I'M DEFINITELY WRONG, OR IT MEANS SOMETHING HILARIOUS.
DEFINITELY THE FORMER.
YEAH, PROBABLY.
UM. I DID NOT THINK YOU'D BE LAUGHING. WHICH SEEMS LIKE IT SHOULD BE BETTER THAN YELLING... BUT SOMEHOW *IS NOT?*
SORRY... I JUST... I'M NO SURE WHY YO THINK YOU CA ONLY BE IN O BAND AT A TIME?
WAIT. WHAT?
I MEAN, YES, IT'S GOOD YOU CONFESSED BECAUSE YOU DEFINITELY CANNOT BE IN A *SECRET* BAND...
...WELL, NOT WITHOUT ME CALLING YOU A TRAITOR AND LIAR PERSON AND TEARING YOUR HEAD OFF.
BUT YOU CAN DEFINITEL HAVE A SI PROJECT THAT'S JU *SMART.*

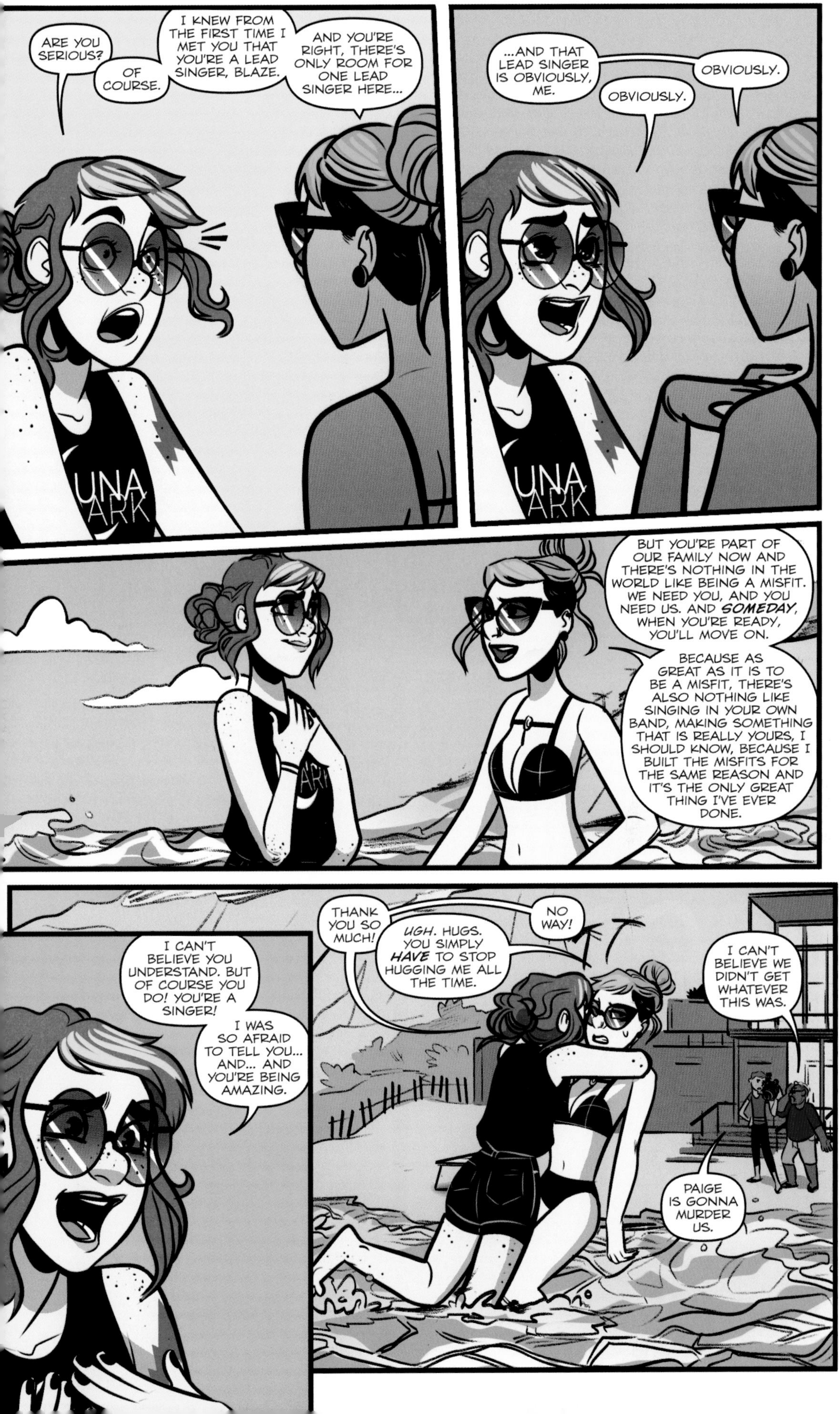
ARE YOU SERIOUS?
OF COURSE.
I KNEW FROM THE FIRST TIME I MET YOU THAT YOU'RE A LEAD SINGER, BLAZE.
AND YOU'RE RIGHT, THERE'S ONLY ROOM FOR ONE LEAD SINGER HERE...
...AND THAT LEAD SINGER IS OBVIOUSLY, ME.
OBVIOUSLY.
OBVIOUSLY.
UNA
ARK
BUT YOU'RE PART OF OUR FAMILY NOW AND THERE'S NOTHING IN THE WORLD LIKE BEING A MISFIT. WE NEED YOU, AND YOU NEED US. AND SOMEDAY, WHEN YOU'RE READY, YOU'LL MOVE ON.
BECAUSE AS GREAT AS IT IS TO BE A MISFIT, THERE'S ALSO NOTHING LIKE SINGING IN YOUR OWN BAND, MAKING SOMETHING THAT IS REALLY YOURS, I SHOULD KNOW, BECAUSE I BUILT THE MISFITS FOR THE SAME REASON AND IT'S THE ONLY GREAT THING I'VE EVER DONE.
I CAN'T BELIEVE YOU UNDERSTAND. BUT OF COURSE YOU DO! YOU'RE A SINGER!
I WAS SO AFRAID TO TELL YOU... AND... AND YOU'RE BEING AMAZING.
THANK YOU SO MUCH!
NO WAY!
UGH. HUGS. YOU SIMPLY HAVE TO STOP HUGGING ME ALL THE TIME.
I CAN'T BELIEVE WE DIDN'T GET WHATEVER THIS WAS.
PAIGE IS GONNA MURDER US.

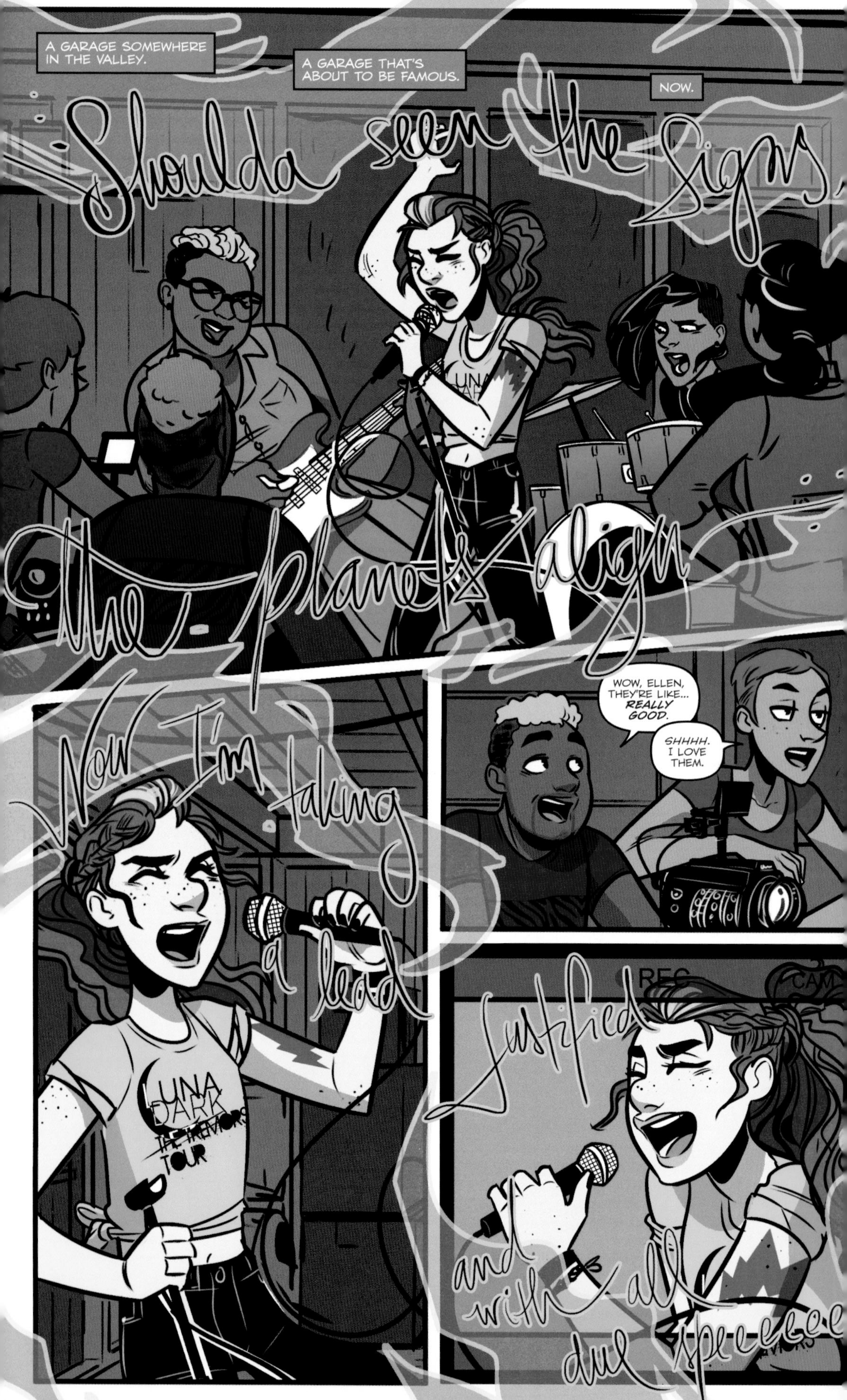
A GARAGE SOMEWHERE IN THE VALLEY.
A GARAGE THAT'S ABOUT TO BE FAMOUS.
NOW.
Shoulda seen the signs,
the planets align
Now I'm taking a lead
WOW, ELLEN, THEY'RE LIKE... *REALLY GOOD*.
SHHHH. I LOVE THEM.
LUNA DARK
THE TREMORS TOUR
REC
CAM
Justified
and with all due speeeee

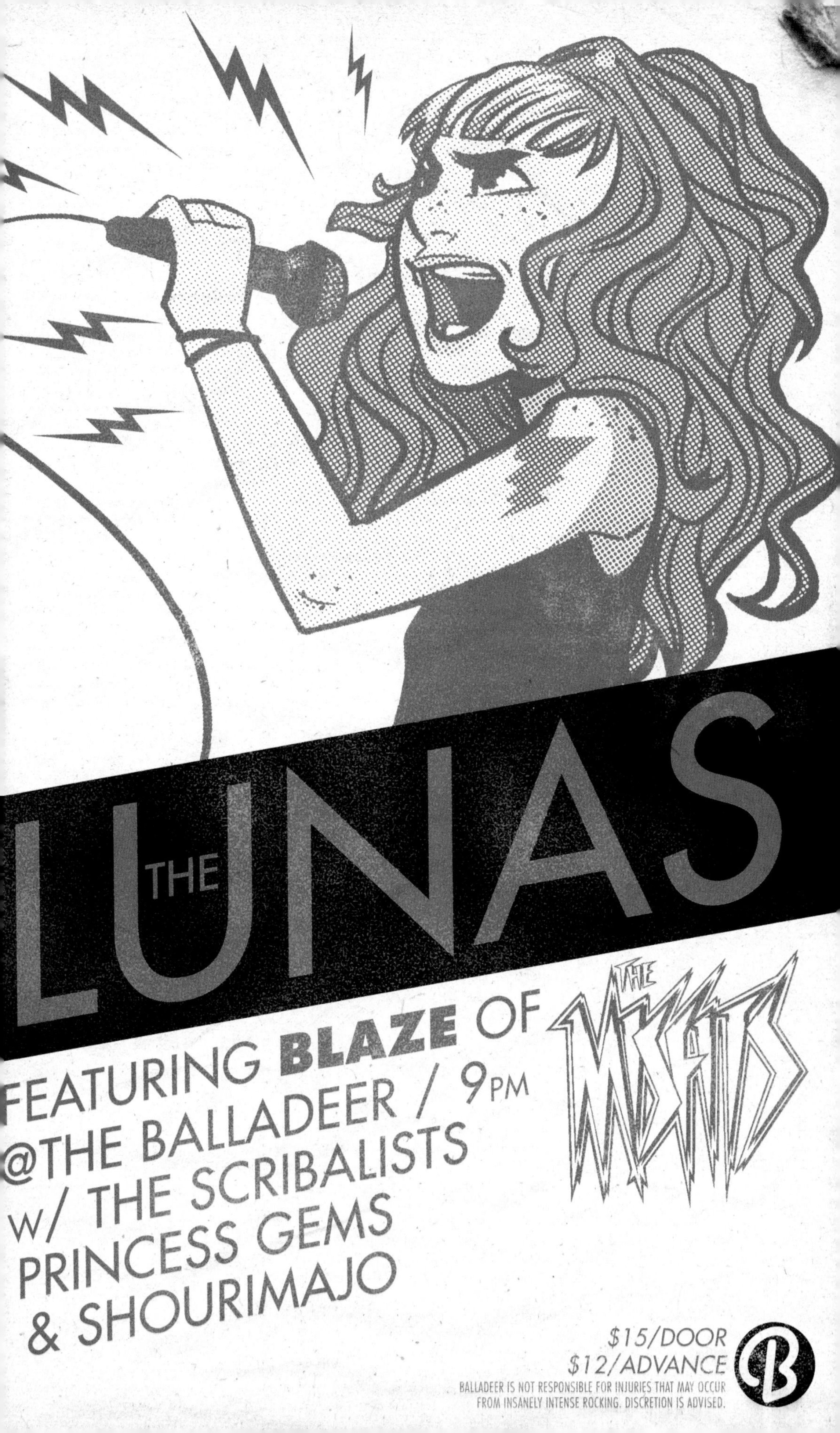
THE LUNAS
FEATURING BLAZE OF THE MISFITS
@THE BALLADEER / 9PM
w/ THE SCRIBALISTS
PRINCESS GEMS
& SHOURIMAJO
$15/DOOR
$12/ADVANCE
BALLADEER IS NOT RESPONSIBLE FOR INJURIES THAT MAY OCCUR FROM INSANELY INTENSE ROCKING. DISCRETION IS ADVISED.

ART M. VICTORIA ROBADO

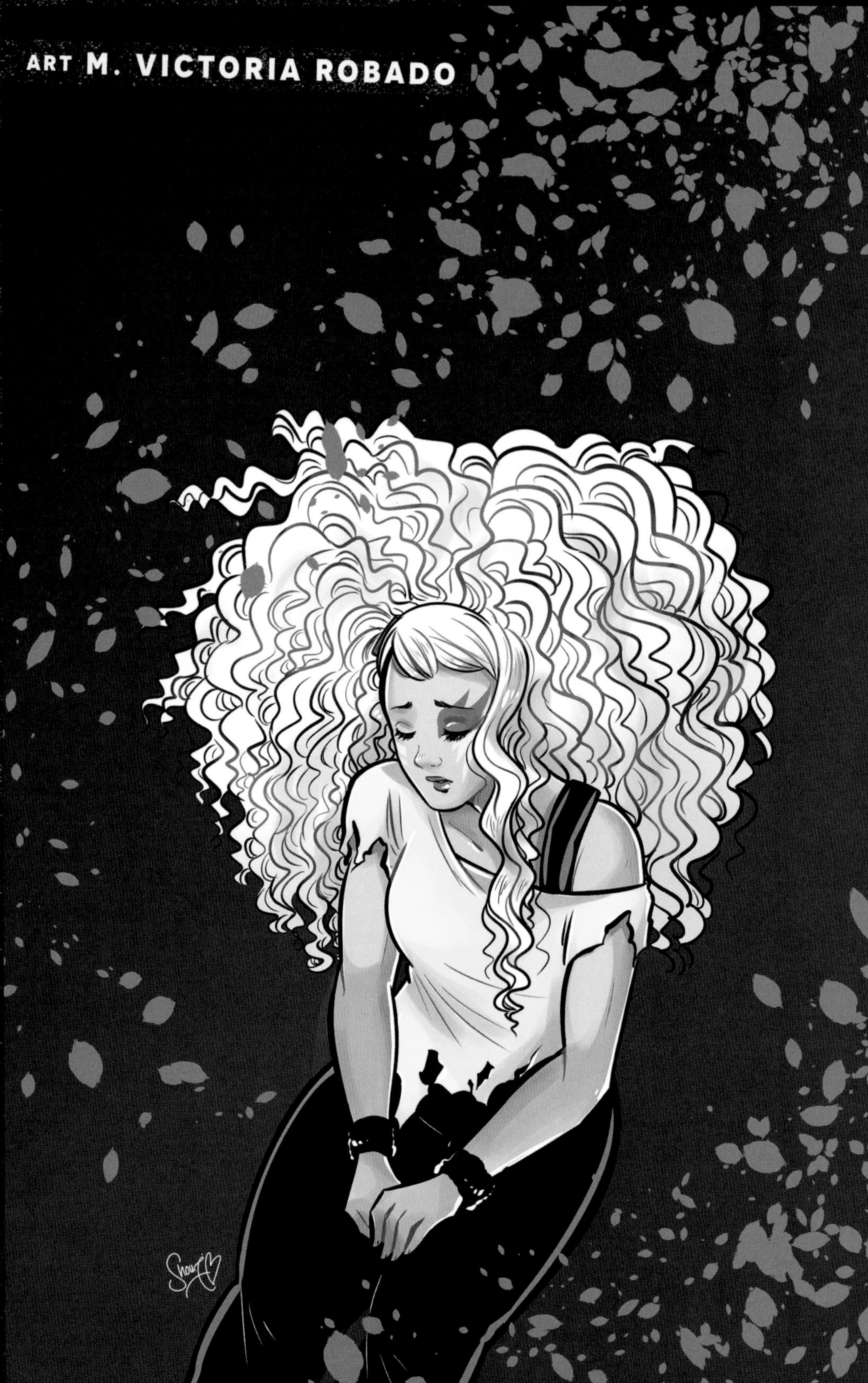

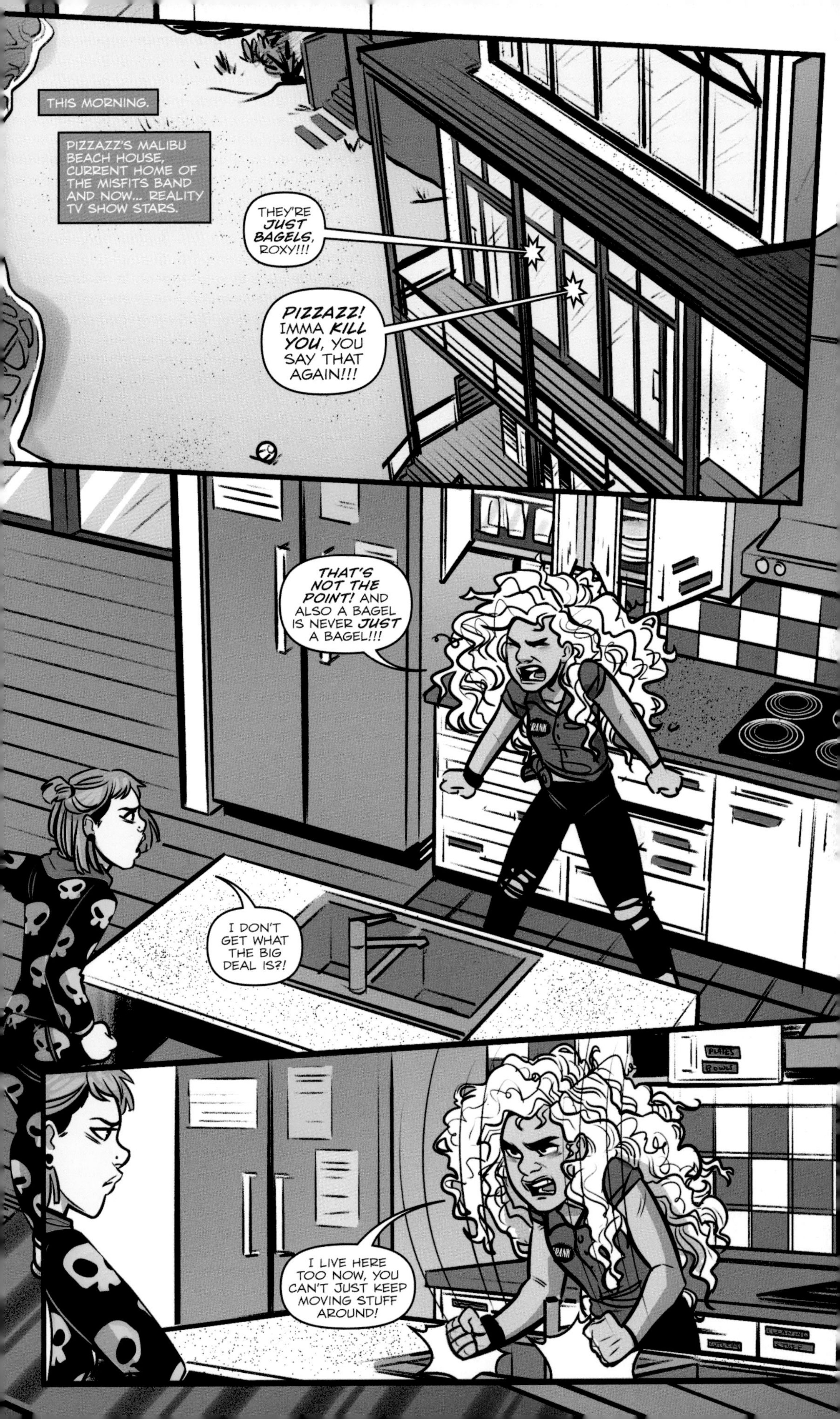
THIS MORNING.
PIZZAZZ'S MALIBU BEACH HOUSE, CURRENT HOME OF THE MISFITS BAND AND NOW... REALITY TV SHOW STARS.
THEY'RE *JUST BAGELS,* ROXY!!!
PIZZAZZ! IMMA *KILL YOU,* YOU SAY THAT AGAIN!!!
THAT'S NOT THE POINT! AND ALSO A BAGEL IS NEVER *JUST* A BAGEL!!!
I DON'T GET WHAT THE BIG DEAL IS?!
I LIVE HERE TOO NOW, YOU CAN'T JUST KEEP MOVING STUFF AROUND!

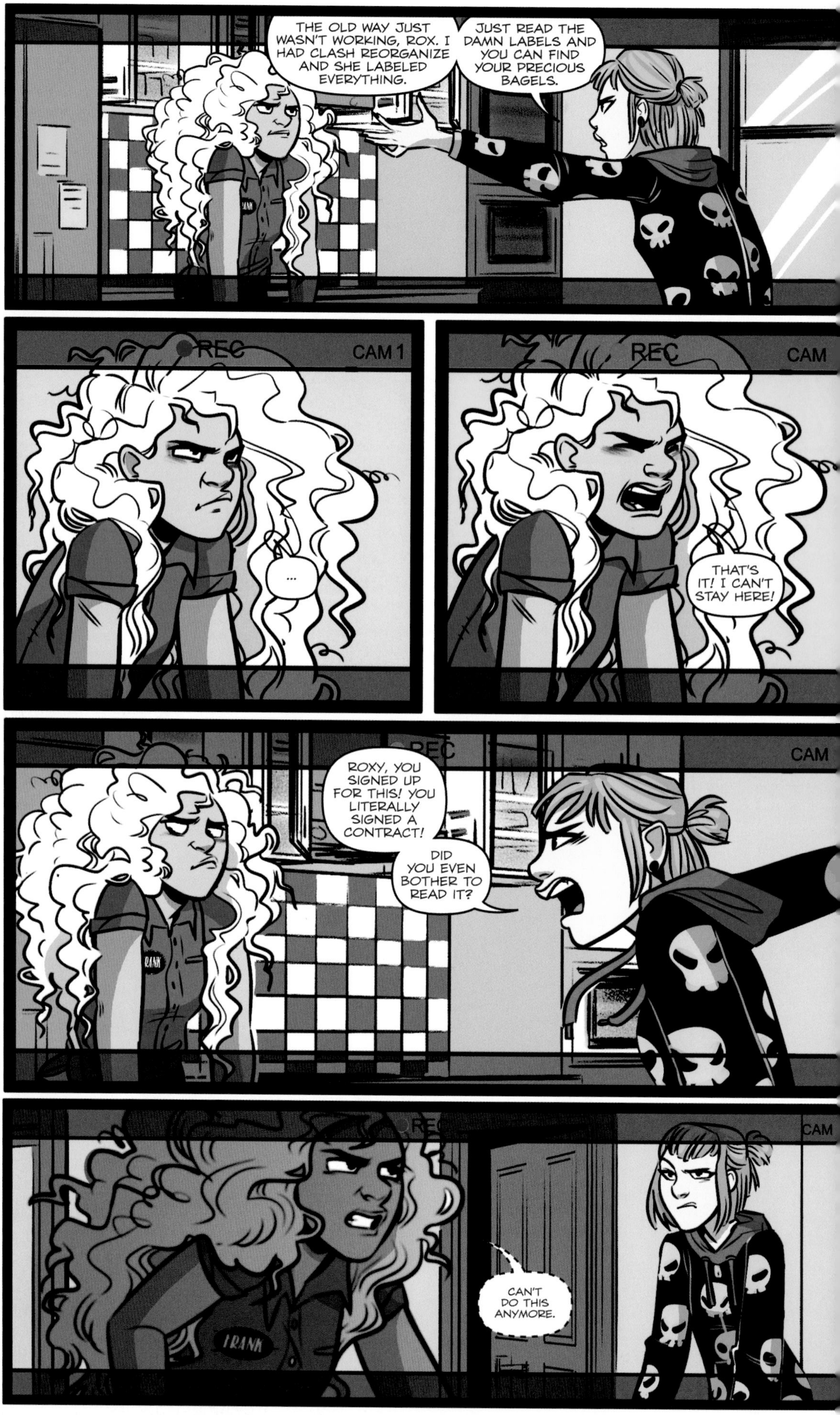
THE OLD WAY JUST WASN'T WORKING, ROX. I HAD CLASH REORGANIZE AND SHE LABELED EVERYTHING.
JUST READ THE DAMN LABELS AND YOU CAN FIND YOUR PRECIOUS BAGELS.
REC
CAM 1
...
REC
CAM
THAT'S IT! I CAN'T STAY HERE!
REC
CAM
ROXY, YOU SIGNED UP FOR THIS! YOU LITERALLY SIGNED A CONTRACT!
DID YOU EVEN BOTHER TO READ IT?
REC
CAM
CAN'T DO THIS ANYMORE.

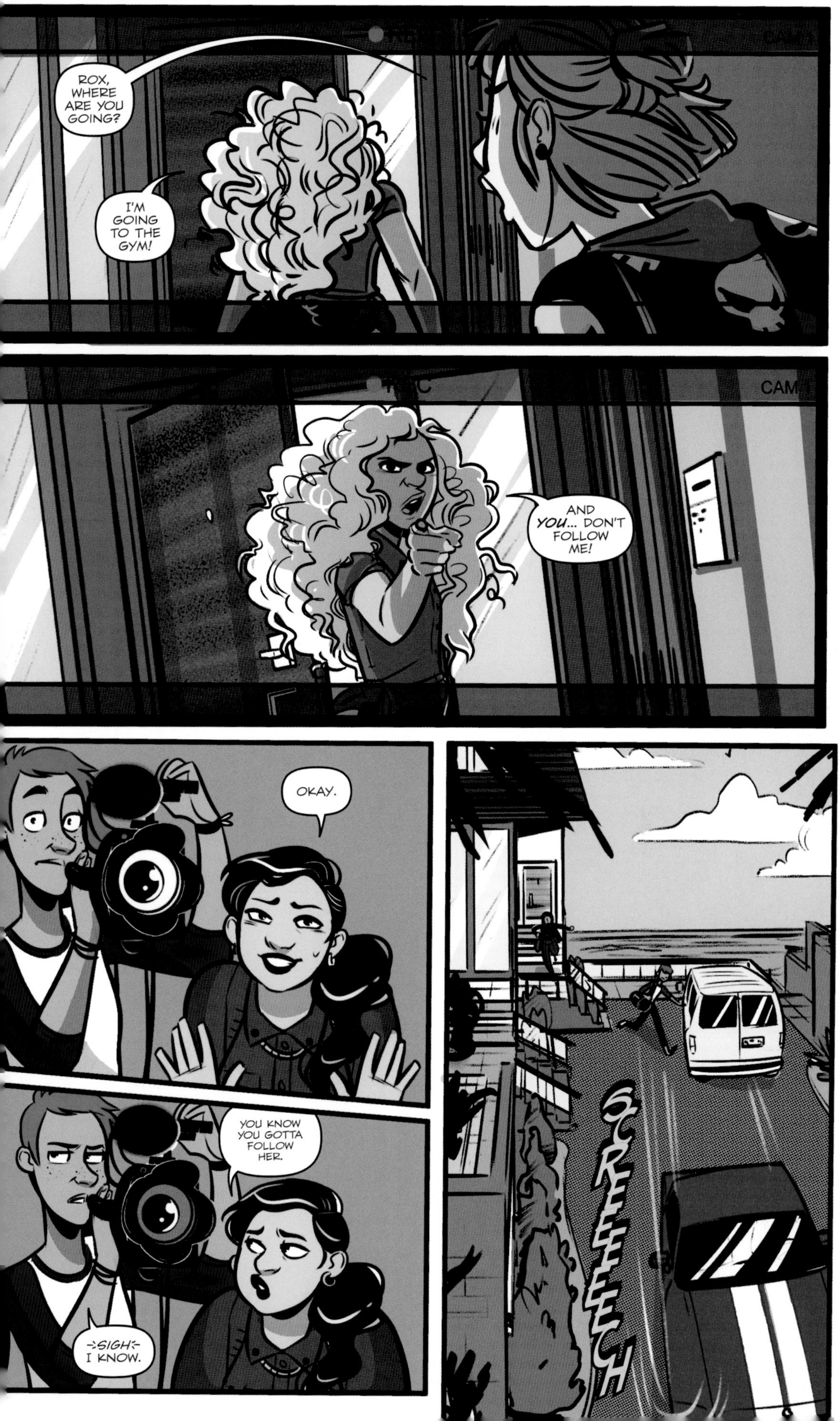
REC
CAM
ROX, WHERE ARE YOU GOING?
I'M GOING TO THE GYM!
REC
CAM 1
AND YOU... DON'T FOLLOW ME!
OKAY.
YOU KNOW YOU GOTTA FOLLOW HER.
-SIGH- I KNOW.
SCREEEEECH

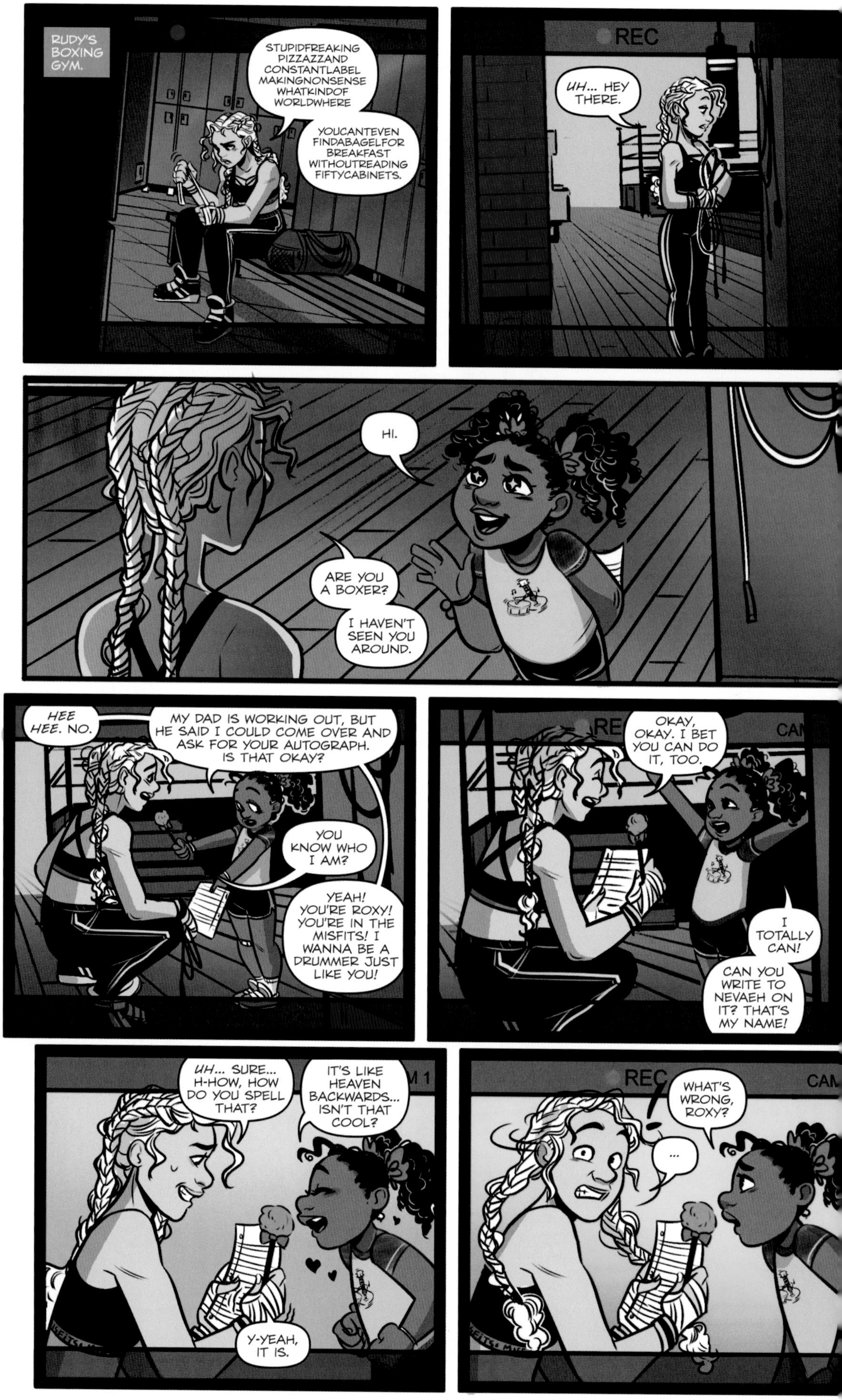
RUDY'S BOXING GYM.
STUPIDFREAKING PIZZAZZAND CONSTANTLABEL MAKINGNONSENSE WHATKINDOF WORLDWHERE
YOUCANTEVEN FINDABAGELFOR BREAKFAST WITHOUTREADING FIFTYCABINETS.
REC
UH... HEY THERE.
HI.
ARE YOU A BOXER?
I HAVEN'T SEEN YOU AROUND.
HEE HEE. NO.
MY DAD IS WORKING OUT, BUT HE SAID I COULD COME OVER AND ASK FOR YOUR AUTOGRAPH. IS THAT OKAY?
YOU KNOW WHO I AM?
YEAH! YOU'RE ROXY! YOU'RE IN THE MISFITS! I WANNA BE A DRUMMER JUST LIKE YOU!
OKAY, OKAY. I BET YOU CAN DO IT, TOO.
I TOTALLY CAN!
CAN YOU WRITE TO NEVAEH ON IT? THAT'S MY NAME!
UH... SURE... H-HOW, HOW DO YOU SPELL THAT?
IT'S LIKE HEAVEN BACKWARDS... ISN'T THAT COOL?
Y-YEAH, IT IS.
REC
!
...
WHAT'S WRONG, ROXY?

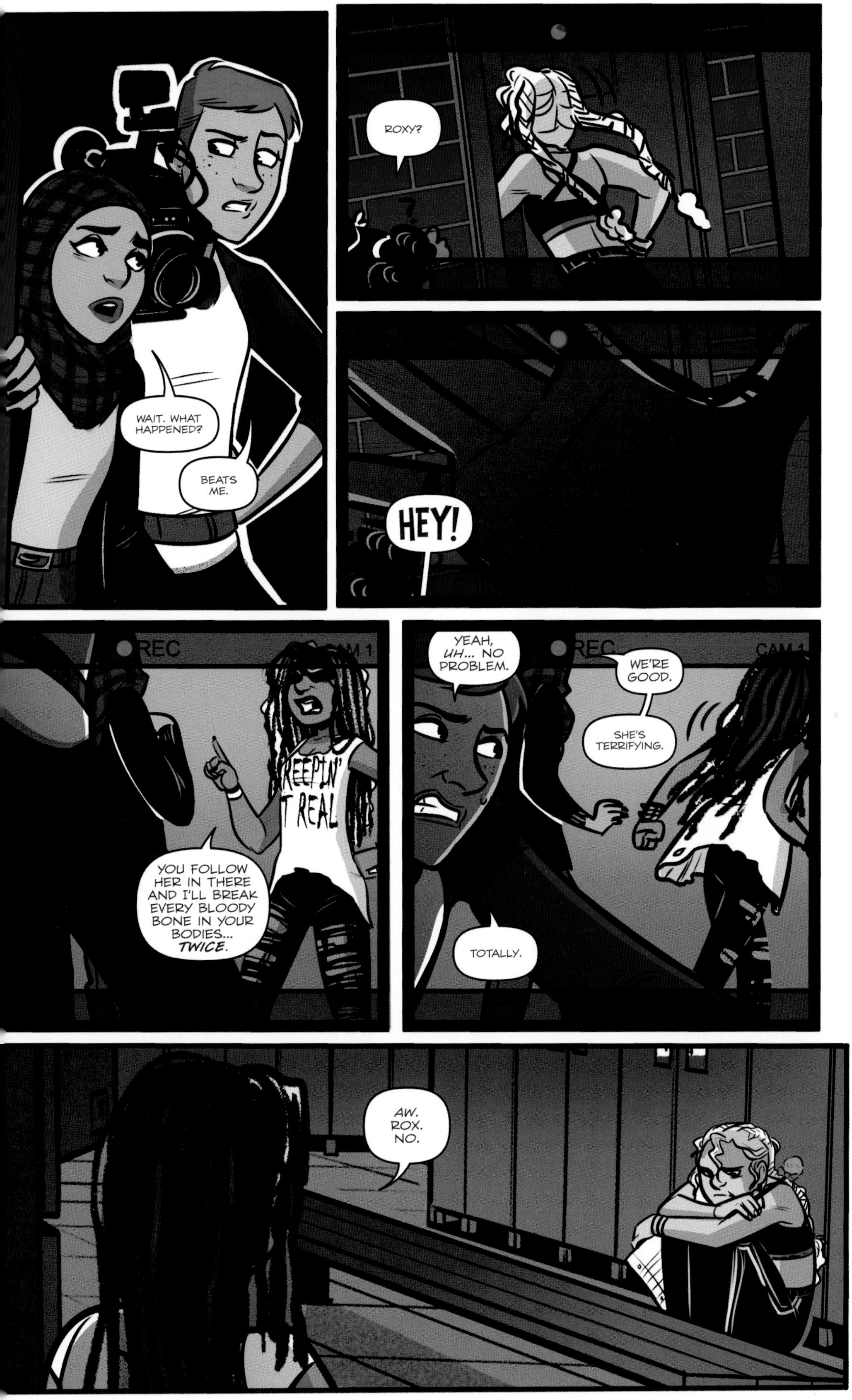
WAIT. WHAT HAPPENED?
BEATS ME.
ROXY?
HEY!
REC
YOU FOLLOW HER IN THERE AND I'LL BREAK EVERY BLOODY BONE IN YOUR BODIES... *TWICE*.
YEAH, *UH*... NO PROBLEM.
WE'RE GOOD.
SHE'S TERRIFYING.
TOTALLY.
AW. ROX. NO.

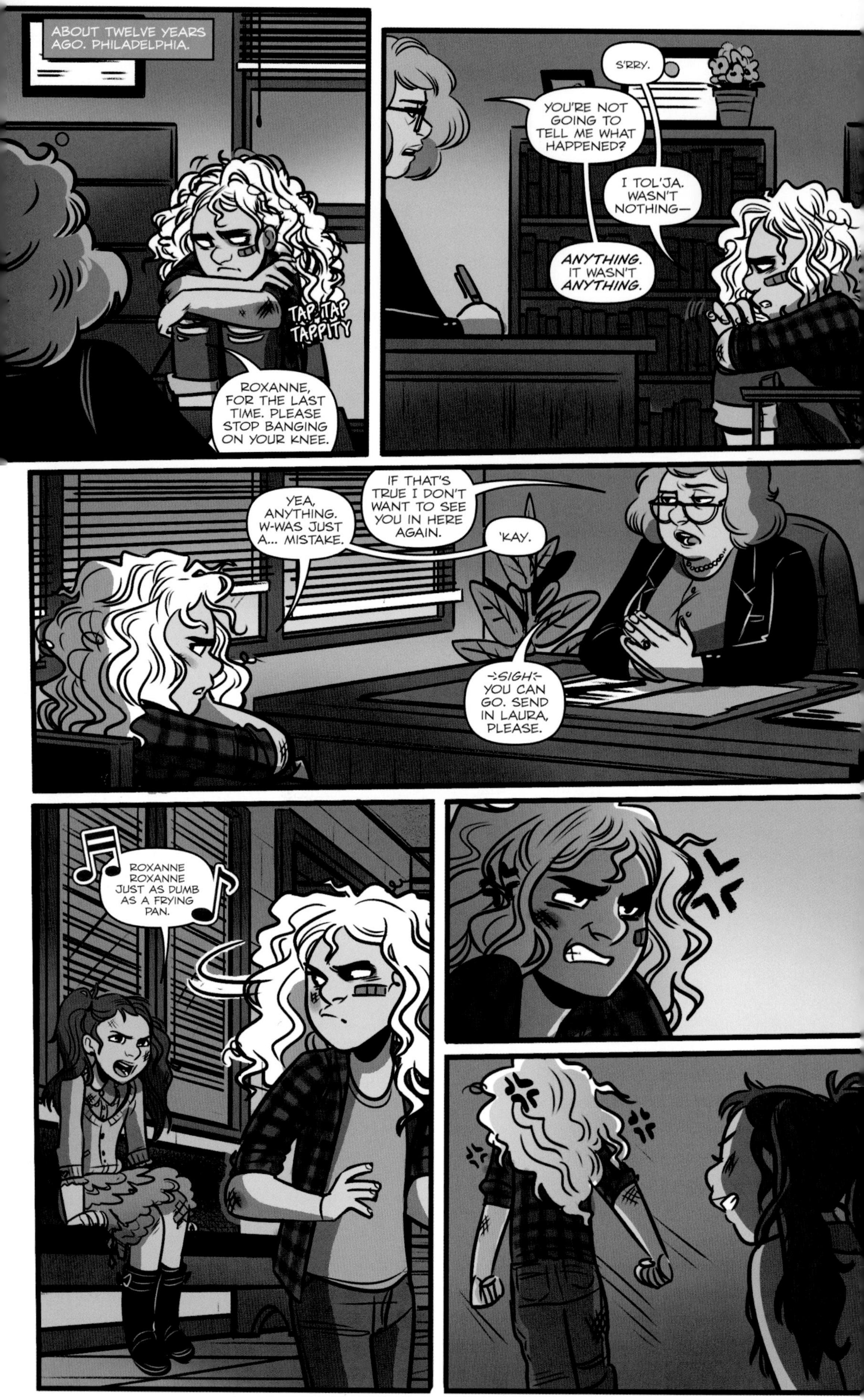
ABOUT TWELVE YEARS AGO. PHILADELPHIA.
TAP TAP TAPPITY
ROXANNE, FOR THE LAST TIME. PLEASE STOP BANGING ON YOUR KNEE.
S'RRY.
YOU'RE NOT GOING TO TELL ME WHAT HAPPENED?
I TOL'JA. WASN'T NOTHING—
ANYTHING. IT WASN'T *ANYTHING*.
YEA, ANYTHING. W-WAS JUST A... MISTAKE.
IF THAT'S TRUE I DON'T WANT TO SEE YOU IN HERE AGAIN.
'KAY.
-SIGH- YOU CAN GO. SEND IN LAURA, PLEASE.
ROXANNE ROXANNE JUST AS DUMB AS A FRYING PAN.

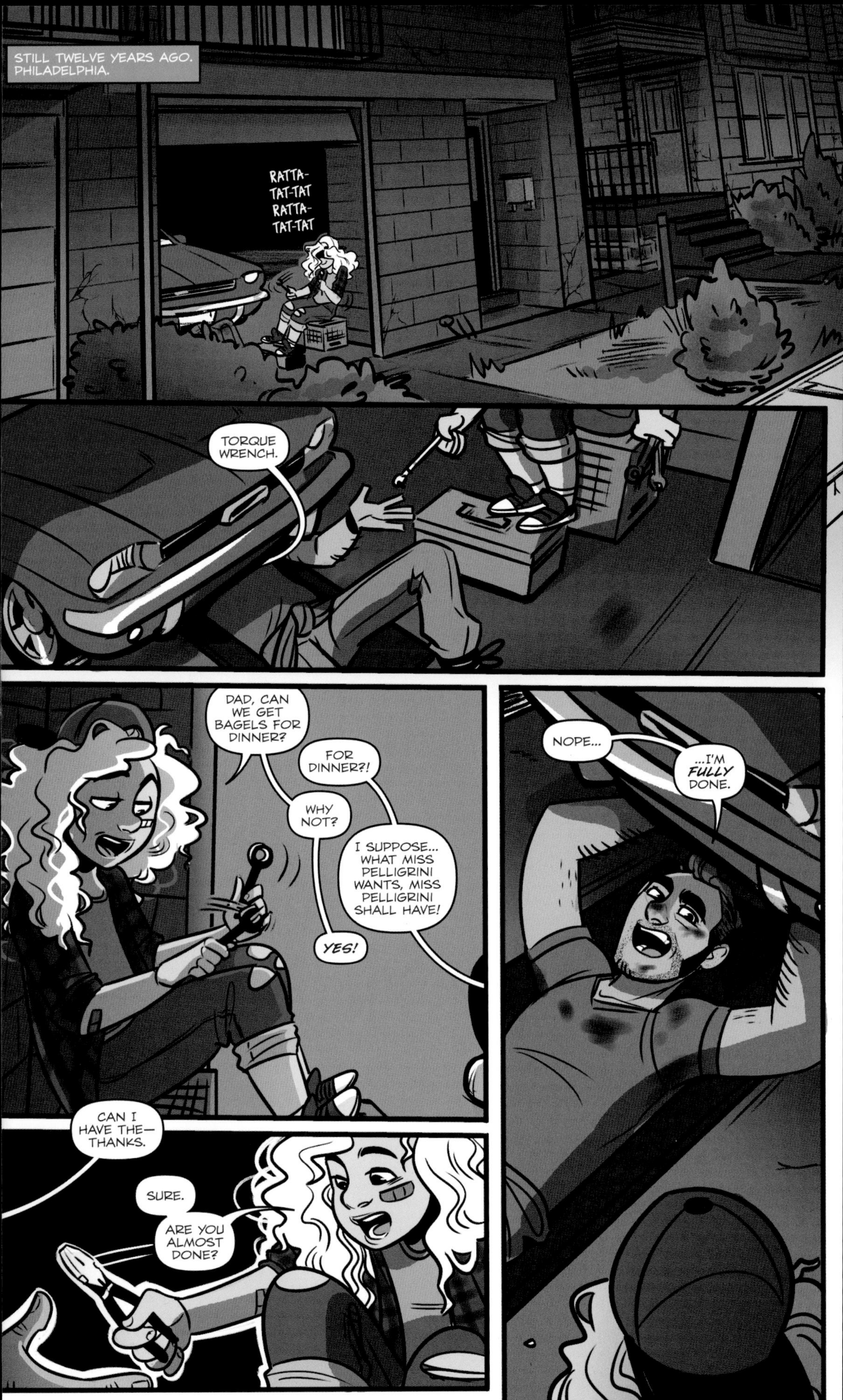
STILL TWELVE YEARS AGO. PHILADELPHIA.
RATTA-TAT-TAT RATTA-TAT-TAT
TORQUE WRENCH.
DAD, CAN WE GET BAGELS FOR DINNER?
FOR DINNER?!
WHY NOT?
I SUPPOSE... WHAT MISS PELLIGRINI WANTS, MISS PELLIGRINI SHALL HAVE!
YES!
NOPE...
...I'M FULLY DONE.
CAN I HAVE THE— THANKS.
SURE.
ARE YOU ALMOST DONE?

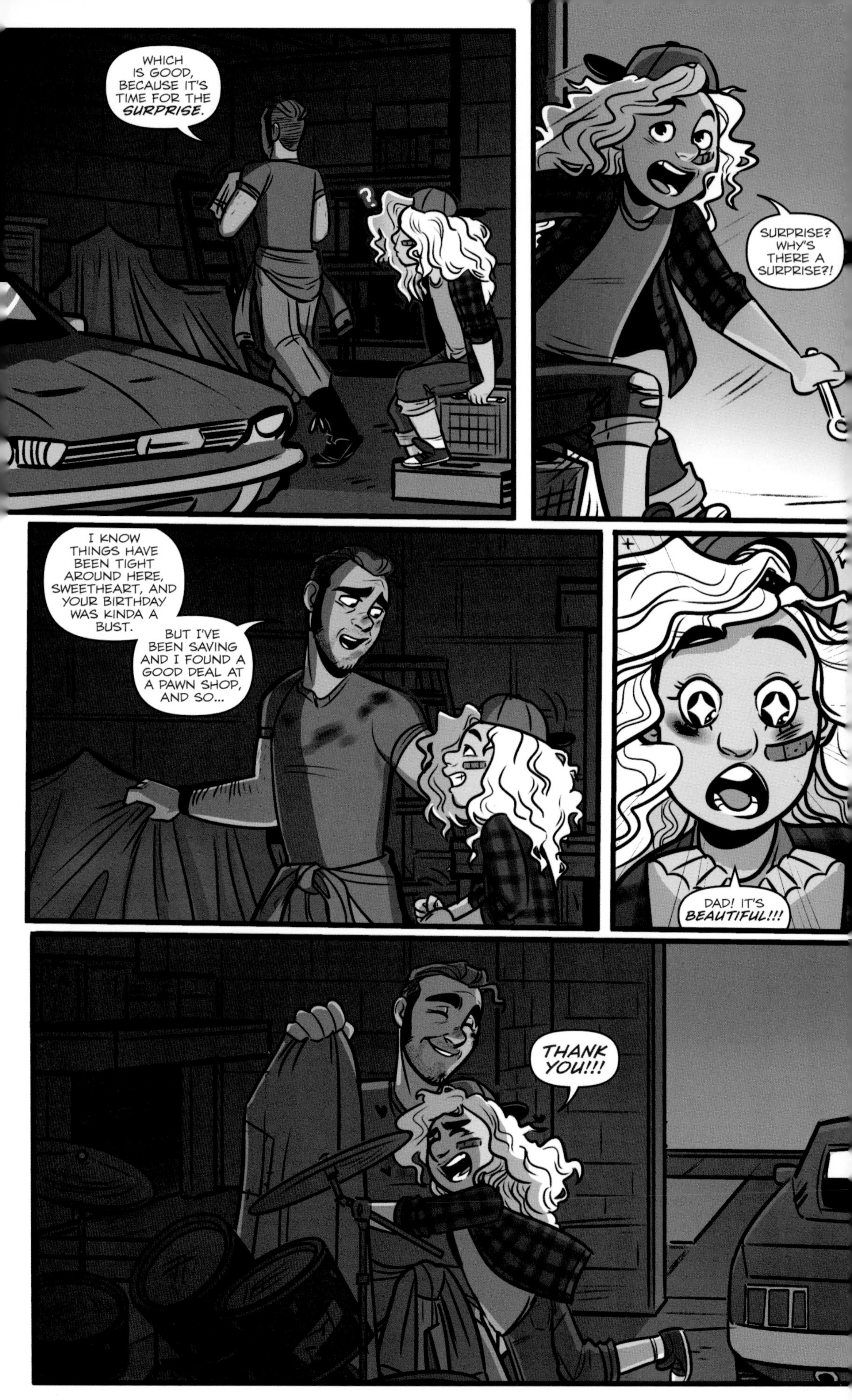

WHICH IS GOOD, BECAUSE IT'S TIME FOR THE *SURPRISE*.
?
SURPRISE? WHY'S THERE A SURPRISE?!
I KNOW THINGS HAVE BEEN TIGHT AROUND HERE, SWEETHEART, AND YOUR BIRTHDAY WAS KINDA A BUST.
BUT I'VE BEEN SAVING AND I FOUND A GOOD DEAL AT A PAWN SHOP, AND SO...
DAD! IT'S *BEAUTIFUL!!!*
THANK YOU!!!

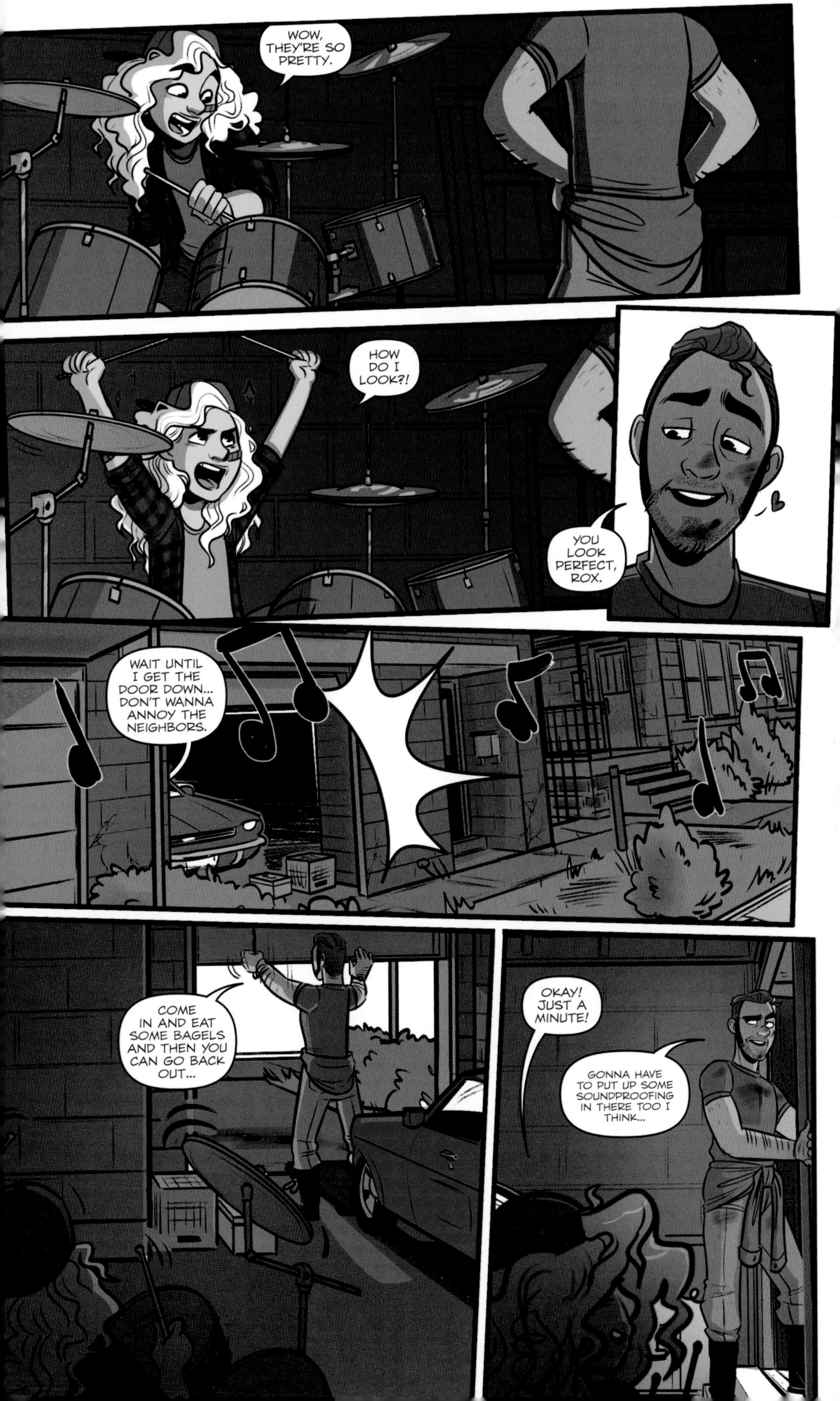
WOW, THEY'RE SO PRETTY.
HOW DO I LOOK?!
YOU LOOK PERFECT, ROX.
WAIT UNTIL I GET THE DOOR DOWN... DON'T WANNA ANNOY THE NEIGHBORS.
COME IN AND EAT SOME BAGELS AND THEN YOU CAN GO BACK OUT...
OKAY! JUST A MINUTE!
GONNA HAVE TO PUT UP SOME SOUNDPROOFING IN THERE TOO I THINK...

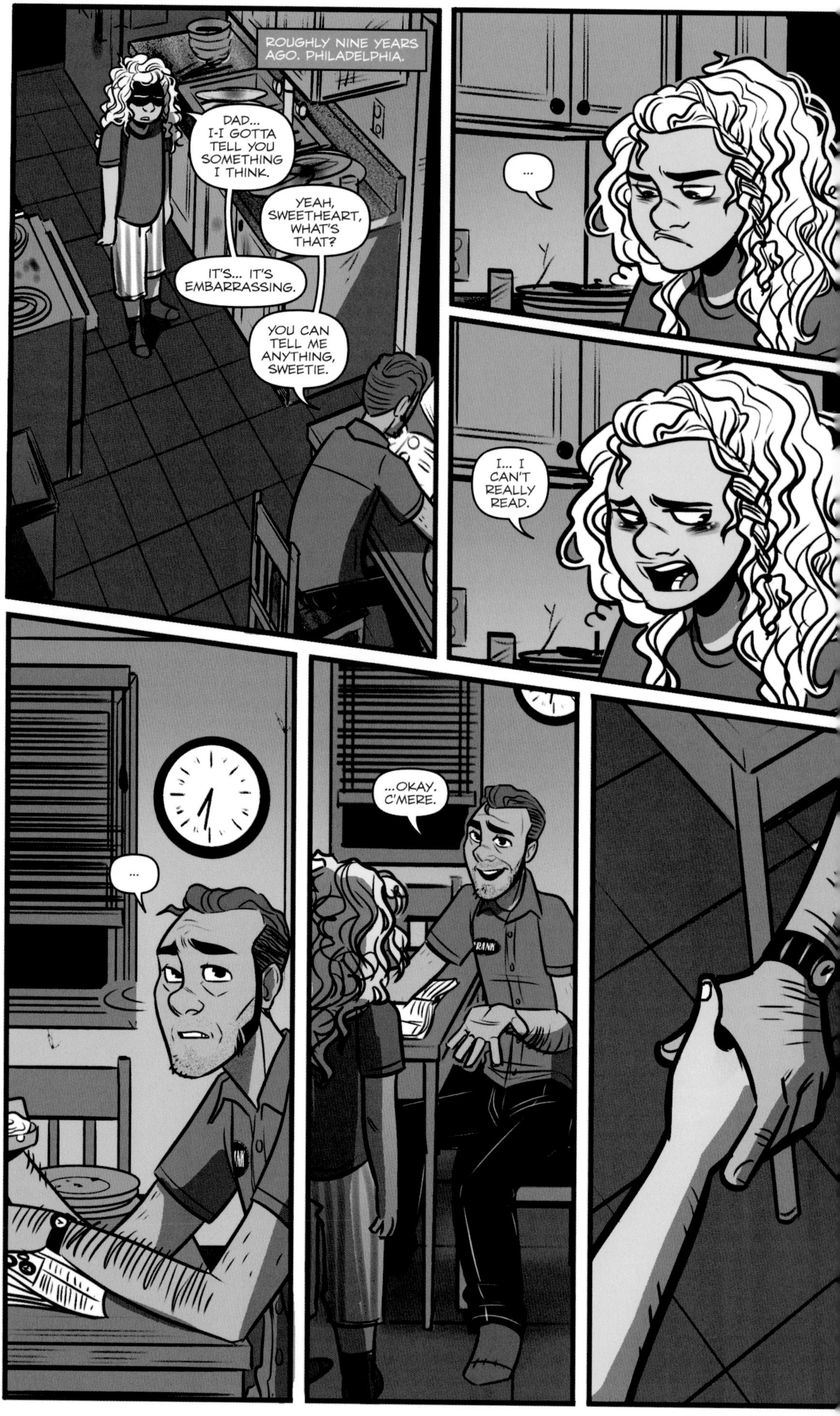
ROUGHLY NINE YEARS AGO. PHILADELPHIA.
DAD... I-I GOTTA TELL YOU SOMETHING I THINK.
YEAH, SWEETHEART, WHAT'S THAT?
IT'S... IT'S EMBARRASSING.
YOU CAN TELL ME ANYTHING, SWEETIE.
...
I... I CAN'T REALLY READ.
...
...OKAY. C'MERE.

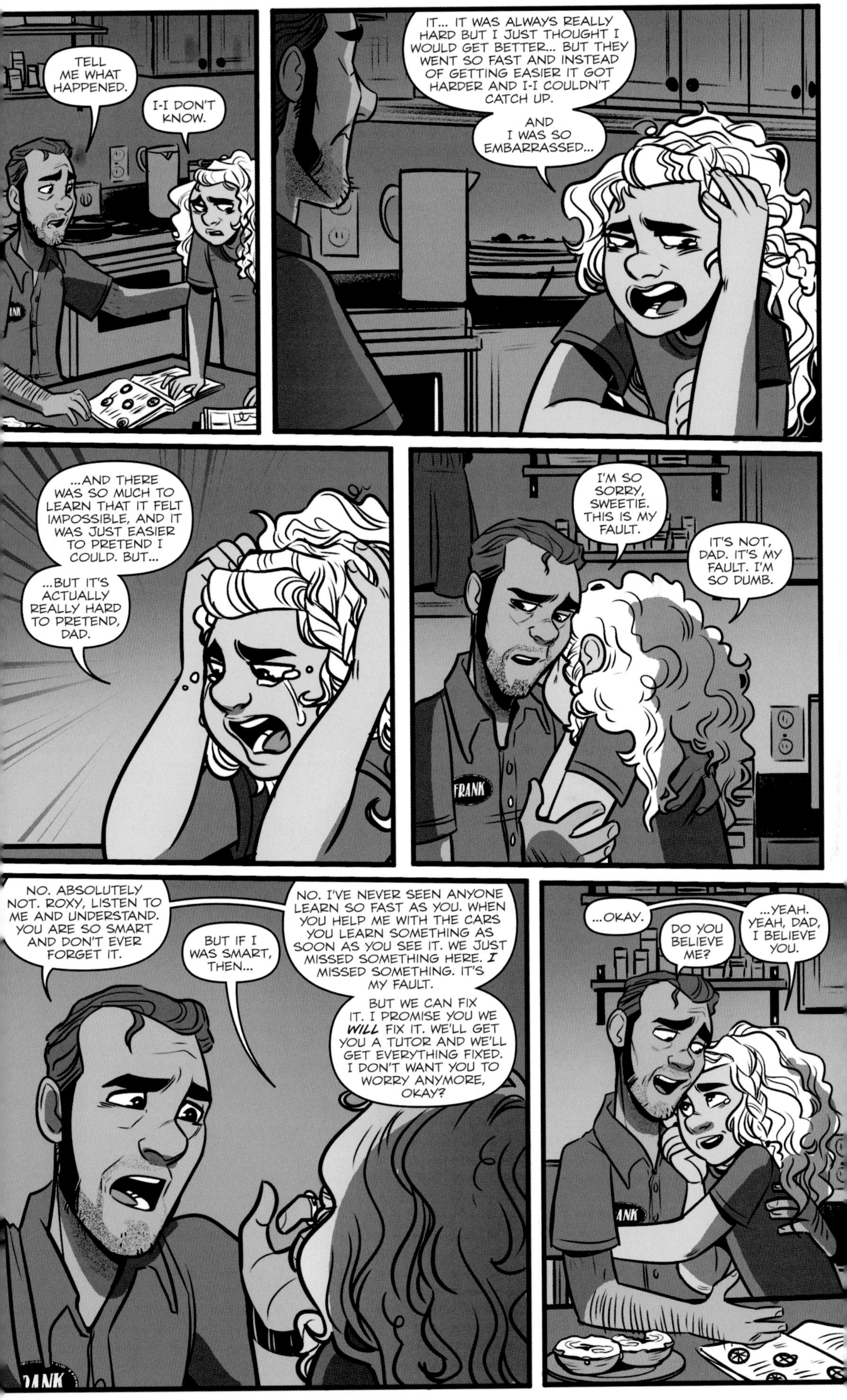
TELL ME WHAT HAPPENED.
I-I DON'T KNOW.
IT... IT WAS ALWAYS REALLY HARD BUT I JUST THOUGHT I WOULD GET BETTER... BUT THEY WENT SO FAST AND INSTEAD OF GETTING EASIER IT GOT HARDER AND I-I COULDN'T CATCH UP.
AND I WAS SO EMBARRASSED...
...AND THERE WAS SO MUCH TO LEARN THAT IT FELT IMPOSSIBLE, AND IT WAS JUST EASIER TO PRETEND I COULD. BUT...
...BUT IT'S ACTUALLY REALLY HARD TO PRETEND, DAD.
I'M SO SORRY, SWEETIE. THIS IS MY FAULT.
IT'S NOT, DAD. IT'S MY FAULT. I'M SO DUMB.
FRANK
NO. ABSOLUTELY NOT. ROXY, LISTEN TO ME AND UNDERSTAND. YOU ARE SO SMART AND DON'T EVER FORGET IT.
BUT IF I WAS SMART, THEN...
NO. I'VE NEVER SEEN ANYONE LEARN SO FAST AS YOU. WHEN YOU HELP ME WITH THE CARS YOU LEARN SOMETHING AS SOON AS YOU SEE IT. WE JUST MISSED SOMETHING HERE. *I* MISSED SOMETHING. IT'S MY FAULT.
BUT WE CAN FIX IT. I PROMISE YOU WE ***WILL*** FIX IT. WE'LL GET YOU A TUTOR AND WE'LL GET EVERYTHING FIXED. I DON'T WANT YOU TO WORRY ANYMORE, OKAY?
...OKAY.
DO YOU BELIEVE ME?
...YEAH. YEAH, DAD, I BELIEVE YOU.

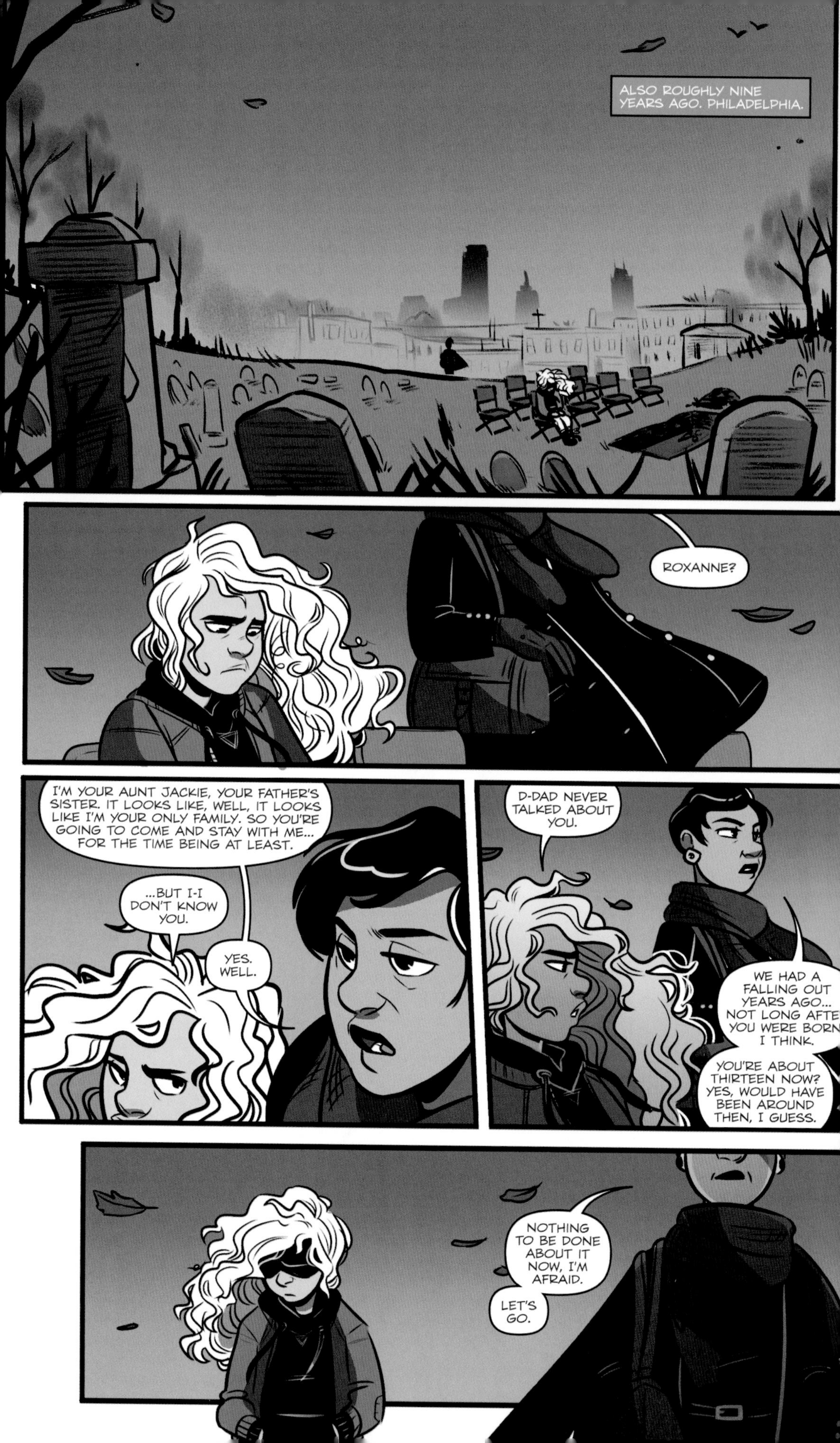
ALSO ROUGHLY NINE YEARS AGO. PHILADELPHIA.
ROXANNE?
I'M YOUR AUNT JACKIE, YOUR FATHER'S SISTER. IT LOOKS LIKE, WELL, IT LOOKS LIKE I'M YOUR ONLY FAMILY. SO YOU'RE GOING TO COME AND STAY WITH ME... FOR THE TIME BEING AT LEAST.
...BUT I-I DON'T KNOW YOU.
YES. WELL.
D-DAD NEVER TALKED ABOUT YOU.
WE HAD A FALLING OUT YEARS AGO... NOT LONG AFTE YOU WERE BORN I THINK.
YOU'RE ABOUT THIRTEEN NOW? YES, WOULD HAVE BEEN AROUND THEN, I GUESS.
NOTHING TO BE DONE ABOUT IT NOW, I'M AFRAID.
LET'S GO.

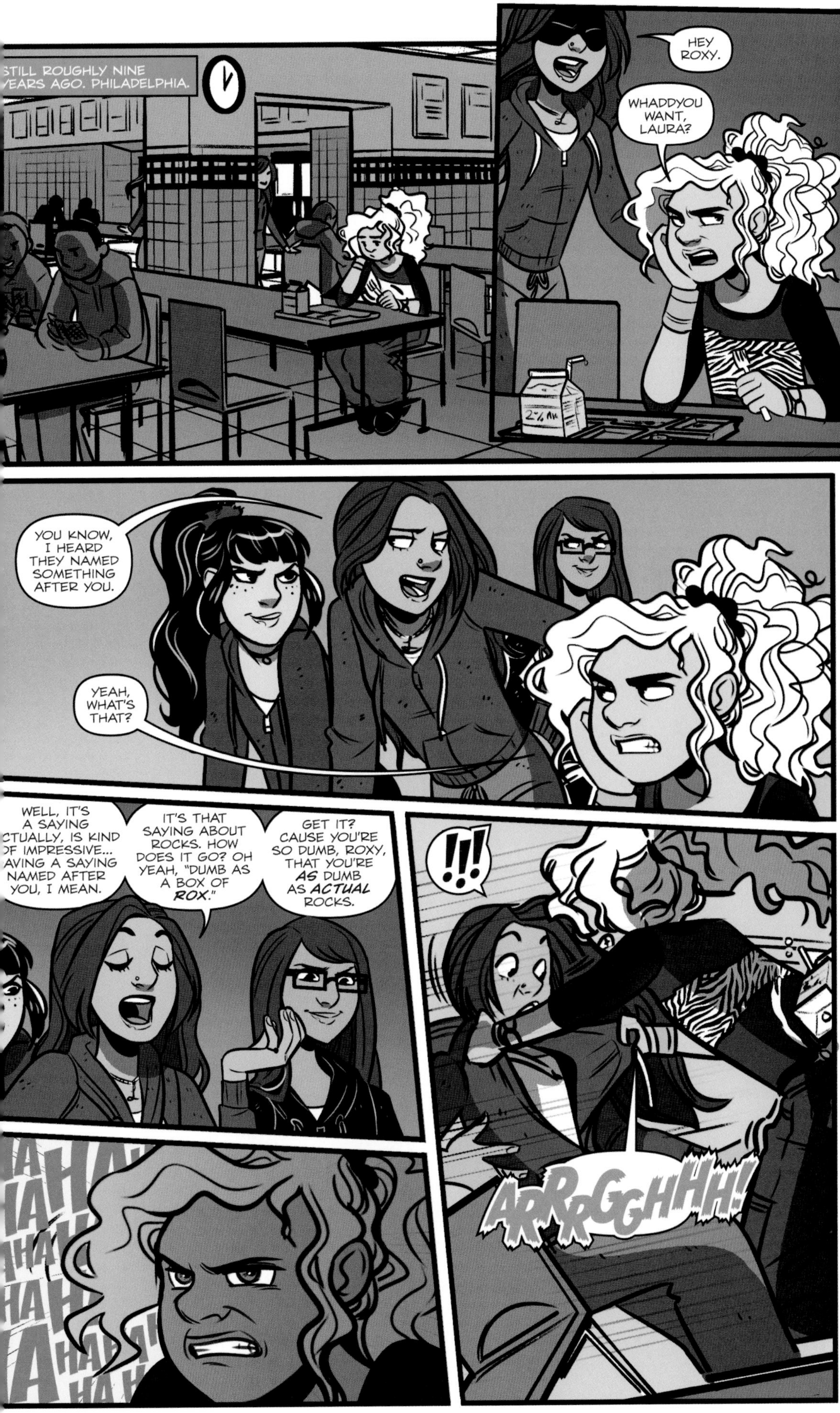

STILL ROUGHLY NINE YEARS AGO. PHILADELPHIA.
HEY ROXY.
WHADDYOU WANT, LAURA?
YOU KNOW, I HEARD THEY NAMED SOMETHING AFTER YOU.
YEAH, WHAT'S THAT?
WELL, IT'S A SAYING CTUALLY, IS KIND F IMPRESSIVE... AVING A SAYING NAMED AFTER YOU, I MEAN.
IT'S THAT SAYING ABOUT ROCKS. HOW DOES IT GO? OH YEAH, "DUMB AS A BOX OF **ROX**."
GET IT? CAUSE YOU'RE SO DUMB, ROXY, THAT YOU'RE ***AS*** DUMB AS ***ACTUAL*** ROCKS.
!!!
HA HA HA HA HA HA
ARRRGGHHH!

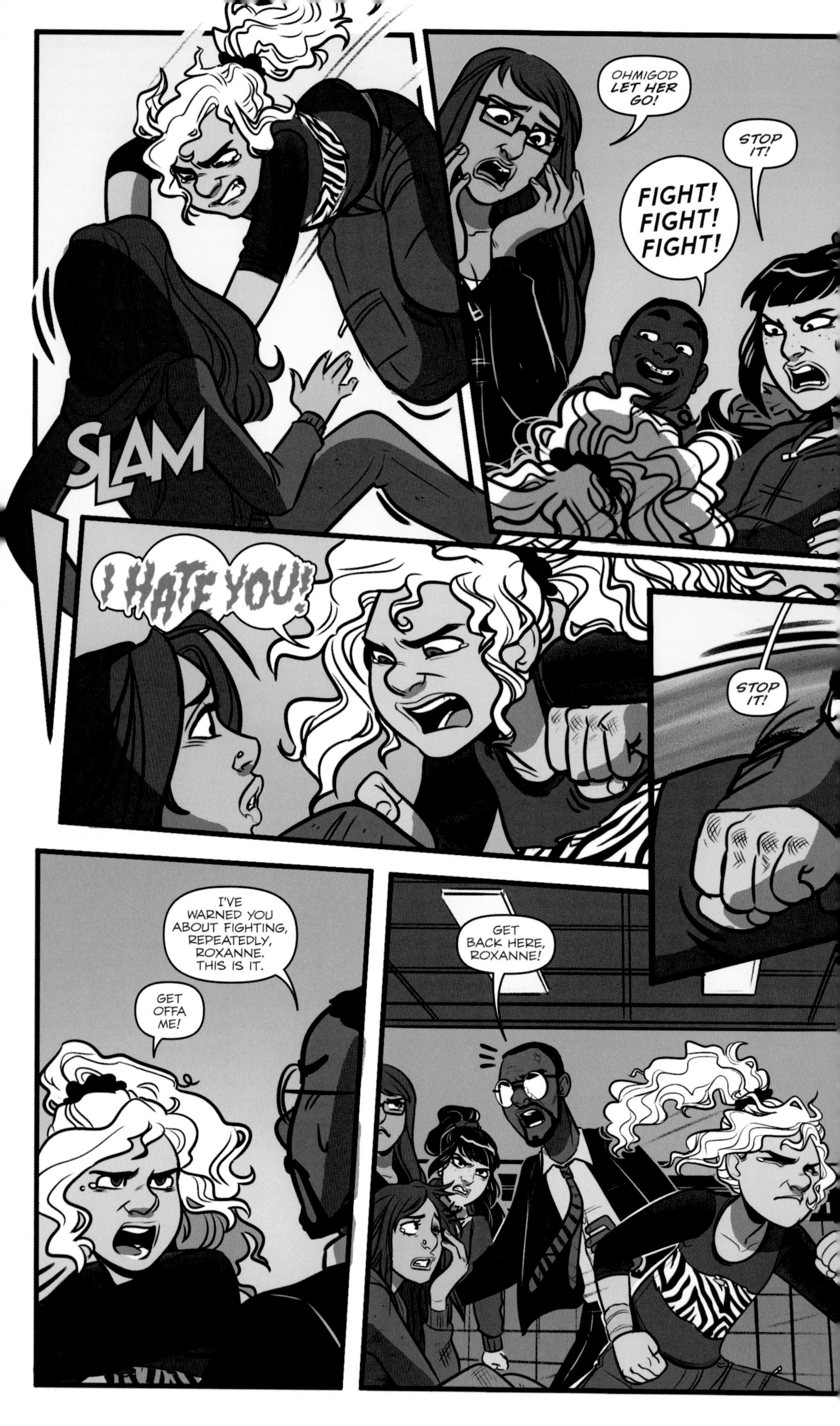
SLAM
OHMIGOD LET HER GO!
STOP IT!
FIGHT! FIGHT! FIGHT!
I HATE YOU!
STOP IT!
I'VE WARNED YOU ABOUT FIGHTING, REPEATEDLY, ROXANNE. THIS IS IT.
GET OFFA ME!
GET BACK HERE, ROXANNE!

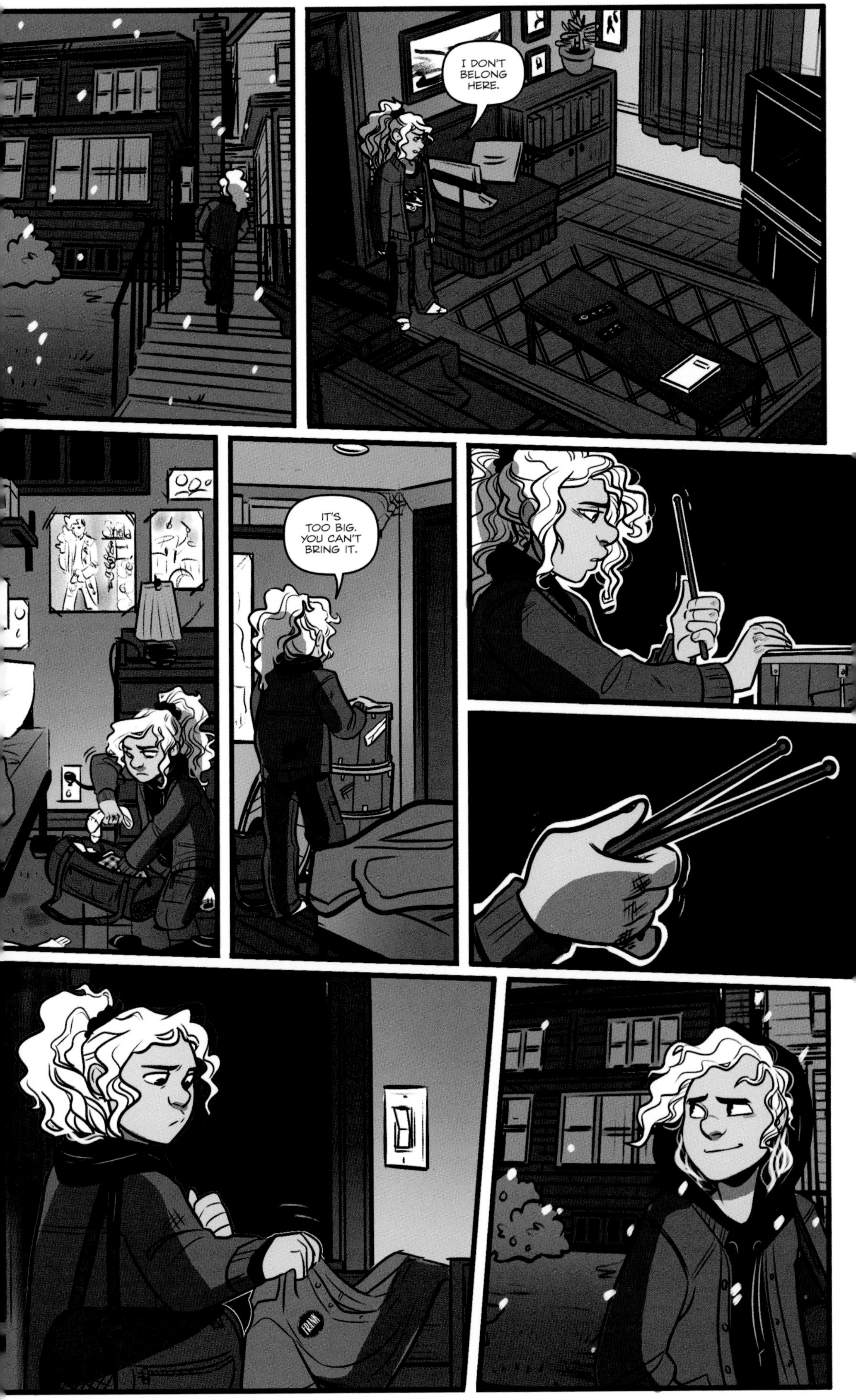
I DON'T BELONG HERE.
IT'S TOO BIG. YOU CAN'T BRING IT.
FRANK

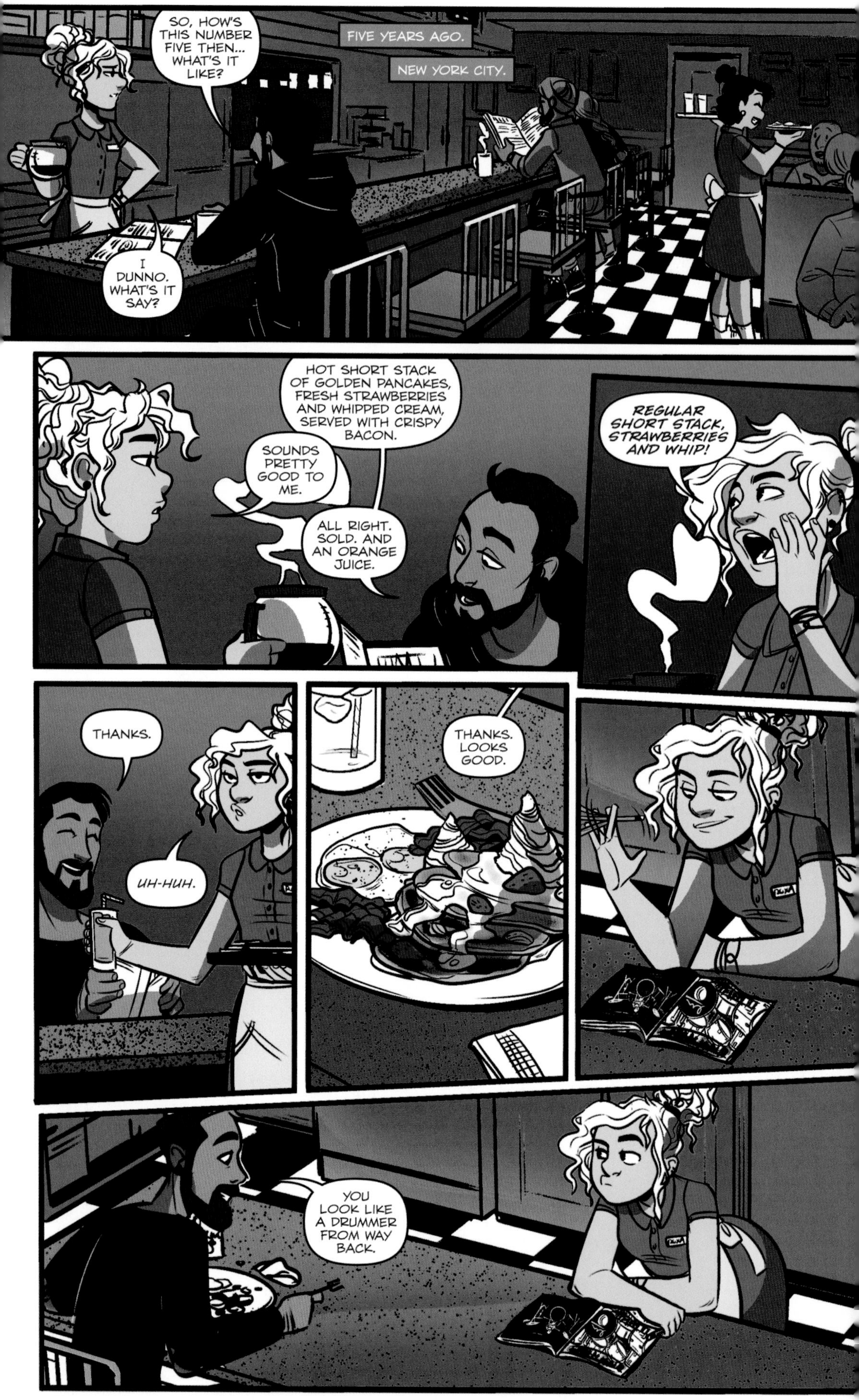
FIVE YEARS AGO.
NEW YORK CITY.
SO, HOW'S THIS NUMBER FIVE THEN... WHAT'S IT LIKE?
I DUNNO. WHAT'S IT SAY?
HOT SHORT STACK OF GOLDEN PANCAKES, FRESH STRAWBERRIES AND WHIPPED CREAM, SERVED WITH CRISPY BACON.
SOUNDS PRETTY GOOD TO ME.
ALL RIGHT. SOLD. AND AN ORANGE JUICE.
REGULAR SHORT STACK, STRAWBERRIES AND WHIP!
THANKS.
UH-HUH.
THANKS. LOOKS GOOD.
YOU LOOK LIKE A DRUMMER FROM WAY BACK.

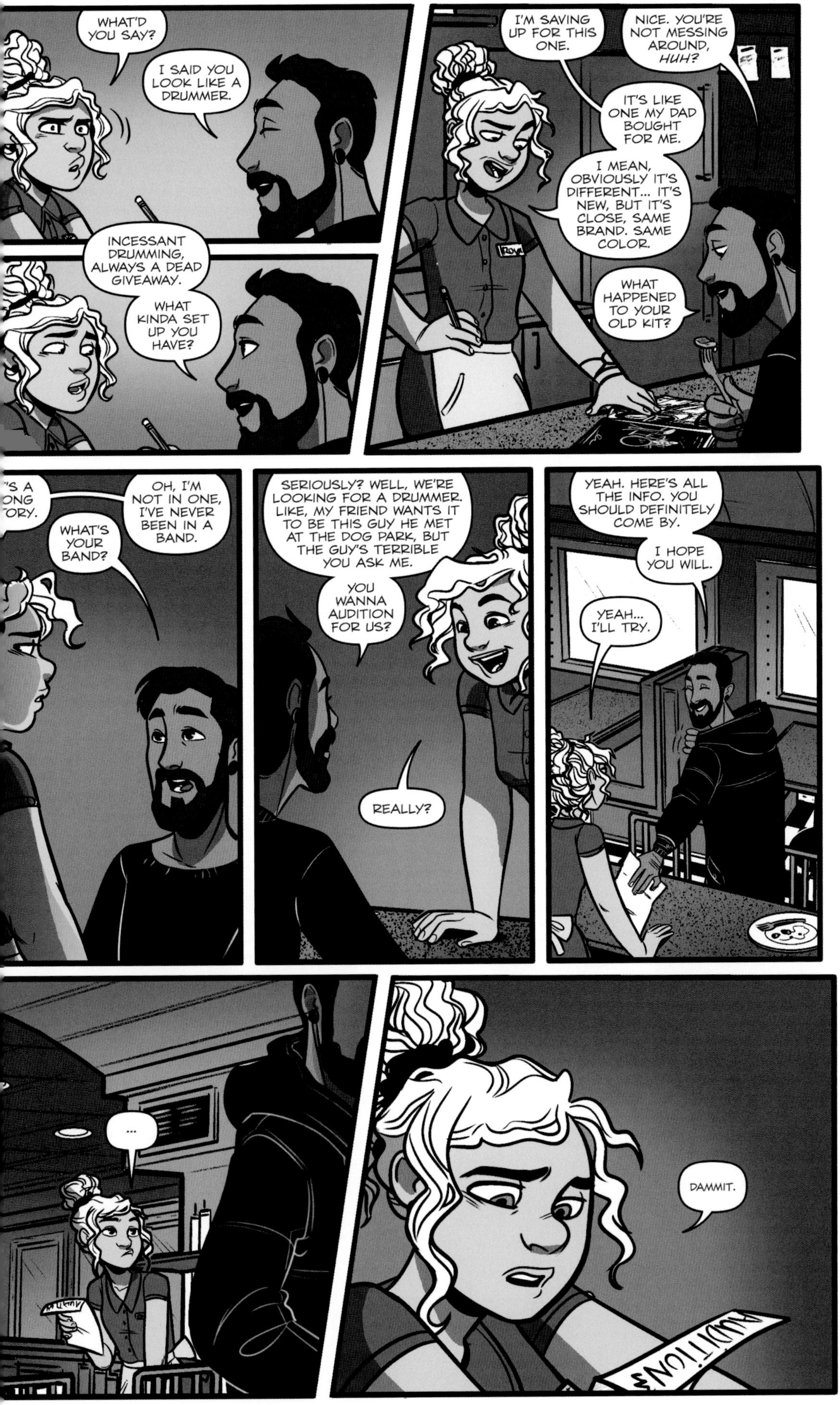
WHAT'D YOU SAY?
I SAID YOU LOOK LIKE A DRUMMER.
INCESSANT DRUMMING, ALWAYS A DEAD GIVEAWAY.
WHAT KINDA SET UP YOU HAVE?
I'M SAVING UP FOR THIS ONE.
NICE. YOU'RE NOT MESSING AROUND, *HUH?*
IT'S LIKE ONE MY DAD BOUGHT FOR ME.
I MEAN, OBVIOUSLY IT'S DIFFERENT... IT'S NEW, BUT IT'S CLOSE, SAME BRAND. SAME COLOR.
WHAT HAPPENED TO YOUR OLD KIT?
'S A ONG TORY.
OH, I'M NOT IN ONE, I'VE NEVER BEEN IN A BAND.
WHAT'S YOUR BAND?
SERIOUSLY? WELL, WE'RE LOOKING FOR A DRUMMER. LIKE, MY FRIEND WANTS IT TO BE THIS GUY HE MET AT THE DOG PARK, BUT THE GUY'S TERRIBLE YOU ASK ME.
YOU WANNA AUDITION FOR US?
REALLY?
YEAH. HERE'S ALL THE INFO. YOU SHOULD DEFINITELY COME BY.
I HOPE YOU WILL.
YEAH... I'LL TRY.
...
DAMMIT.
AUDITIONS

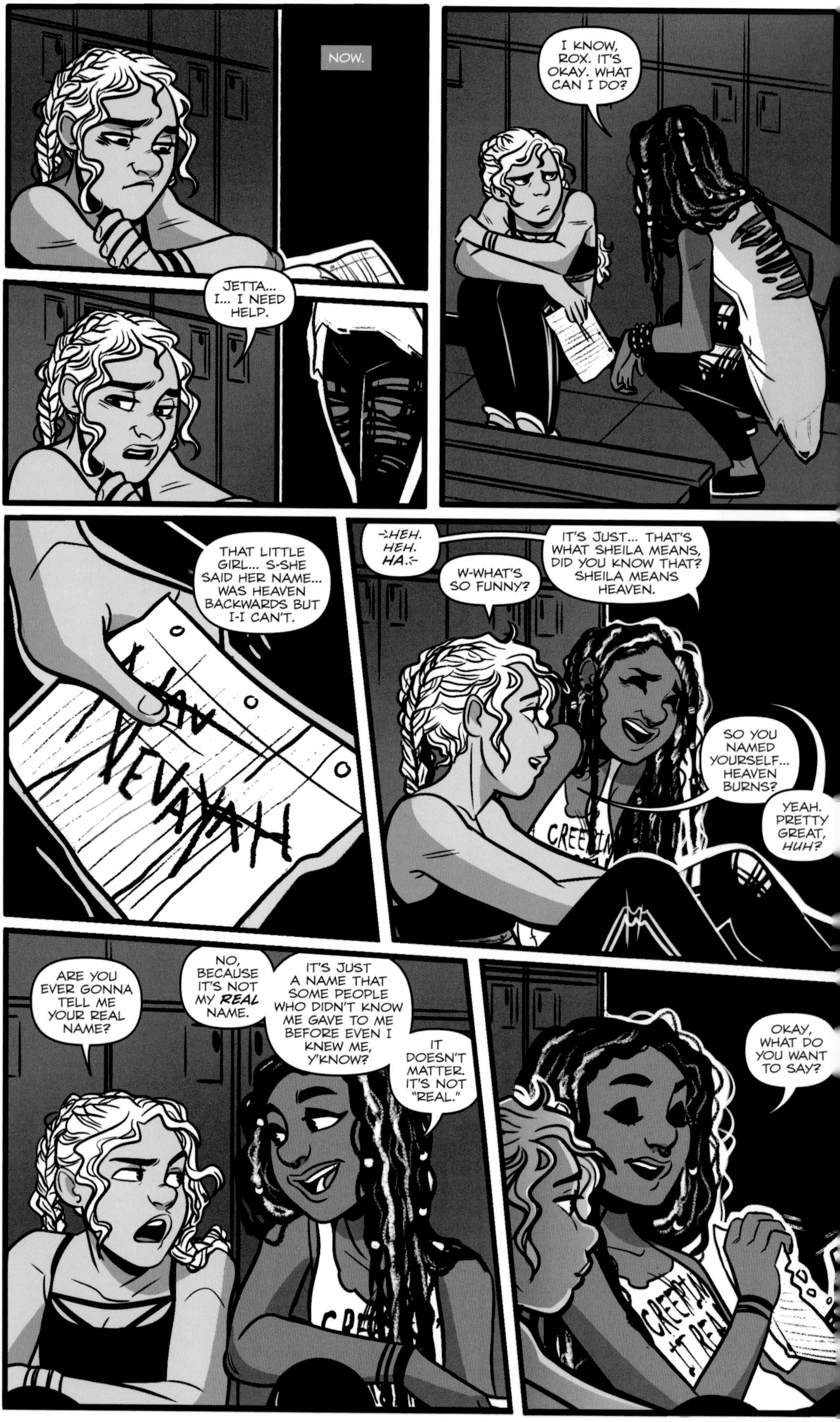

NOW.
JETTA... I... I NEED HELP.
I KNOW, ROX. IT'S OKAY. WHAT CAN I DO?
THAT LITTLE GIRL... S-SHE SAID HER NAME... WAS HEAVEN BACKWARDS BUT I-I CAN'T.
NEVAEH
-HEH. HEH. HA.-
IT'S JUST... THAT'S WHAT SHEILA MEANS, DID YOU KNOW THAT? SHEILA MEANS HEAVEN.
W-WHAT'S SO FUNNY?
SO YOU NAMED YOURSELF... HEAVEN BURNS?
YEAH. PRETTY GREAT, *HUH?*
ARE YOU EVER GONNA TELL ME YOUR REAL NAME?
NO, BECAUSE IT'S NOT MY ***REAL*** NAME.
IT'S JUST A NAME THAT SOME PEOPLE WHO DIDN'T KNOW ME GAVE TO ME BEFORE EVEN I KNEW ME, Y'KNOW?
IT DOESN'T MATTER. IT'S NOT "REAL."
OKAY, WHAT DO YOU WANT TO SAY?

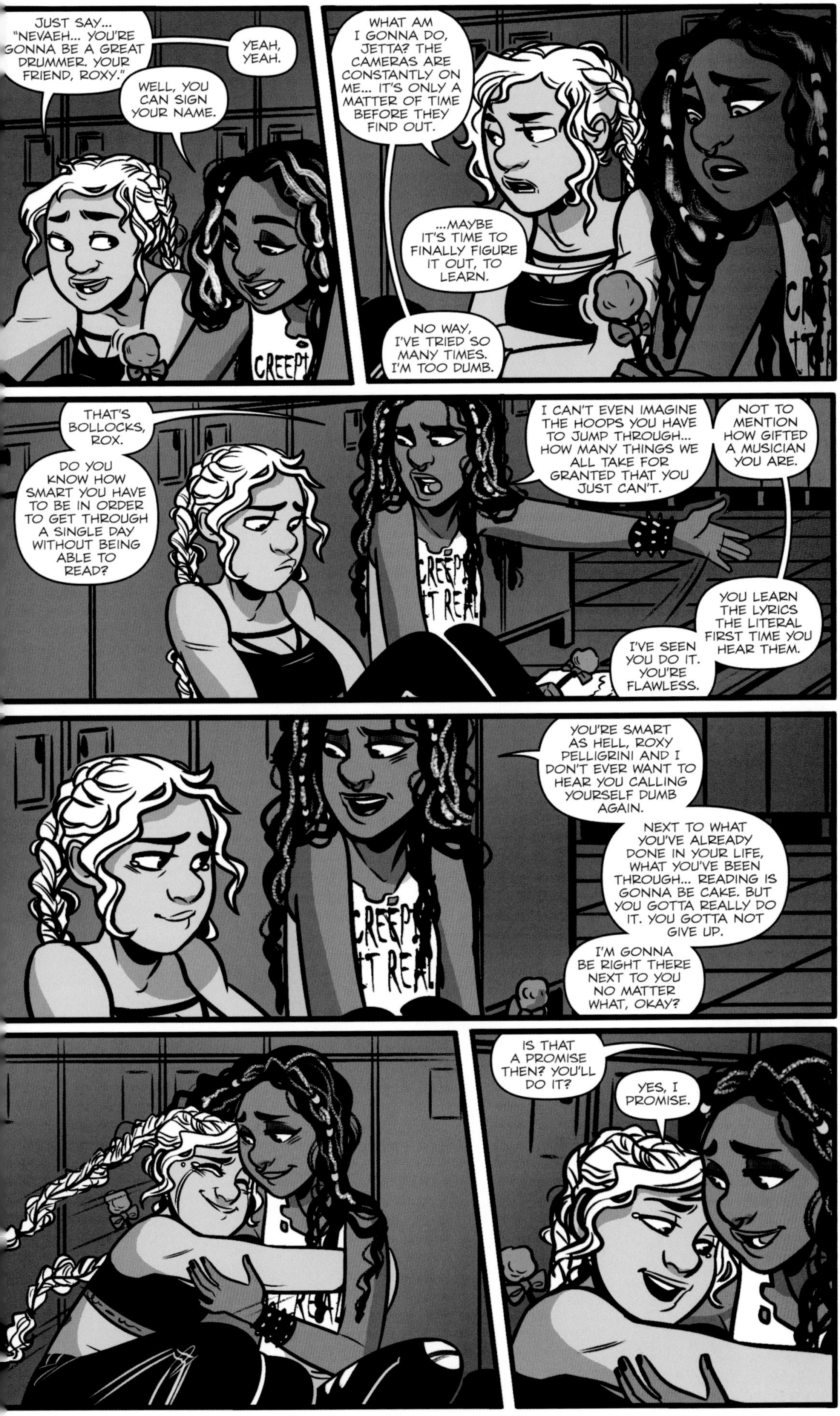
JUST SAY... "NEVAEH... YOU'RE GONNA BE A GREAT DRUMMER. YOUR FRIEND, ROXY."
YEAH, YEAH.
WELL, YOU CAN SIGN YOUR NAME.
CREEP
WHAT AM I GONNA DO, JETTA? THE CAMERAS ARE CONSTANTLY ON ME... IT'S ONLY A MATTER OF TIME BEFORE THEY FIND OUT.
...MAYBE IT'S TIME TO FINALLY FIGURE IT OUT, TO LEARN.
NO WAY, I'VE TRIED SO MANY TIMES. I'M TOO DUMB.
THAT'S BOLLOCKS, ROX.
DO YOU KNOW HOW SMART YOU HAVE TO BE IN ORDER TO GET THROUGH A SINGLE DAY WITHOUT BEING ABLE TO READ?
I CAN'T EVEN IMAGINE THE HOOPS YOU HAVE TO JUMP THROUGH... HOW MANY THINGS WE ALL TAKE FOR GRANTED THAT YOU JUST CAN'T.
NOT TO MENTION HOW GIFTED A MUSICIAN YOU ARE.
YOU LEARN THE LYRICS THE LITERAL FIRST TIME YOU HEAR THEM.
I'VE SEEN YOU DO IT. YOU'RE FLAWLESS.
YOU'RE SMART AS HELL, ROXY PELLIGRINI AND I DON'T EVER WANT TO HEAR YOU CALLING YOURSELF DUMB AGAIN.
NEXT TO WHAT YOU'VE ALREADY DONE IN YOUR LIFE, WHAT YOU'VE BEEN THROUGH... READING IS GONNA BE CAKE. BUT YOU GOTTA REALLY DO IT. YOU GOTTA NOT GIVE UP.
I'M GONNA BE RIGHT THERE NEXT TO YOU NO MATTER WHAT, OKAY?
IS THAT A PROMISE THEN? YOU'LL DO IT?
YES, I PROMISE.

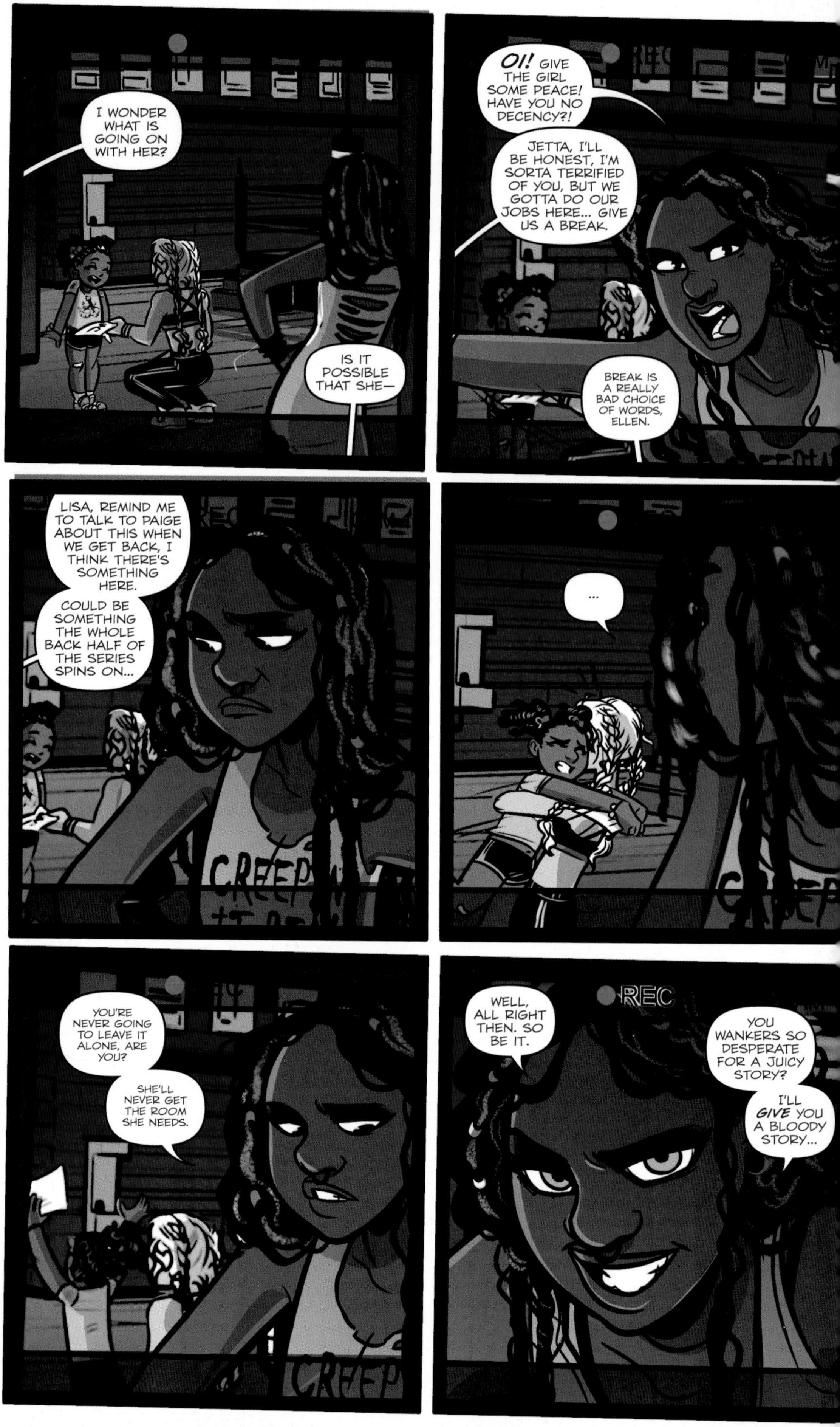
I WONDER WHAT IS GOING ON WITH HER?
IS IT POSSIBLE THAT SHE—
OI! GIVE THE GIRL SOME PEACE! HAVE YOU NO DECENCY?!
JETTA, I'LL BE HONEST, I'M SORTA TERRIFIED OF YOU, BUT WE GOTTA DO OUR JOBS HERE... GIVE US A BREAK.
BREAK IS A REALLY BAD CHOICE OF WORDS, ELLEN.
LISA, REMIND ME TO TALK TO PAIGE ABOUT THIS WHEN WE GET BACK, I THINK THERE'S SOMETHING HERE.
COULD BE SOMETHING THE WHOLE BACK HALF OF THE SERIES SPINS ON...
CREEP
...
YOU'RE NEVER GOING TO LEAVE IT ALONE, ARE YOU?
SHE'LL NEVER GET THE ROOM SHE NEEDS.
REC
WELL, ALL RIGHT THEN. SO BE IT.
YOU WANKERS SO DESPERATE FOR A JUICY STORY?
I'LL *GIVE* YOU A BLOODY STORY...

AUGUST 4–6 • SANTA ANA, CA • $TBD

the **MISFITS** • **MANIC TUESDAYS**
the **SLIPPERY SUBJECTS** • **FORMAL FRIDAYS**
SAM WISE and the CHARLIES • **CHIFF**
THOM THOM CLUB • **AGENT ONGE**
DOMO ARIGATO ROBADO • **5-GUITAR BAND**
GIBBYS • **TED ADAMS BLUES CATASTROPHE**
UNICORN • **RYALL FOR ONE** • **TRIPLE DAGGER**
HURONS • **SIMON EYES** • **MOWJIRA** • **DUBS**
TALKING MARCI MARCI • **BOBBY BOBBINS**
LT. DANG • the **JV's** • **UNFAIR SUPERPOWERS**
LANDSTRIDER • **BEDFORD DRIVE** • **RAPTAZ**
S.C.B. • **WOODFORD BROWNLEE** • **CERA SI**
UYETAKERS • **LONG LUNCH** • **MEIS KNEES**
HANK ON THE BANK • **POP PROJECT** • **NOT TESLA**
YPICAL GIL • **BARLINERS** • **TIPPED IN** • **LAST WALT**
URLATER • **THAT'S AMAURI** • **TIME CHEETAHS** • **FIL**
the **WAREHOUSE GIRLS** • **COLD SLITHER** • **GENTLEMEN GHOSTS**
ANADIAN TYPERWRITER • **TUNAK TUN** • **SHEVLIN DIRT** • **DELARE**
the **EYE SINGER** • **HATE SO REAL** • **MIKEAGE** • **SAGNASTY**
DR. SCHMEE • **HORSHACKS** • **REBOUNDERS** • **SEEING BREAD**
5-MINUTEMEN • the **INSANGELS** • **AYA and EMI** • **MUAMS**

ART M. VICTORIA ROBADO

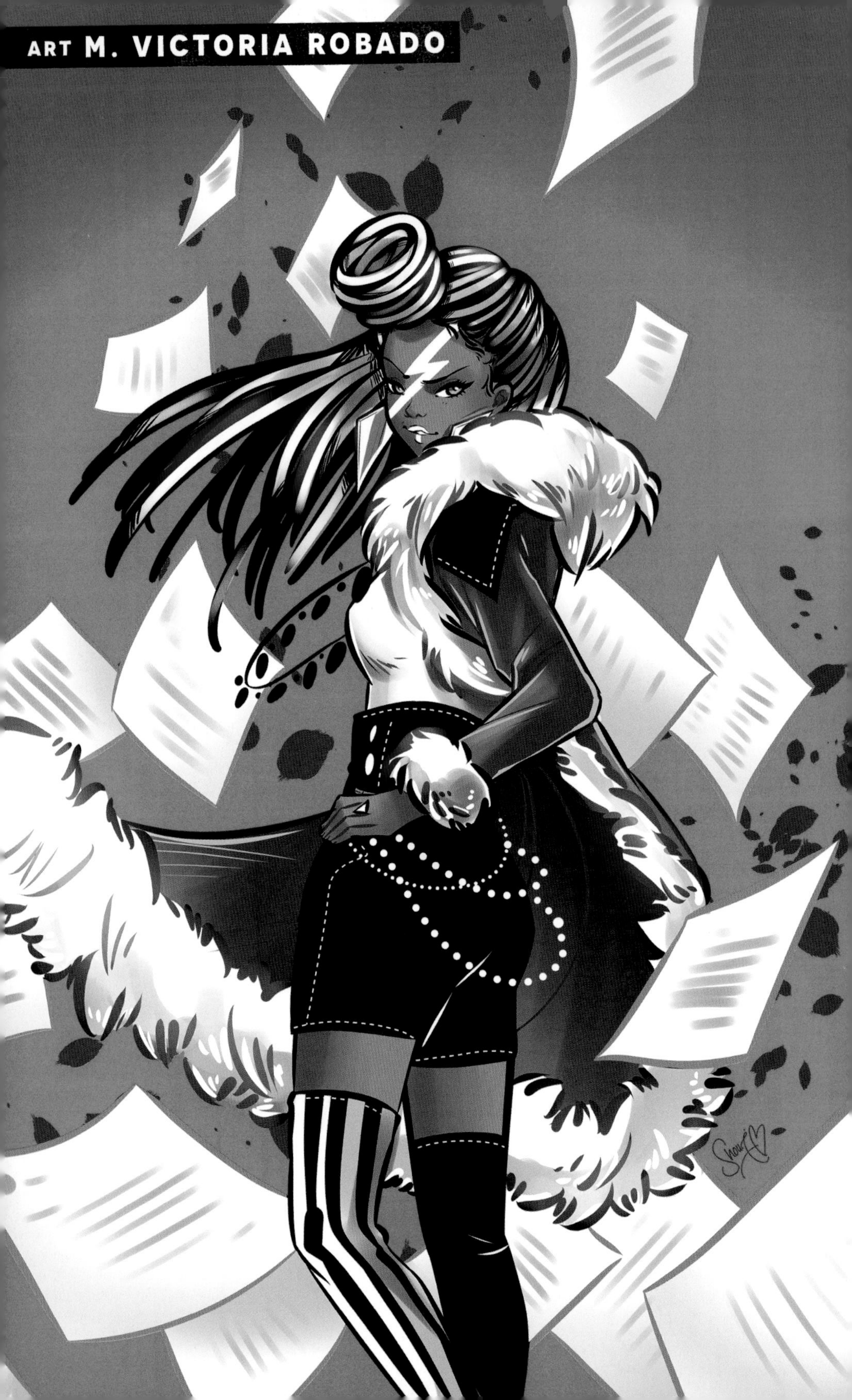

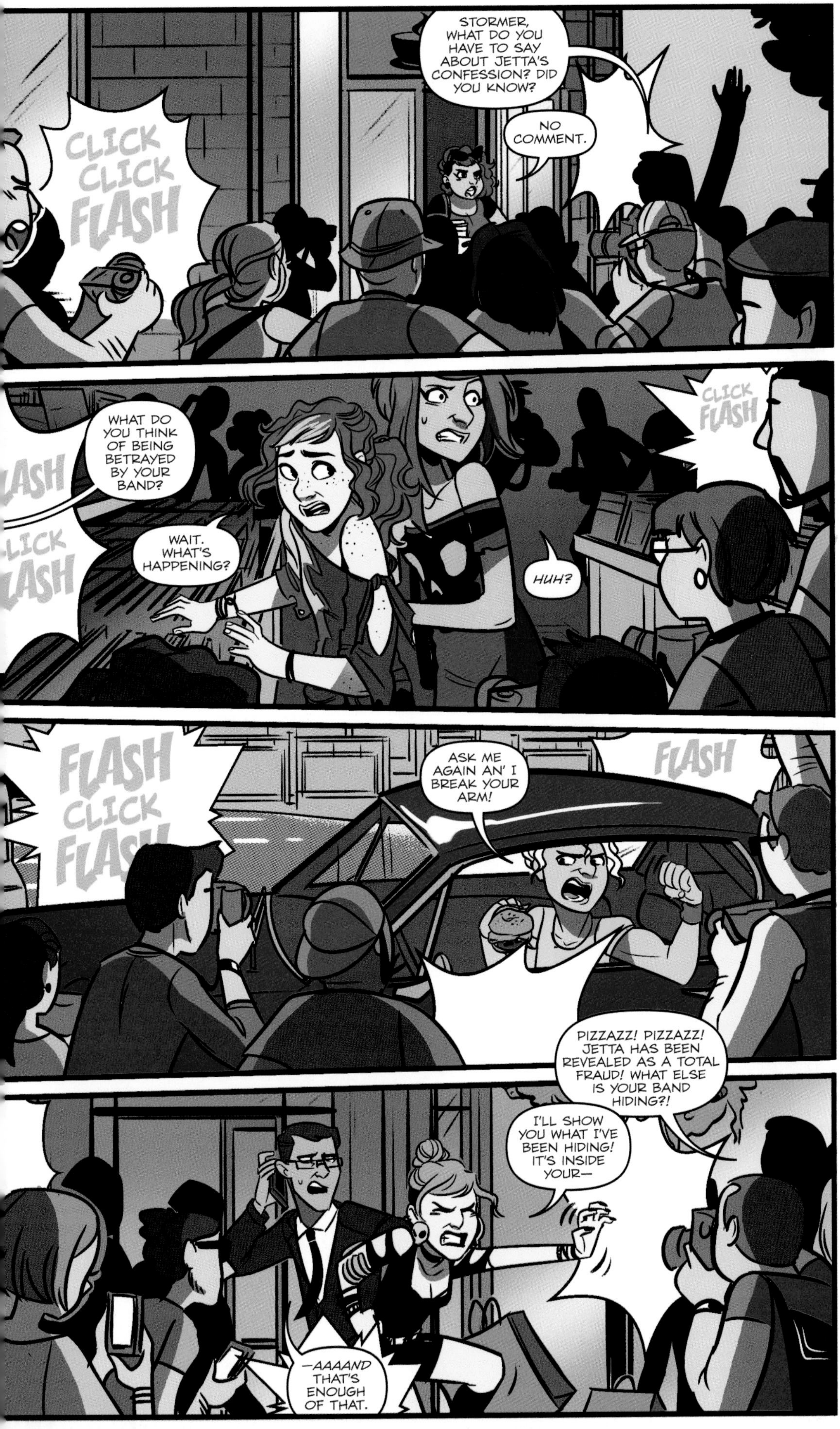

CLICK CLICK FLASH
STORMER, WHAT DO YOU HAVE TO SAY ABOUT JETTA'S CONFESSION? DID YOU KNOW?
NO COMMENT.
WHAT DO YOU THINK OF BEING BETRAYED BY YOUR BAND?
CLICK FLASH
WAIT. WHAT'S HAPPENING?
HUH?
FLASH CLICK FLASH
FLASH
ASK ME AGAIN AN' I BREAK YOUR ARM!
PIZZAZZ! PIZZAZZ! JETTA HAS BEEN REVEALED AS A TOTAL FRAUD! WHAT ELSE IS YOUR BAND HIDING?!
I'LL SHOW YOU WHAT I'VE BEEN HIDING! IT'S INSIDE YOUR—
—AAAAND THAT'S ENOUGH OF THAT.

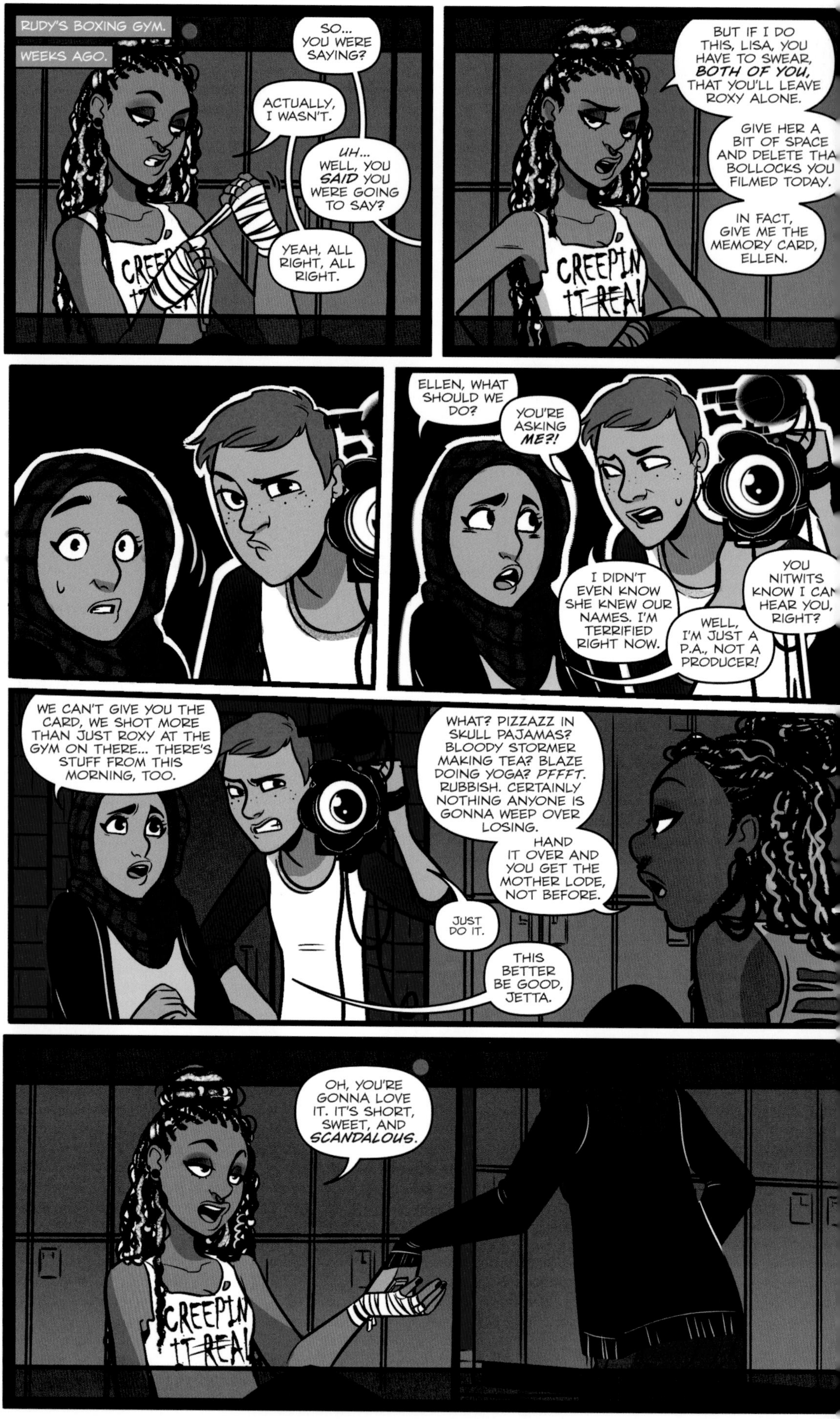
RUDY'S BOXING GYM.
WEEKS AGO.
SO... YOU WERE SAYING?
ACTUALLY, I WASN'T.
UH... WELL, YOU SAID YOU WERE GOING TO SAY?
YEAH, ALL RIGHT, ALL RIGHT.
BUT IF I DO THIS, LISA, YOU HAVE TO SWEAR, BOTH OF YOU, THAT YOU'LL LEAVE ROXY ALONE.
GIVE HER A BIT OF SPACE AND DELETE THA BOLLOCKS YOU FILMED TODAY.
IN FACT, GIVE ME THE MEMORY CARD, ELLEN.
ELLEN, WHAT SHOULD WE DO?
YOU'RE ASKING ME?!
I DIDN'T EVEN KNOW SHE KNEW OUR NAMES. I'M TERRIFIED RIGHT NOW.
WELL, I'M JUST A P.A., NOT A PRODUCER!
YOU NITWITS KNOW I CAN HEAR YOU, RIGHT?
WE CAN'T GIVE YOU THE CARD, WE SHOT MORE THAN JUST ROXY AT THE GYM ON THERE... THERE'S STUFF FROM THIS MORNING, TOO.
WHAT? PIZZAZZ IN SKULL PAJAMAS? BLOODY STORMER MAKING TEA? BLAZE DOING YOGA? PFFFT. RUBBISH. CERTAINLY NOTHING ANYONE IS GONNA WEEP OVER LOSING.
HAND IT OVER AND YOU GET THE MOTHER LODE, NOT BEFORE.
JUST DO IT.
THIS BETTER BE GOOD, JETTA.
OH, YOU'RE GONNA LOVE IT. IT'S SHORT, SWEET, AND SCANDALOUS.

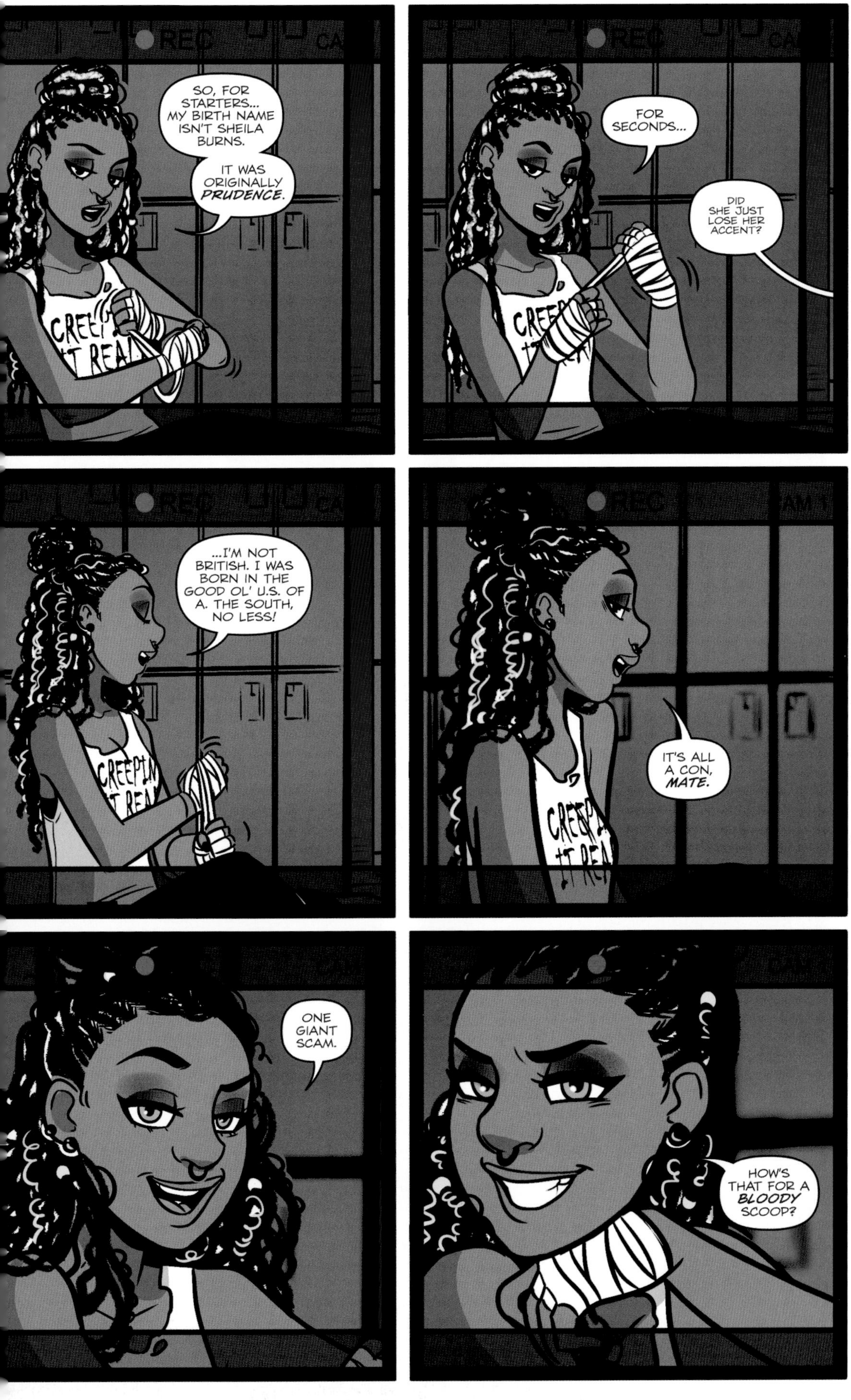
REC
SO, FOR STARTERS... MY BIRTH NAME ISN'T SHEILA BURNS.
IT WAS ORIGINALLY *PRUDENCE*.
CREEPIN' IT REAL
REC
FOR SECONDS...
DID SHE JUST LOSE HER ACCENT?
REC
...I'M NOT BRITISH. I WAS BORN IN THE GOOD OL' U.S. OF A. THE SOUTH, NO LESS!
CREEPIN' IT REAL
REC
IT'S ALL A CON, *MATE*.
ONE GIANT SCAM.
HOW'S THAT FOR A *BLOODY* SCOOP?

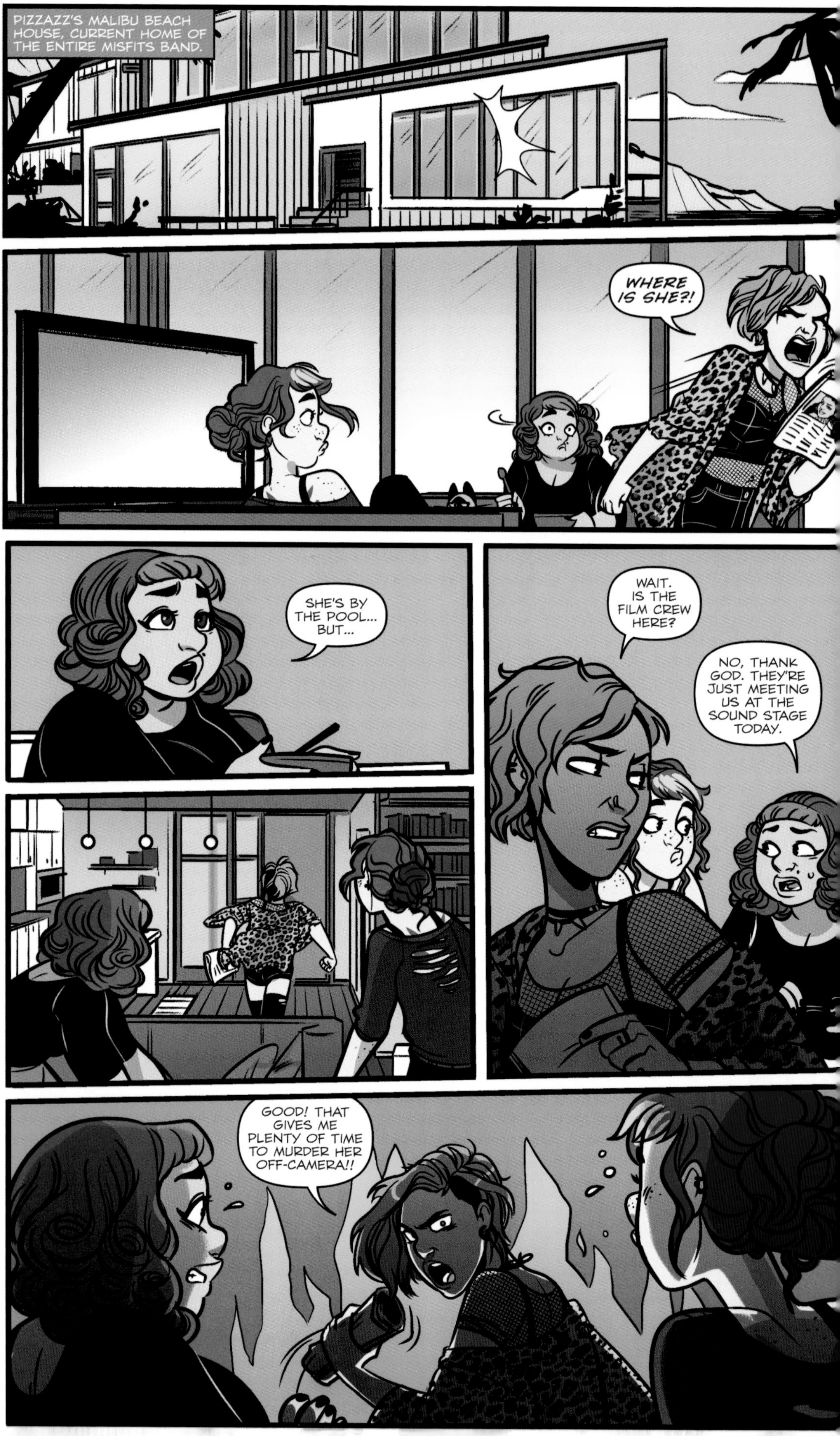
PIZZAZZ'S MALIBU BEACH HOUSE, CURRENT HOME OF THE ENTIRE MISFITS BAND.
WHERE IS SHE?!
SHE'S BY THE POOL... BUT...
WAIT. IS THE FILM CREW HERE?
NO, THANK GOD. THEY'RE JUST MEETING US AT THE SOUND STAGE TODAY.
GOOD! THAT GIVES ME PLENTY OF TIME TO MURDER HER OFF-CAMERA!!

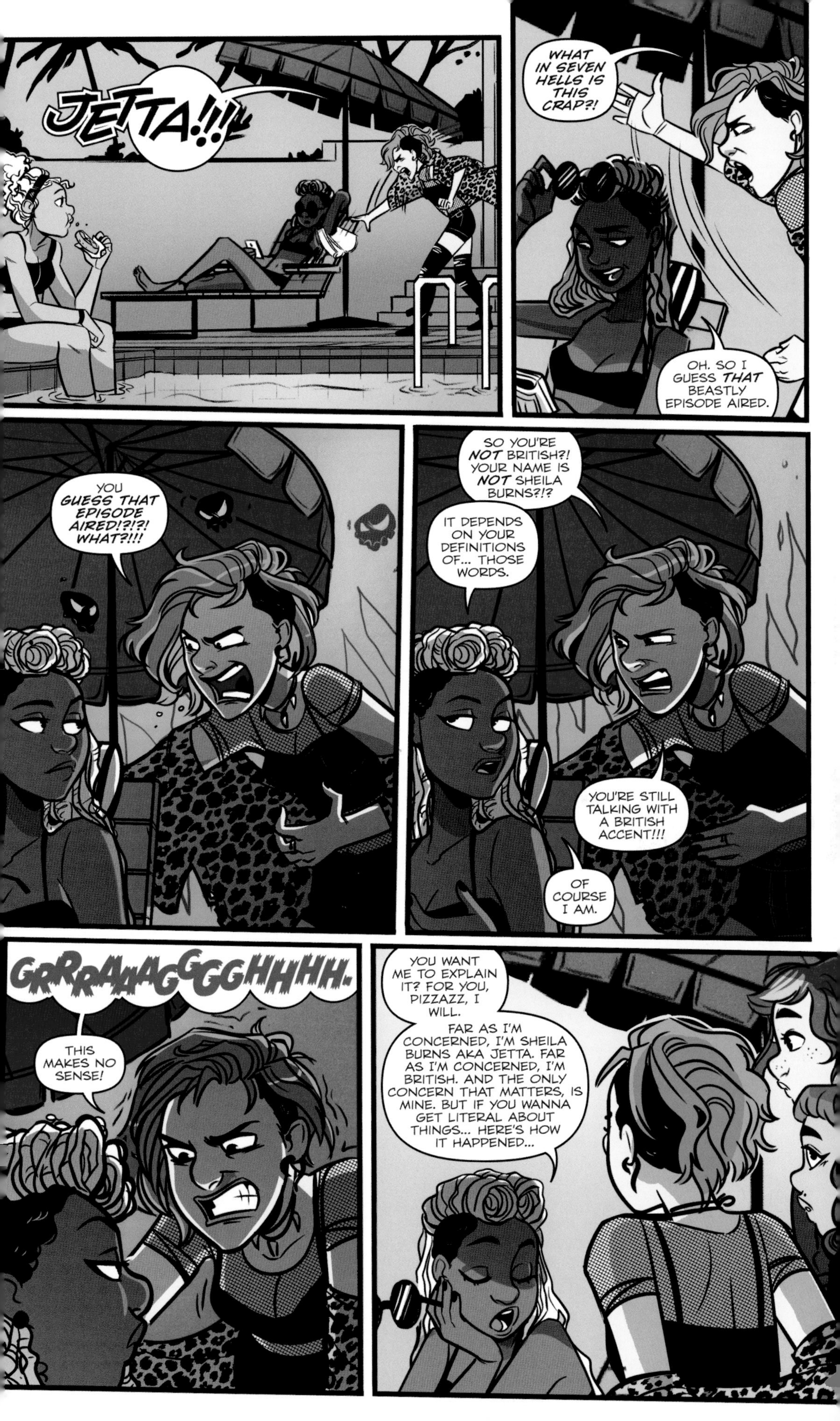
JETTA!!!
WHAT IN SEVEN HELLS IS THIS CRAP?!
OH. SO I GUESS THAT BEASTLY EPISODE AIRED.
YOU GUESS THAT EPISODE AIRED!?!?! WHAT?!!!
SO YOU'RE NOT BRITISH?! YOUR NAME IS NOT SHEILA BURNS?!?
IT DEPENDS ON YOUR DEFINITIONS OF... THOSE WORDS.
YOU'RE STILL TALKING WITH A BRITISH ACCENT!!!
OF COURSE I AM.
GRRRAAAGGGGHHHH.
THIS MAKES NO SENSE!
YOU WANT ME TO EXPLAIN IT? FOR YOU, PIZZAZZ, I WILL.
FAR AS I'M CONCERNED, I'M SHEILA BURNS AKA JETTA. FAR AS I'M CONCERNED, I'M BRITISH. AND THE ONLY CONCERN THAT MATTERS, IS MINE. BUT IF YOU WANNA GET LITERAL ABOUT THINGS... HERE'S HOW IT HAPPENED...

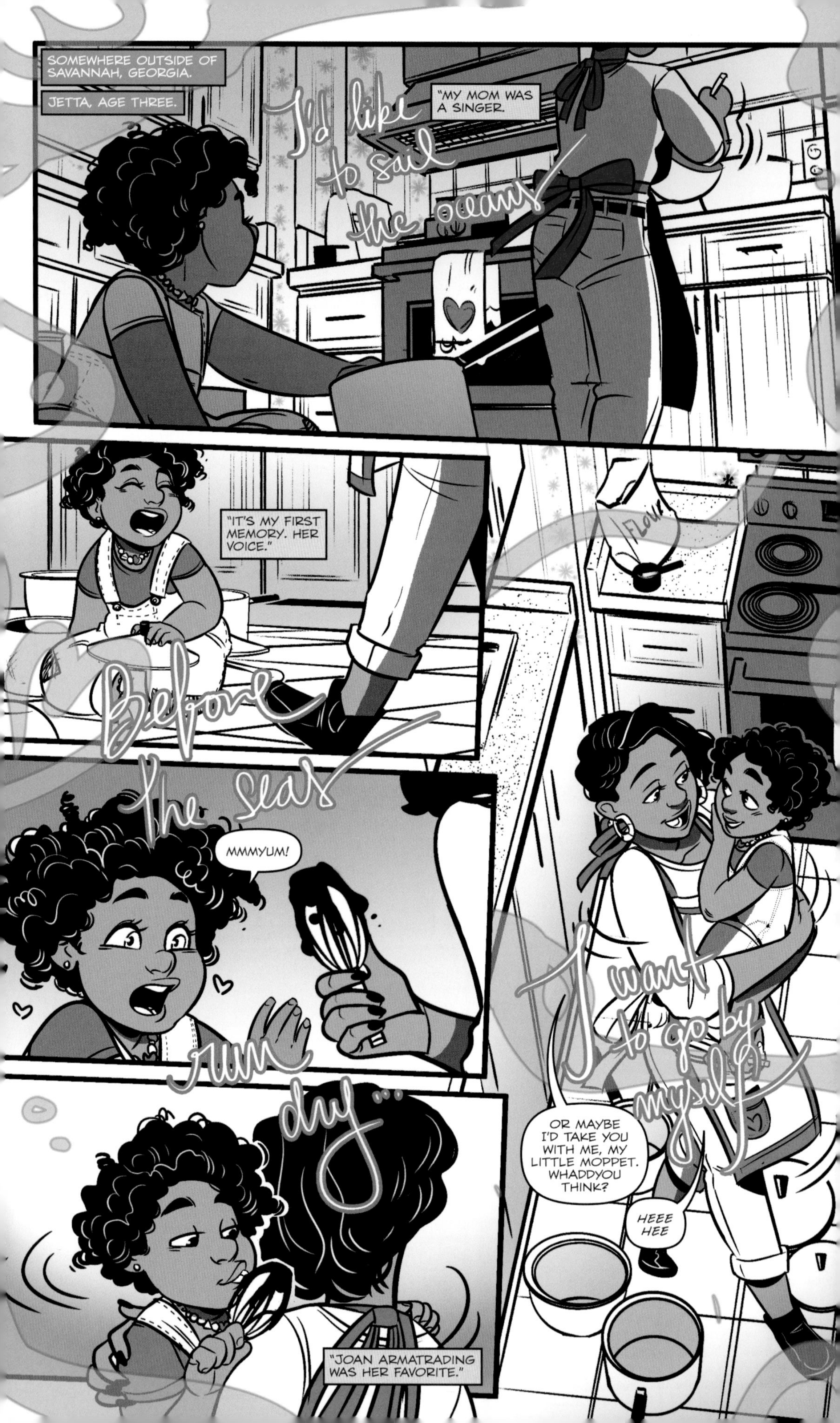

SOMEWHERE OUTSIDE OF SAVANNAH, GEORGIA.
JETTA, AGE THREE.
"MY MOM WAS A SINGER.
I'd like to sail the oceans
"IT'S MY FIRST MEMORY. HER VOICE."
Before the seas
MMMYUM!
run dry...
"JOAN ARMATRADING WAS HER FAVORITE."
I want to go by myself
OR MAYBE I'D TAKE YOU WITH ME, MY LITTLE MOPPET. WHADDYOU THINK?
HEEE HEE

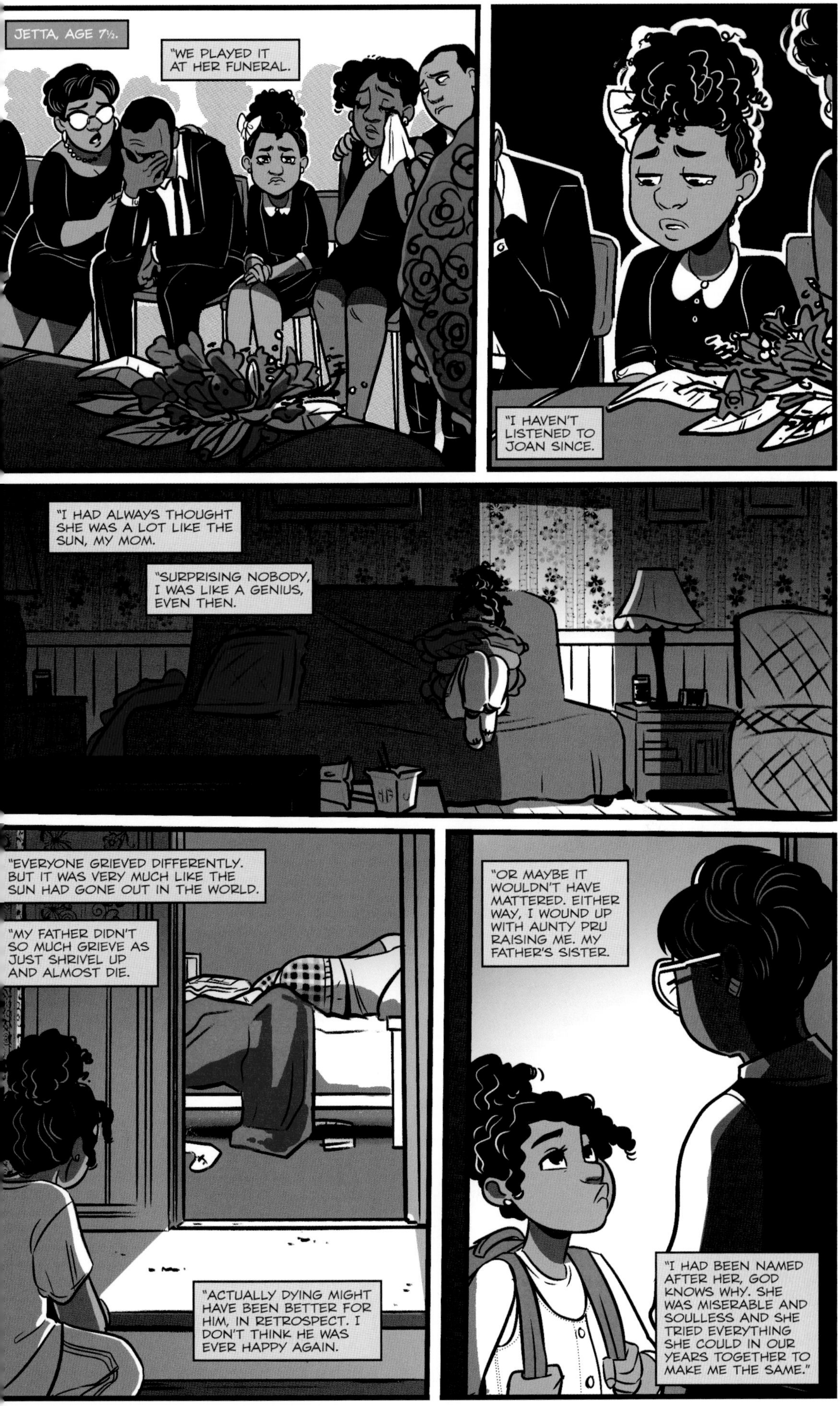
JETTA, AGE 7½.
"WE PLAYED IT AT HER FUNERAL.
"I HAVEN'T LISTENED TO JOAN SINCE.
"I HAD ALWAYS THOUGHT SHE WAS A LOT LIKE THE SUN, MY MOM.
"SURPRISING NOBODY, I WAS LIKE A GENIUS, EVEN THEN.
"EVERYONE GRIEVED DIFFERENTLY. BUT IT WAS VERY MUCH LIKE THE SUN HAD GONE OUT IN THE WORLD.
"MY FATHER DIDN'T SO MUCH GRIEVE AS JUST SHRIVEL UP AND ALMOST DIE.
"ACTUALLY DYING MIGHT HAVE BEEN BETTER FOR HIM, IN RETROSPECT. I DON'T THINK HE WAS EVER HAPPY AGAIN.
"OR MAYBE IT WOULDN'T HAVE MATTERED. EITHER WAY, I WOUND UP WITH AUNTY PRU RAISING ME. MY FATHER'S SISTER.
"I HAD BEEN NAMED AFTER HER, GOD KNOWS WHY. SHE WAS MISERABLE AND SOULLESS AND SHE TRIED EVERYTHING SHE COULD IN OUR YEARS TOGETHER TO MAKE ME THE SAME."

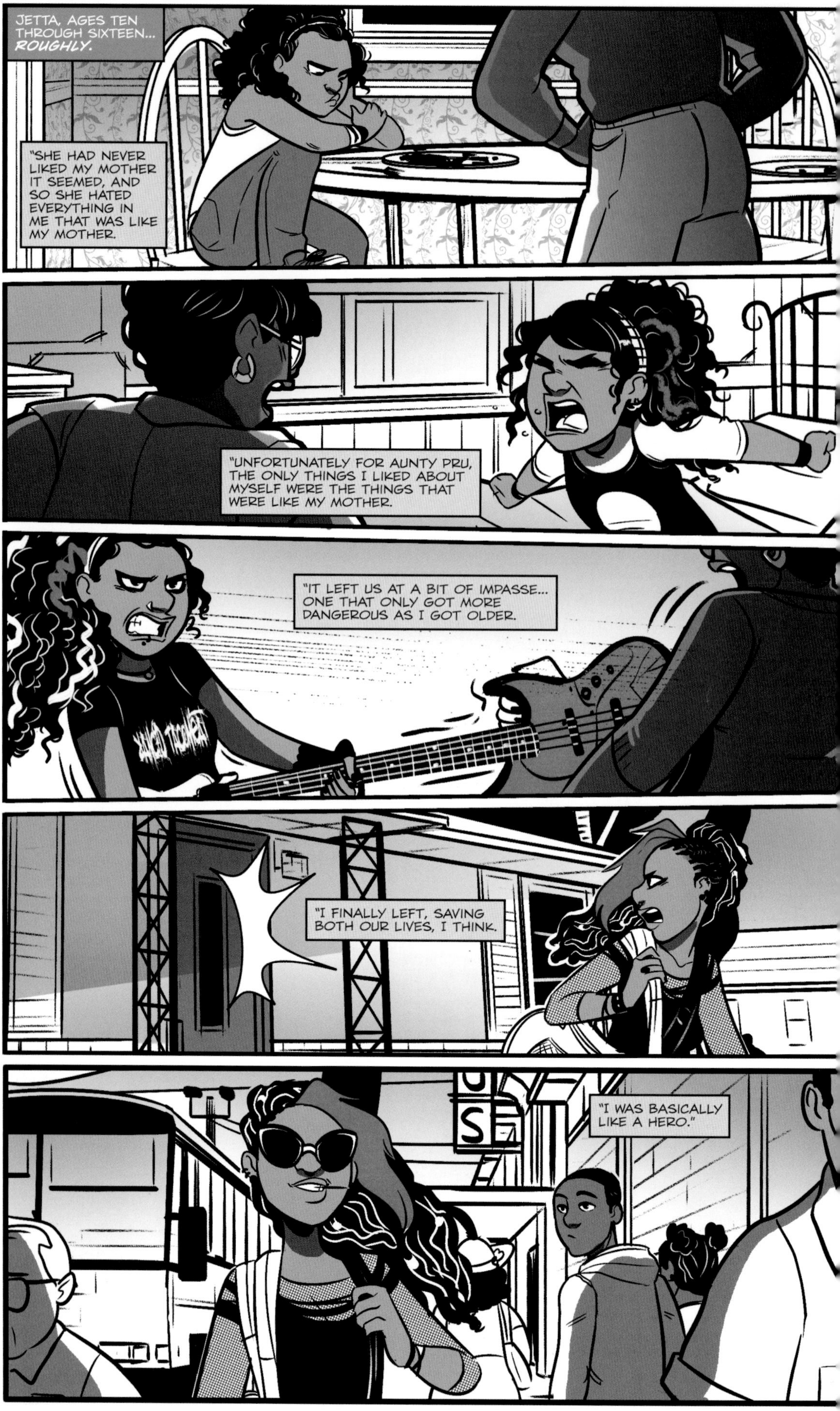
JETTA, AGES TEN THROUGH SIXTEEN... *ROUGHLY.*
"SHE HAD NEVER LIKED MY MOTHER IT SEEMED, AND SO SHE HATED EVERYTHING IN ME THAT WAS LIKE MY MOTHER.
"UNFORTUNATELY FOR AUNTY PRU, THE ONLY THINGS I LIKED ABOUT MYSELF WERE THE THINGS THAT WERE LIKE MY MOTHER.
"IT LEFT US AT A BIT OF IMPASSE... ONE THAT ONLY GOT MORE DANGEROUS AS I GOT OLDER.
"I FINALLY LEFT, SAVING BOTH OUR LIVES, I THINK.
"I WAS BASICALLY LIKE A HERO."

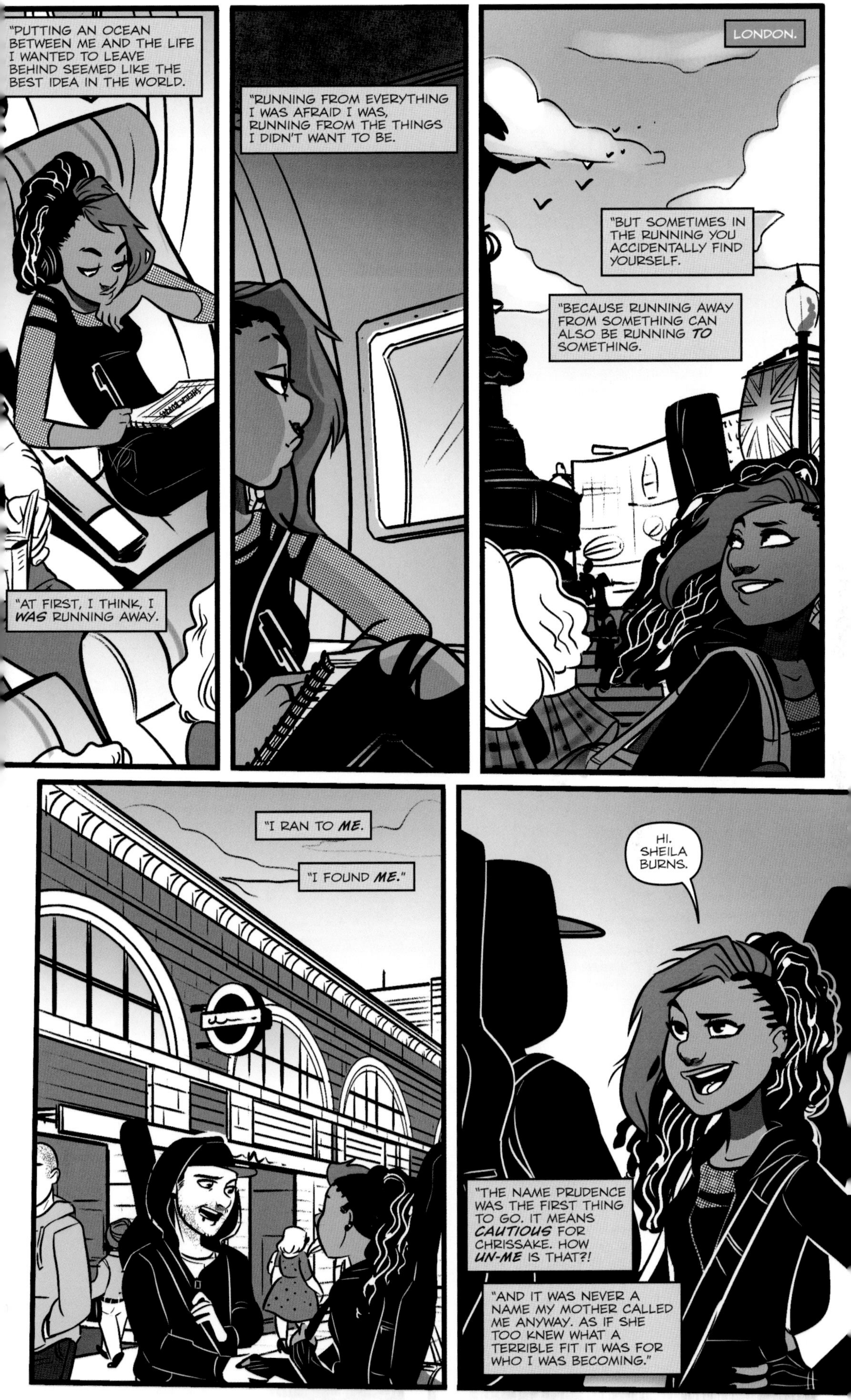
"PUTTING AN OCEAN BETWEEN ME AND THE LIFE I WANTED TO LEAVE BEHIND SEEMED LIKE THE BEST IDEA IN THE WORLD.
"AT FIRST, I THINK, I WAS RUNNING AWAY.
"RUNNING FROM EVERYTHING I WAS AFRAID I WAS, RUNNING FROM THE THINGS I DIDN'T WANT TO BE.
LONDON.
"BUT SOMETIMES IN THE RUNNING YOU ACCIDENTALLY FIND YOURSELF.
"BECAUSE RUNNING AWAY FROM SOMETHING CAN ALSO BE RUNNING TO SOMETHING.
"I RAN TO ME.
"I FOUND ME."
HI. SHEILA BURNS.
"THE NAME PRUDENCE WAS THE FIRST THING TO GO. IT MEANS CAUTIOUS FOR CHRISSAKE. HOW UN-ME IS THAT?!
"AND IT WAS NEVER A NAME MY MOTHER CALLED ME ANYWAY. AS IF SHE TOO KNEW WHAT A TERRIBLE FIT IT WAS FOR WHO I WAS BECOMING."

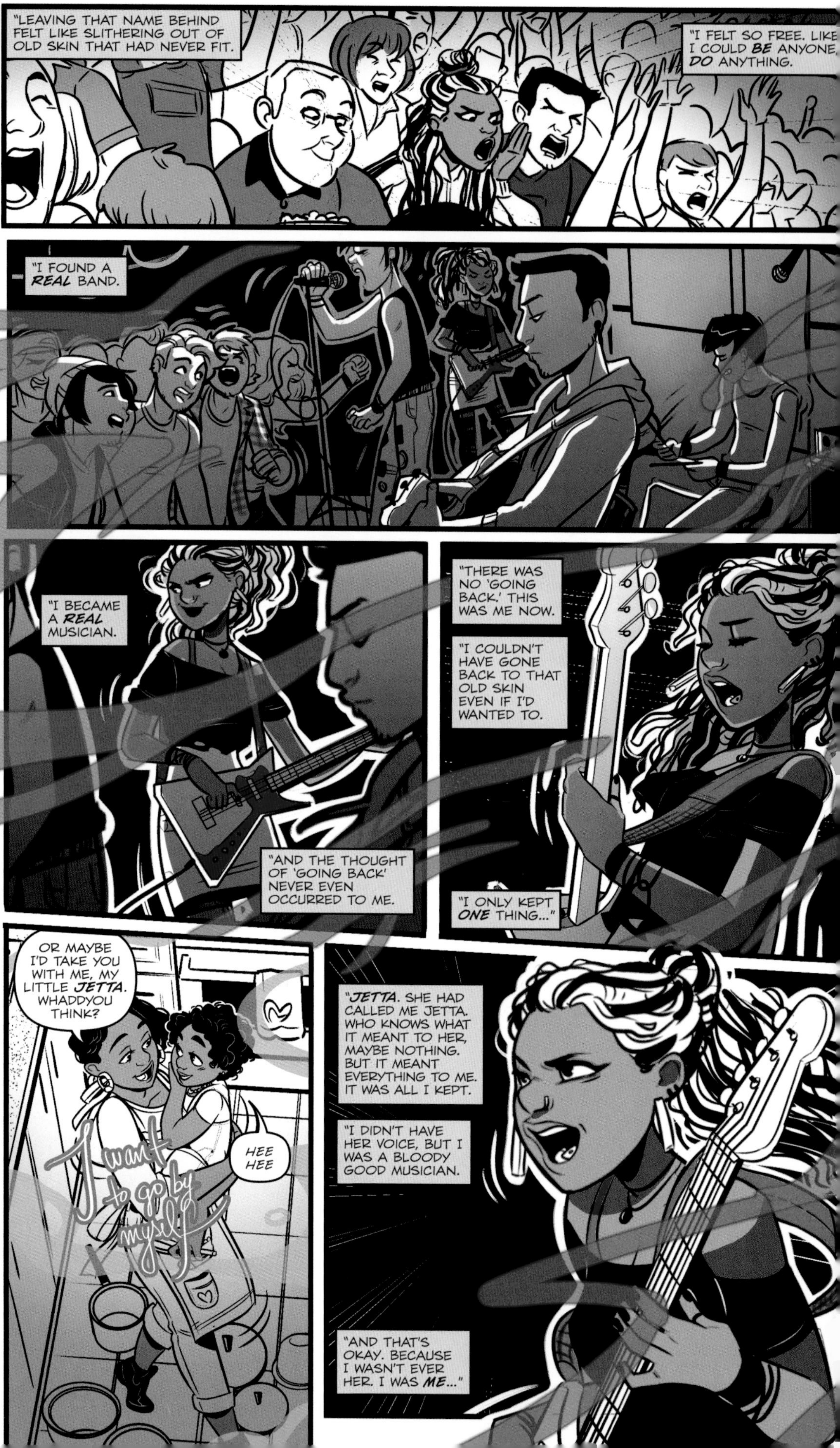
"LEAVING THAT NAME BEHIND FELT LIKE SLITHERING OUT OF OLD SKIN THAT HAD NEVER FIT.
"I FELT SO FREE. LIKE I COULD BE ANYONE, DO ANYTHING.
"I FOUND A REAL BAND.
"I BECAME A REAL MUSICIAN.
"AND THE THOUGHT OF 'GOING BACK' NEVER EVEN OCCURRED TO ME.
"THERE WAS NO 'GOING BACK.' THIS WAS ME NOW.
"I COULDN'T HAVE GONE BACK TO THAT OLD SKIN EVEN IF I'D WANTED TO.
"I ONLY KEPT ONE THING..."
OR MAYBE I'D TAKE YOU WITH ME, MY LITTLE JETTA. WHADDYOU THINK?
HEE HEE
I want to go by myself
"JETTA. SHE HAD CALLED ME JETTA. WHO KNOWS WHAT IT MEANT TO HER, MAYBE NOTHING. BUT IT MEANT EVERYTHING TO ME. IT WAS ALL I KEPT.
"I DIDN'T HAVE HER VOICE, BUT I WAS A BLOODY GOOD MUSICIAN.
"AND THAT'S OKAY. BECAUSE I WASN'T EVER HER. I WAS ME..."

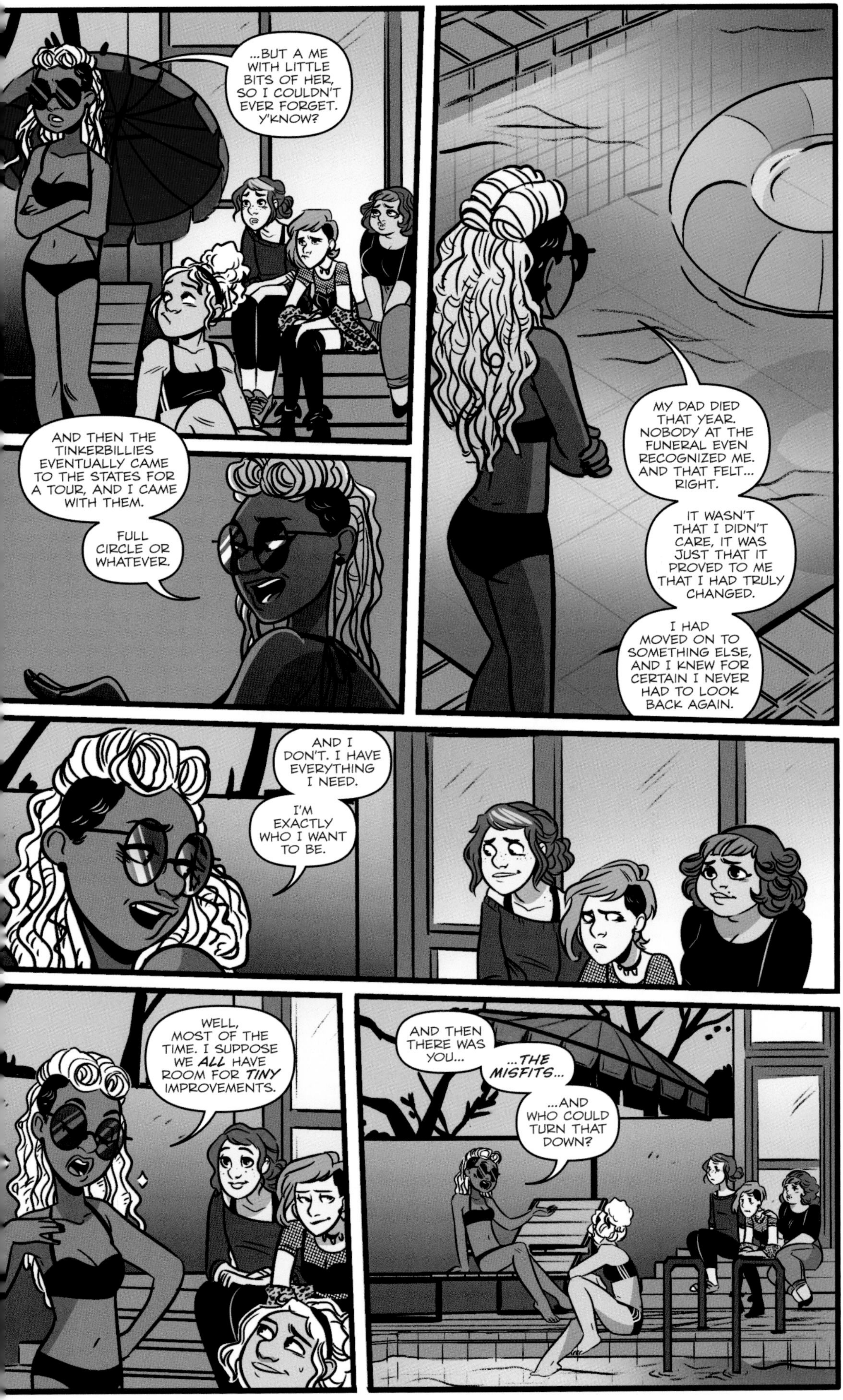
...BUT A ME WITH LITTLE BITS OF HER, SO I COULDN'T EVER FORGET. Y'KNOW?
AND THEN THE TINKERBILLIES EVENTUALLY CAME TO THE STATES FOR A TOUR, AND I CAME WITH THEM.
FULL CIRCLE OR WHATEVER.
MY DAD DIED THAT YEAR. NOBODY AT THE FUNERAL EVEN RECOGNIZED ME. AND THAT FELT... RIGHT.
IT WASN'T THAT I DIDN'T CARE, IT WAS JUST THAT IT PROVED TO ME THAT I HAD TRULY CHANGED.
I HAD MOVED ON TO SOMETHING ELSE, AND I KNEW FOR CERTAIN I NEVER HAD TO LOOK BACK AGAIN.
AND I DON'T. I HAVE EVERYTHING I NEED.
I'M EXACTLY WHO I WANT TO BE.
WELL, MOST OF THE TIME. I SUPPOSE WE ALL HAVE ROOM FOR TINY IMPROVEMENTS.
AND THEN THERE WAS YOU...
...THE MISFITS...
...AND WHO COULD TURN THAT DOWN?

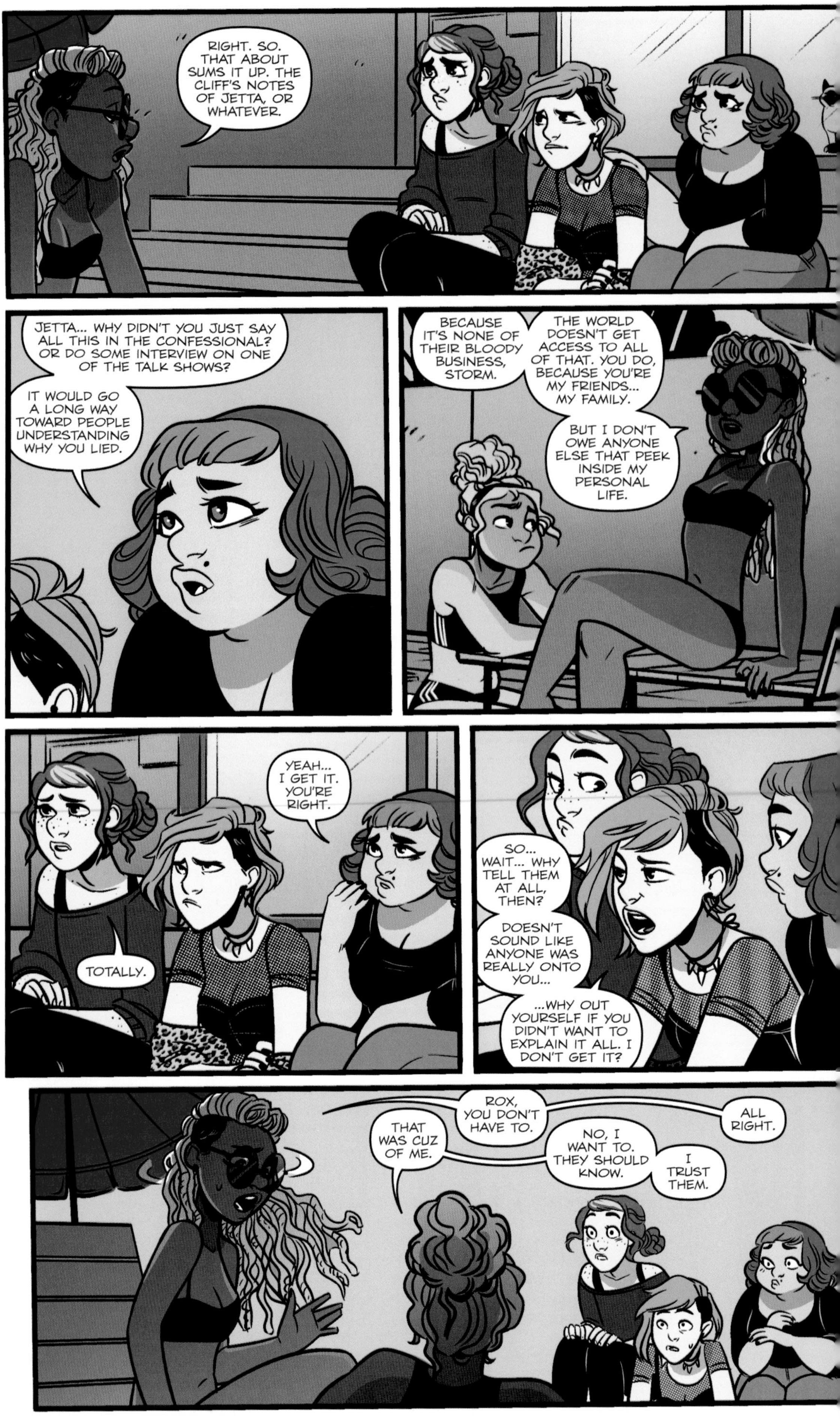
RIGHT. SO. THAT ABOUT SUMS IT UP. THE CLIFF'S NOTES OF JETTA, OR WHATEVER.
JETTA... WHY DIDN'T YOU JUST SAY ALL THIS IN THE CONFESSIONAL? OR DO SOME INTERVIEW ON ONE OF THE TALK SHOWS?
IT WOULD GO A LONG WAY TOWARD PEOPLE UNDERSTANDING WHY YOU LIED.
BECAUSE IT'S NONE OF THEIR BLOODY BUSINESS, STORM.
THE WORLD DOESN'T GET ACCESS TO ALL OF THAT. YOU DO, BECAUSE YOU'RE MY FRIENDS... MY FAMILY.
BUT I DON'T OWE ANYONE ELSE THAT PEEK INSIDE MY PERSONAL LIFE.
YEAH... I GET IT. YOU'RE RIGHT.
TOTALLY.
SO... WAIT... WHY TELL THEM AT ALL, THEN?
DOESN'T SOUND LIKE ANYONE WAS REALLY ONTO YOU...
...WHY OUT YOURSELF IF YOU DIDN'T WANT TO EXPLAIN IT ALL. I DON'T GET IT?
THAT WAS CUZ OF ME.
ROX, YOU DON'T HAVE TO.
NO, I WANT TO. THEY SHOULD KNOW.
I TRUST THEM.
ALL RIGHT.

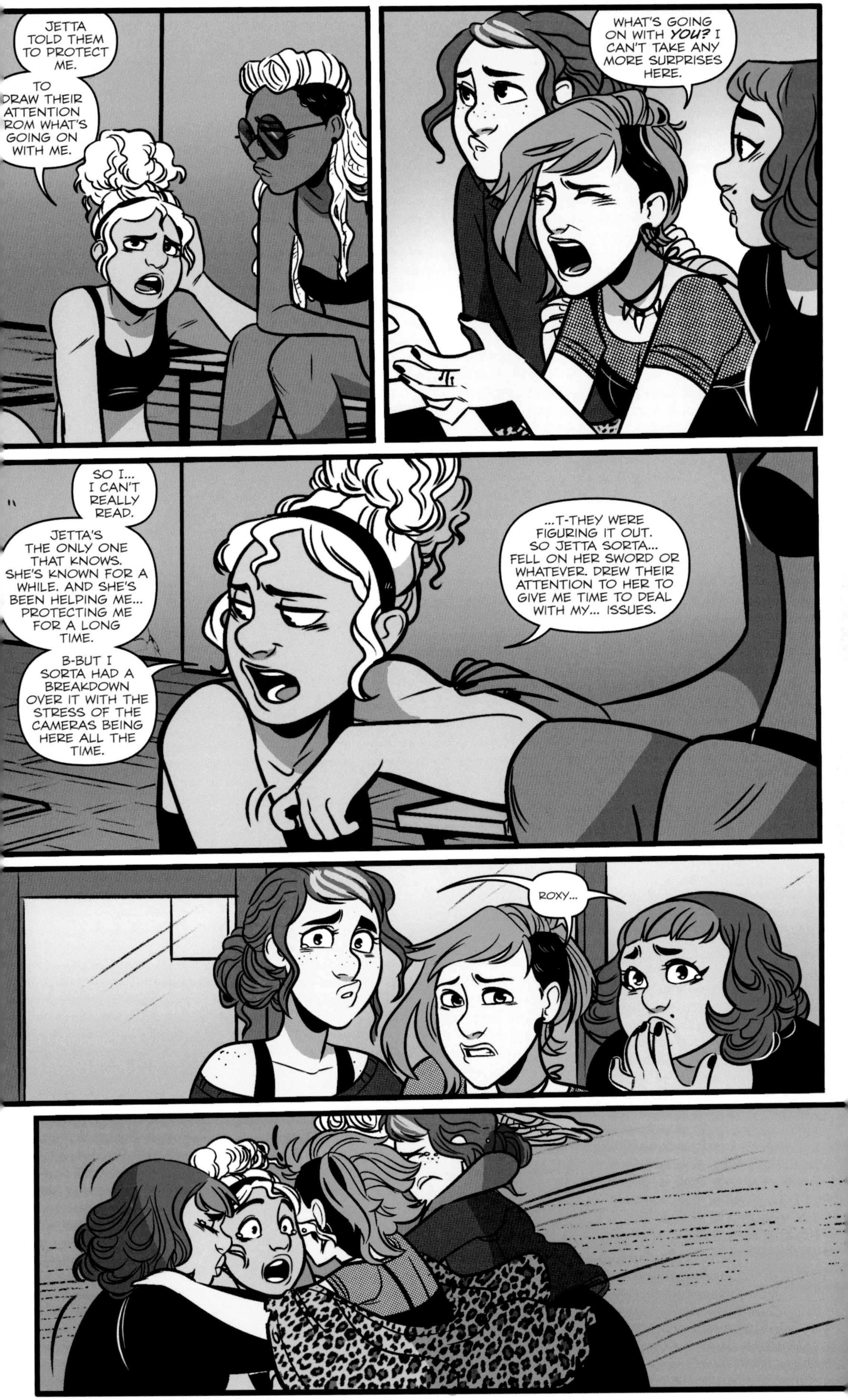
JETTA TOLD THEM TO PROTECT ME.
TO DRAW THEIR ATTENTION ROM WHAT'S GOING ON WITH ME.
WHAT'S GOING ON WITH *YOU?* I CAN'T TAKE ANY MORE SURPRISES HERE.
SO I... I CAN'T REALLY READ.
JETTA'S THE ONLY ONE THAT KNOWS. SHE'S KNOWN FOR A WHILE. AND SHE'S BEEN HELPING ME... PROTECTING ME FOR A LONG TIME.
B-BUT I SORTA HAD A BREAKDOWN OVER IT WITH THE STRESS OF THE CAMERAS BEING HERE ALL THE TIME.
...T-THEY WERE FIGURING IT OUT. SO JETTA SORTA... FELL ON HER SWORD OR WHATEVER. DREW THEIR ATTENTION TO HER TO GIVE ME TIME TO DEAL WITH MY... ISSUES.
ROXY...

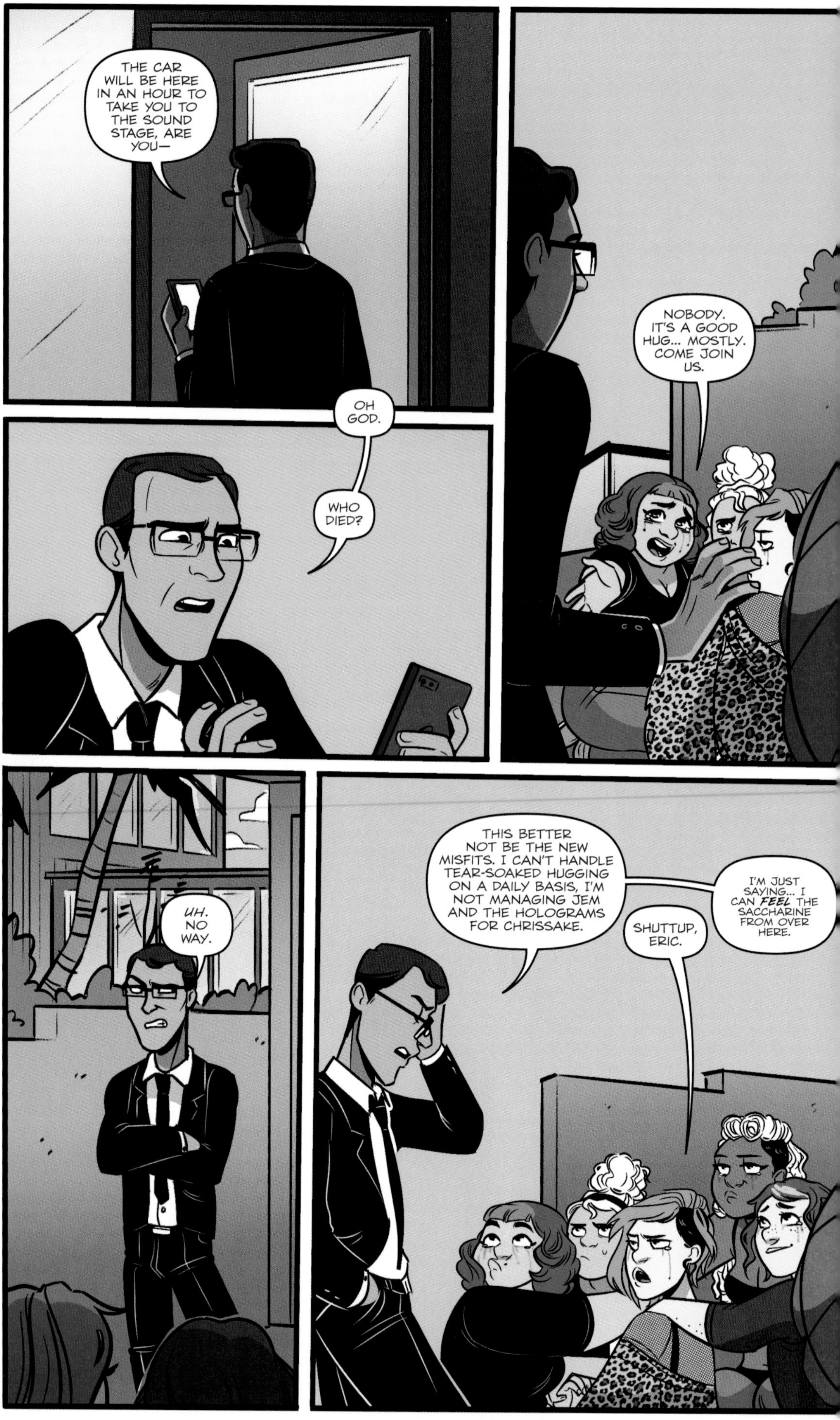
THE CAR WILL BE HERE IN AN HOUR TO TAKE YOU TO THE SOUND STAGE, ARE YOU—
OH GOD.
WHO DIED?
NOBODY. IT'S A GOOD HUG... MOSTLY. COME JOIN US.
UH. NO WAY.
THIS BETTER NOT BE THE NEW MISFITS. I CAN'T HANDLE TEAR-SOAKED HUGGING ON A DAILY BASIS, I'M NOT MANAGING JEM AND THE HOLOGRAMS FOR CHRISSAKE.
SHUTTUP, ERIC.
I'M JUST SAYING... I CAN *FEEL* THE SACCHARINE FROM OVER HERE.

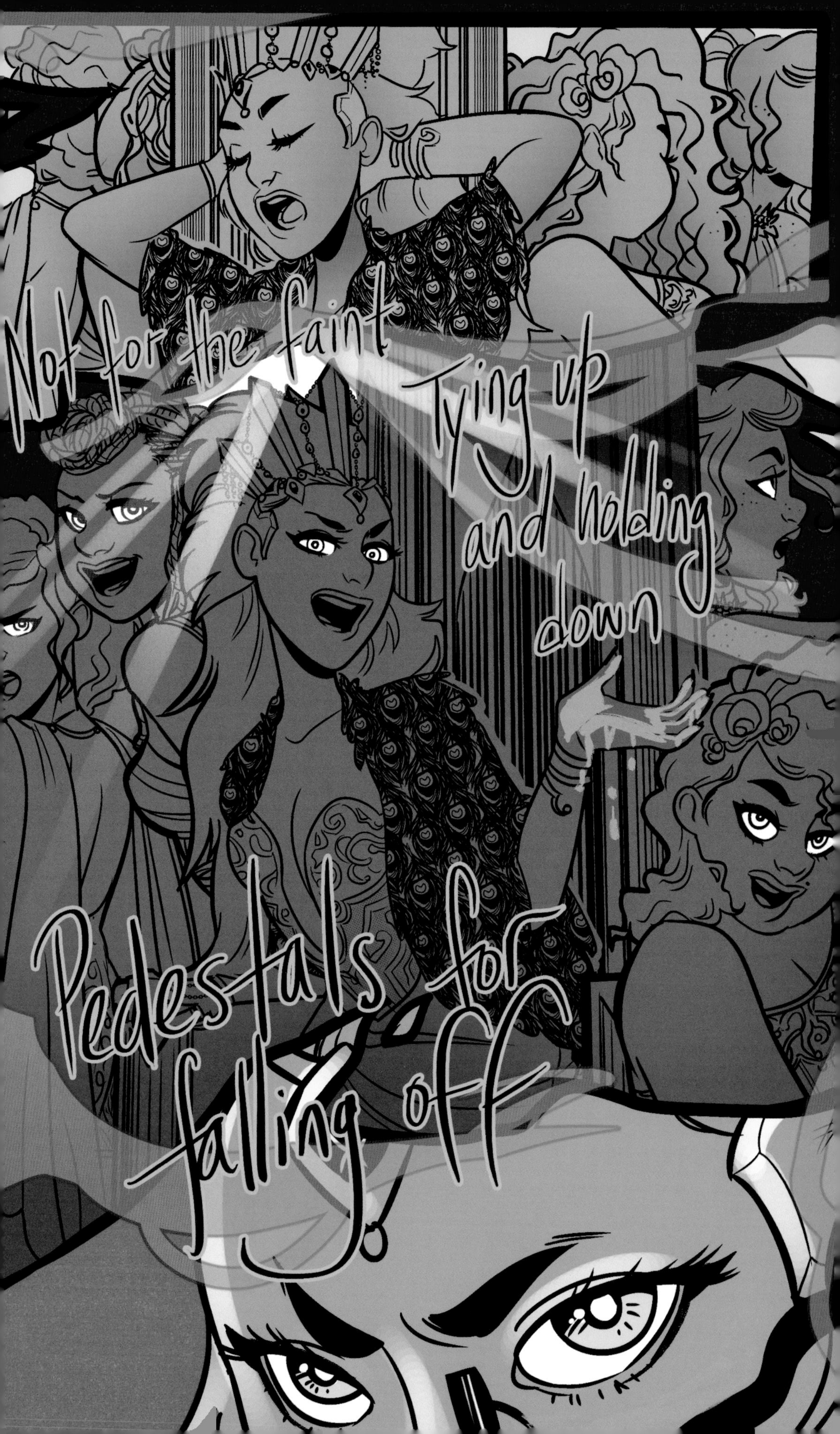
Not for the faint
Tying up and holding down
Pedestals for falling off

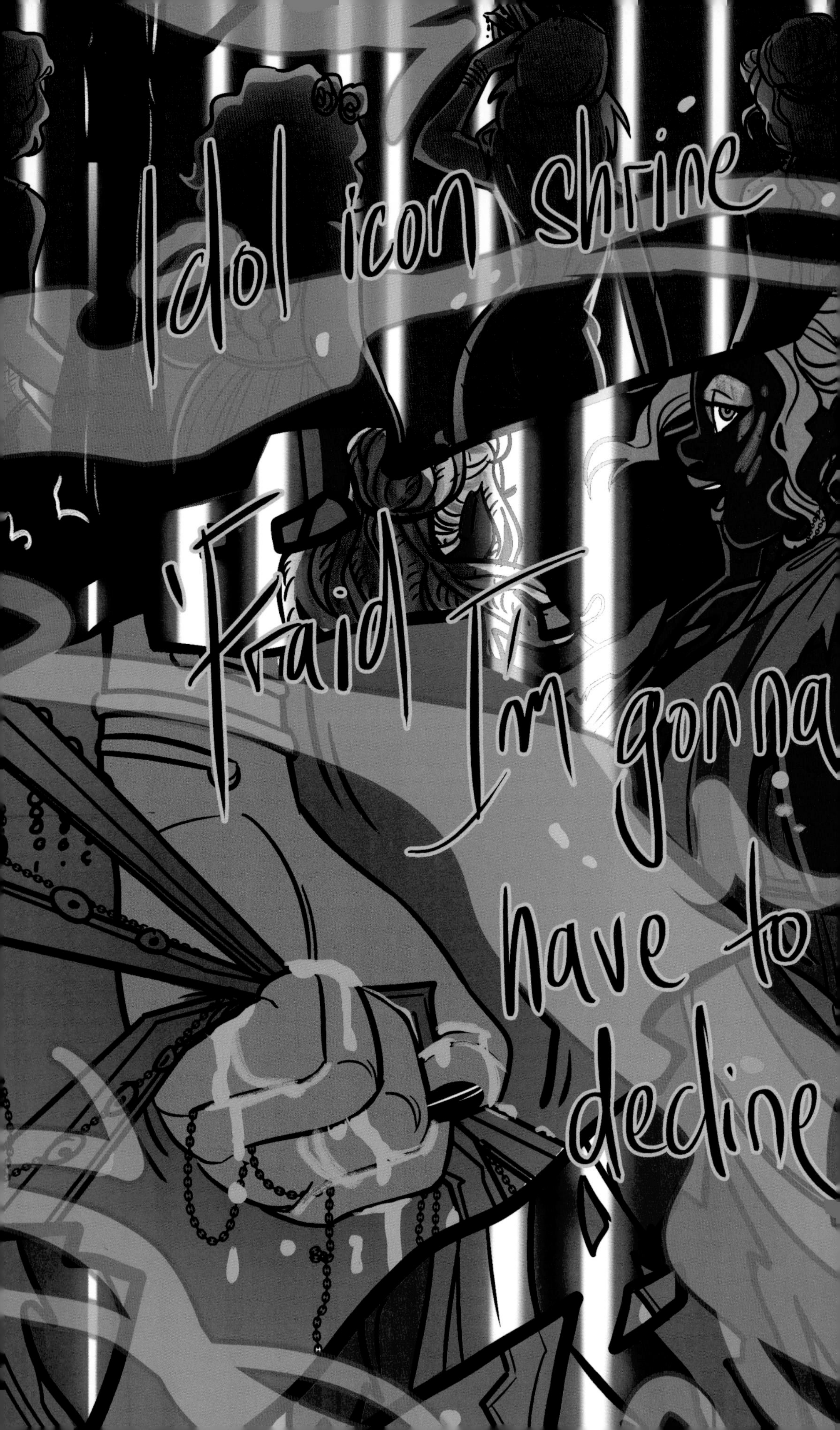
Idol icon shrine
'Fraid I'm gonna
have to
decline

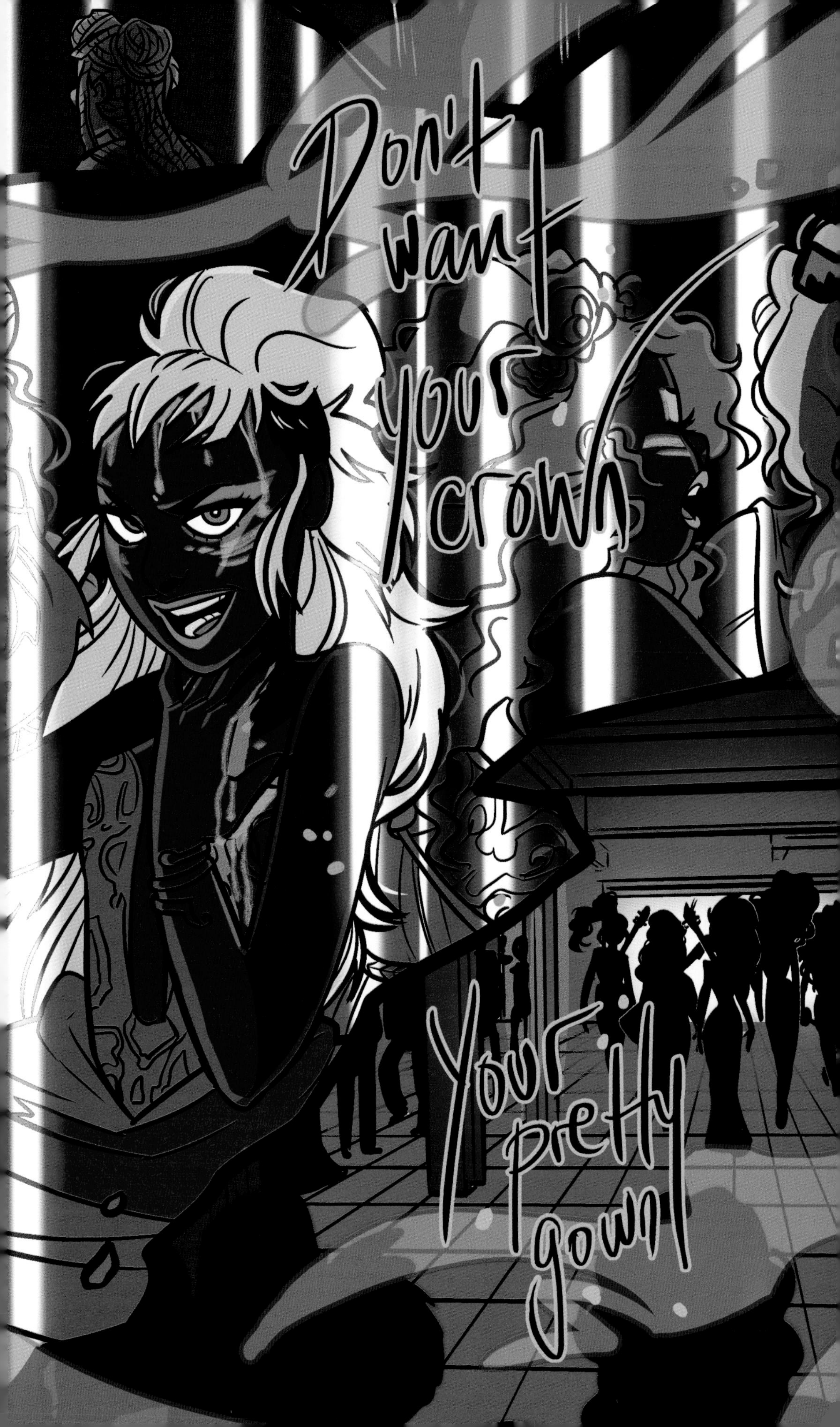
Don't want your crown
Your pretty gown

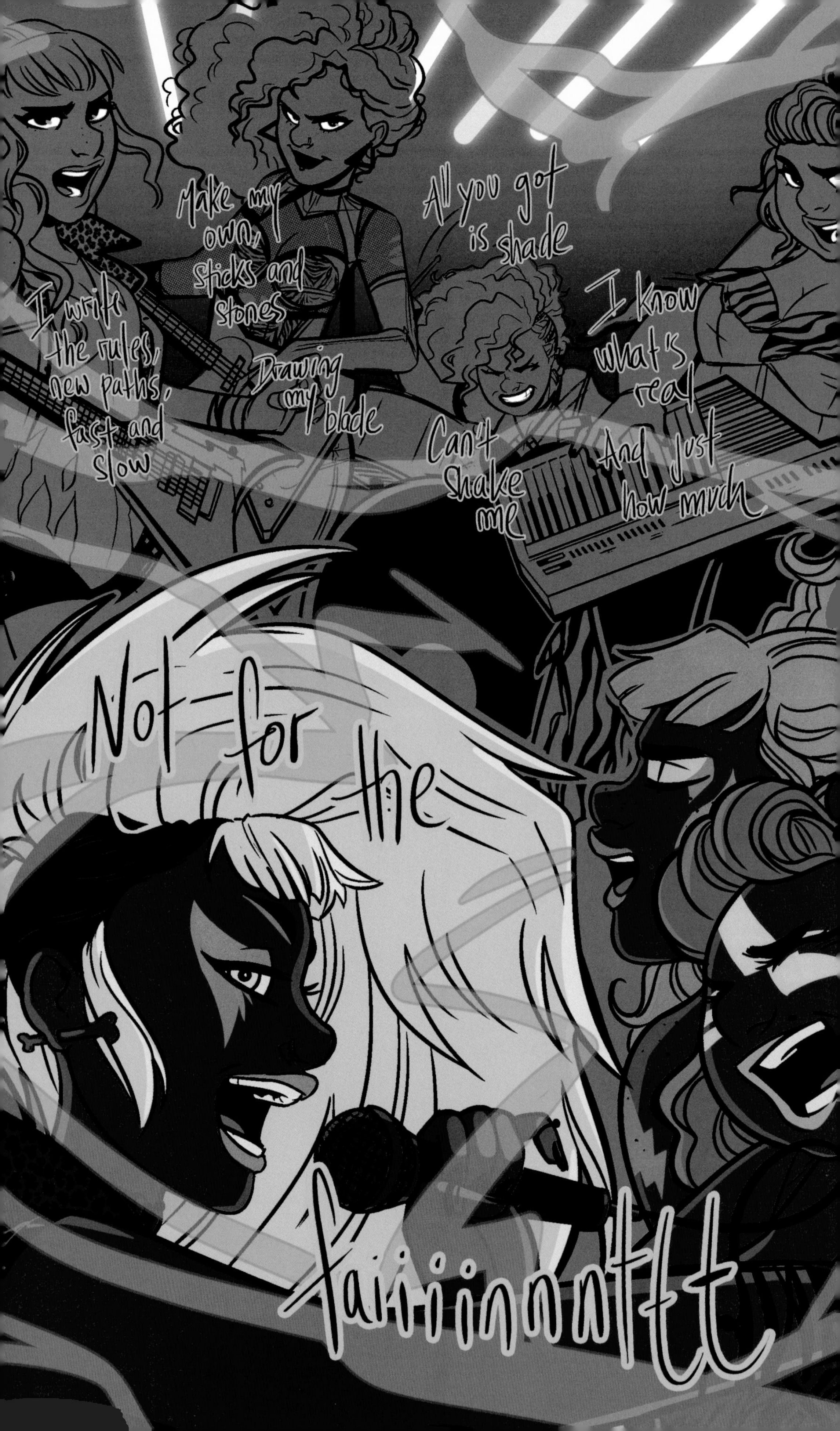
I write the rules, new paths, fast and slow
Make my own, sticks and stones
Drawing my blade
All you got is shade
Can't shake me
I know what's real
And just how much
Not for the
faiiinnnttt

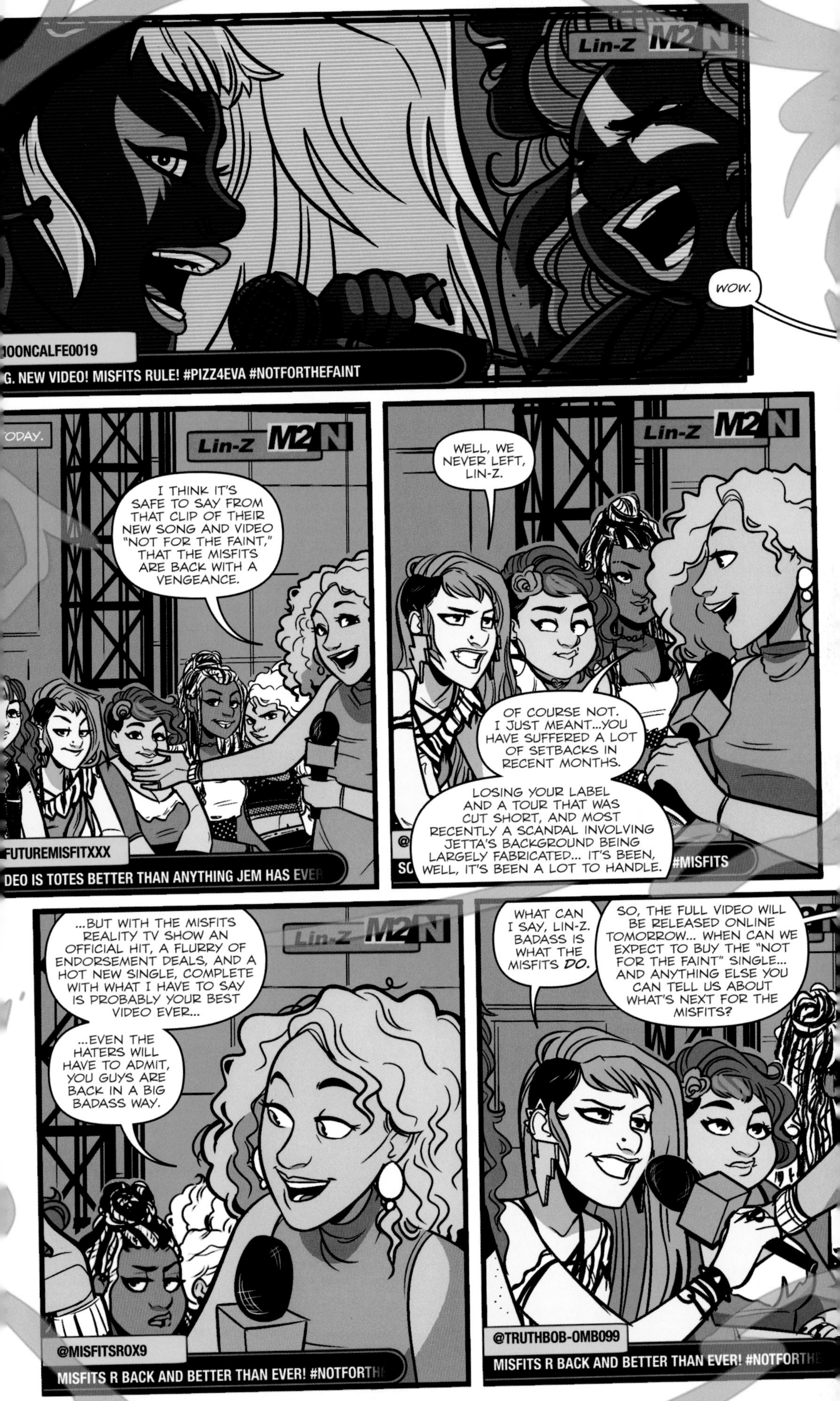
Lin-Z M2N
WOW.
OONCALFE0019
G. NEW VIDEO! MISFITS RULE! #PIZZ4EVA #NOTFORTHEFAINT
ODAY.
Lin-Z M2N
I THINK IT'S SAFE TO SAY FROM THAT CLIP OF THEIR NEW SONG AND VIDEO "NOT FOR THE FAINT," THAT THE MISFITS ARE BACK WITH A VENGEANCE.
FUTUREMISFITXXX
DEO IS TOTES BETTER THAN ANYTHING JEM HAS EVE
Lin-Z M2N
WELL, WE NEVER LEFT, LIN-Z.
OF COURSE NOT. I JUST MEANT...YOU HAVE SUFFERED A LOT OF SETBACKS IN RECENT MONTHS.
LOSING YOUR LABEL AND A TOUR THAT WAS CUT SHORT, AND MOST RECENTLY A SCANDAL INVOLVING JETTA'S BACKGROUND BEING LARGELY FABRICATED... IT'S BEEN, WELL, IT'S BEEN A LOT TO HANDLE.
#MISFITS
Lin-Z M2N
...BUT WITH THE MISFITS REALITY TV SHOW AN OFFICIAL HIT, A FLURRY OF ENDORSEMENT DEALS, AND A HOT NEW SINGLE, COMPLETE WITH WHAT I HAVE TO SAY IS PROBABLY YOUR BEST VIDEO EVER...
...EVEN THE HATERS WILL HAVE TO ADMIT, YOU GUYS ARE BACK IN A BIG BADASS WAY.
@MISFITSROX9
MISFITS R BACK AND BETTER THAN EVER! #NOTFORTH
WHAT CAN I SAY, LIN-Z. BADASS IS WHAT THE MISFITS DO.
SO, THE FULL VIDEO WILL BE RELEASED ONLINE TOMORROW... WHEN CAN WE EXPECT TO BUY THE "NOT FOR THE FAINT" SINGLE... AND ANYTHING ELSE YOU CAN TELL US ABOUT WHAT'S NEXT FOR THE MISFITS?
@TRUTHBOB-OMB099
MISFITS R BACK AND BETTER THAN EVER! #NOTFORTH

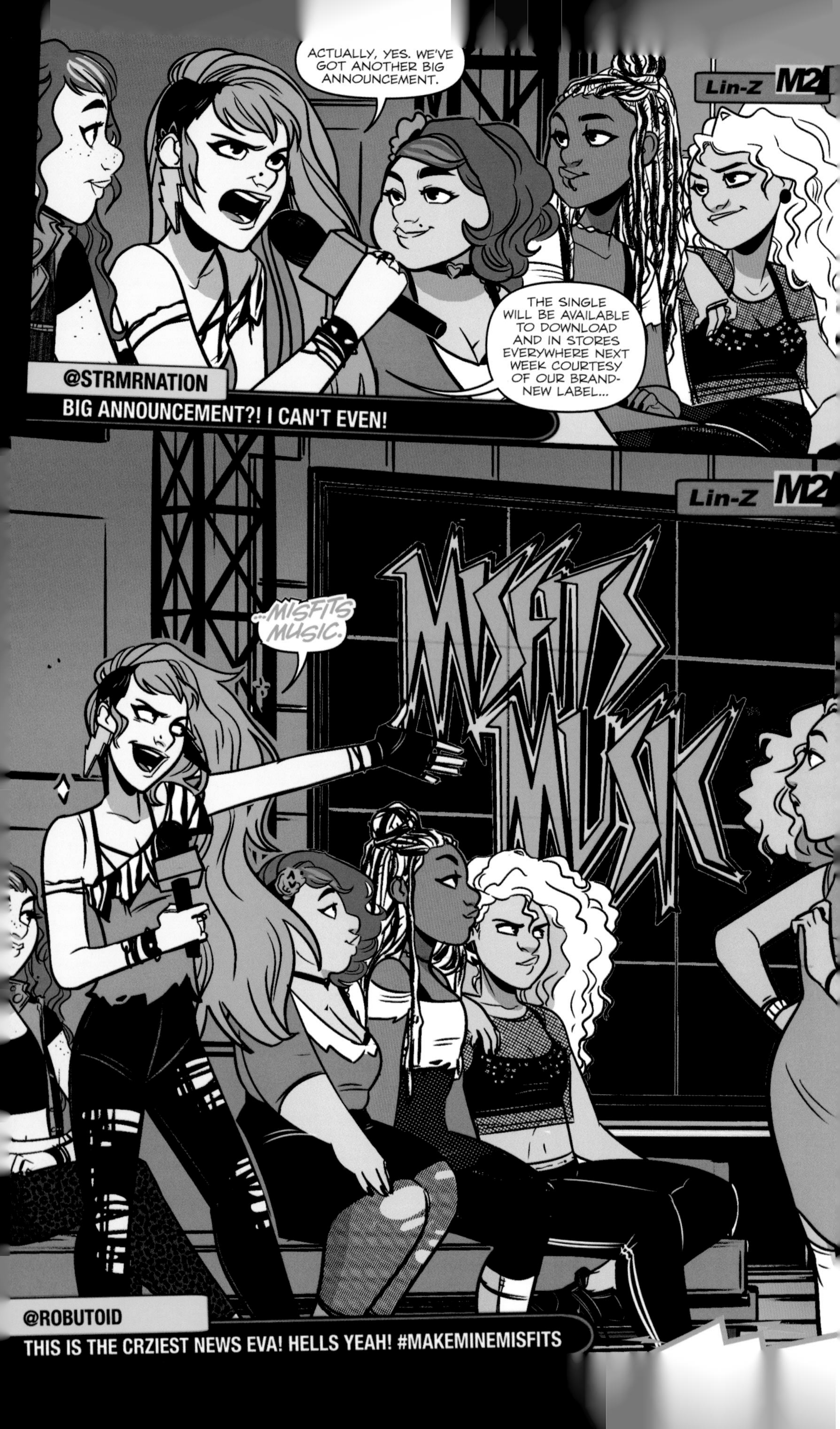
ACTUALLY, YES. WE'VE GOT ANOTHER BIG ANNOUNCEMENT.
Lin-Z
M2
THE SINGLE WILL BE AVAILABLE TO DOWNLOAD AND IN STORES EVERYWHERE NEXT WEEK COURTESY OF OUR BRAND-NEW LABEL...
@STRMRNATION
BIG ANNOUNCEMENT?! I CAN'T EVEN!
Lin-Z
M2
...MISFITS MUSIC.
MISFITS MUSIC
@ROBUTOID
THIS IS THE CRZIEST NEWS EVA! HELLS YEAH! #MAKEMINEMISFITS

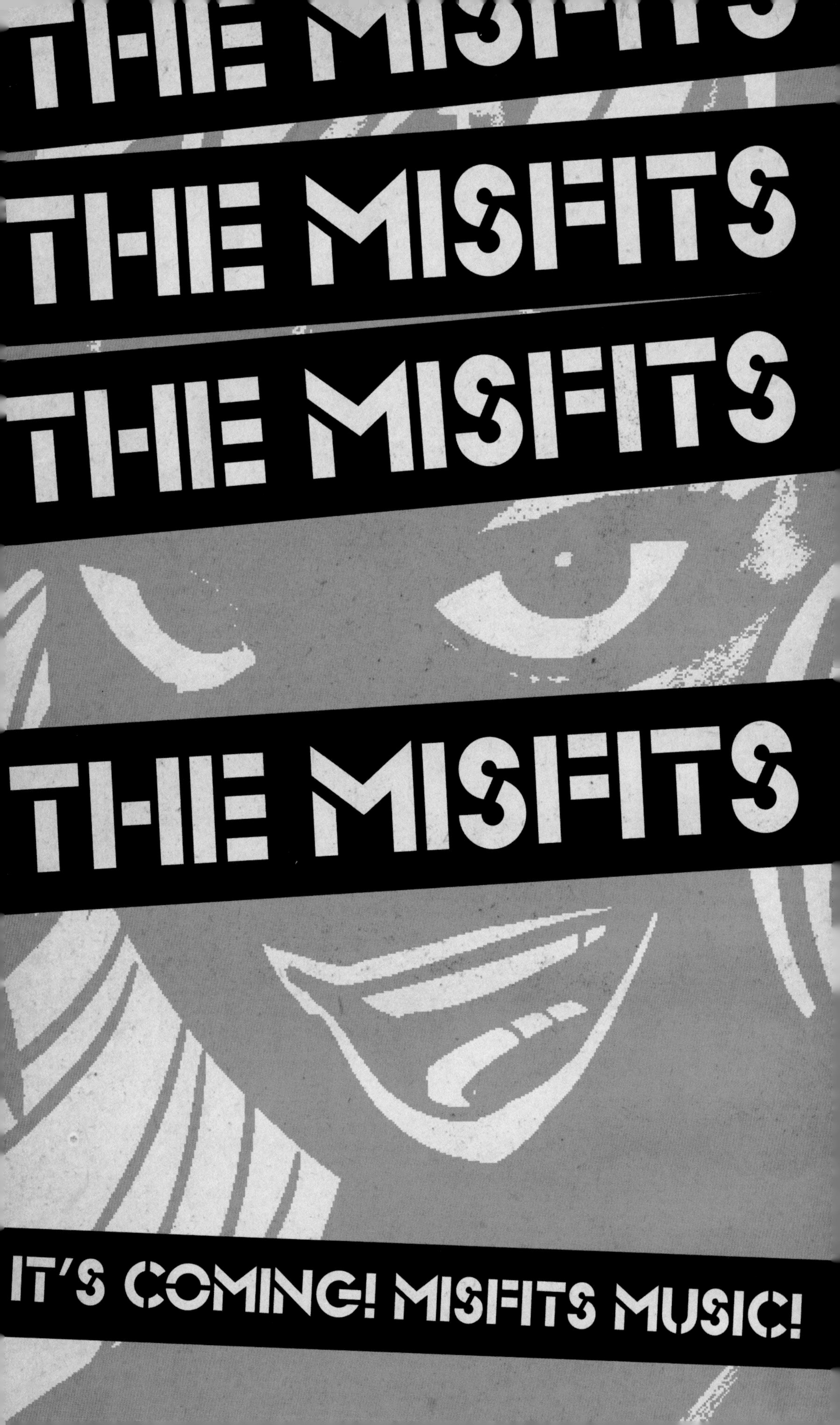
THE MISFITS
THE MISFITS
THE MISFITS
IT'S COMING! MISFITS MUSIC!

ART JENN ST-ONGE

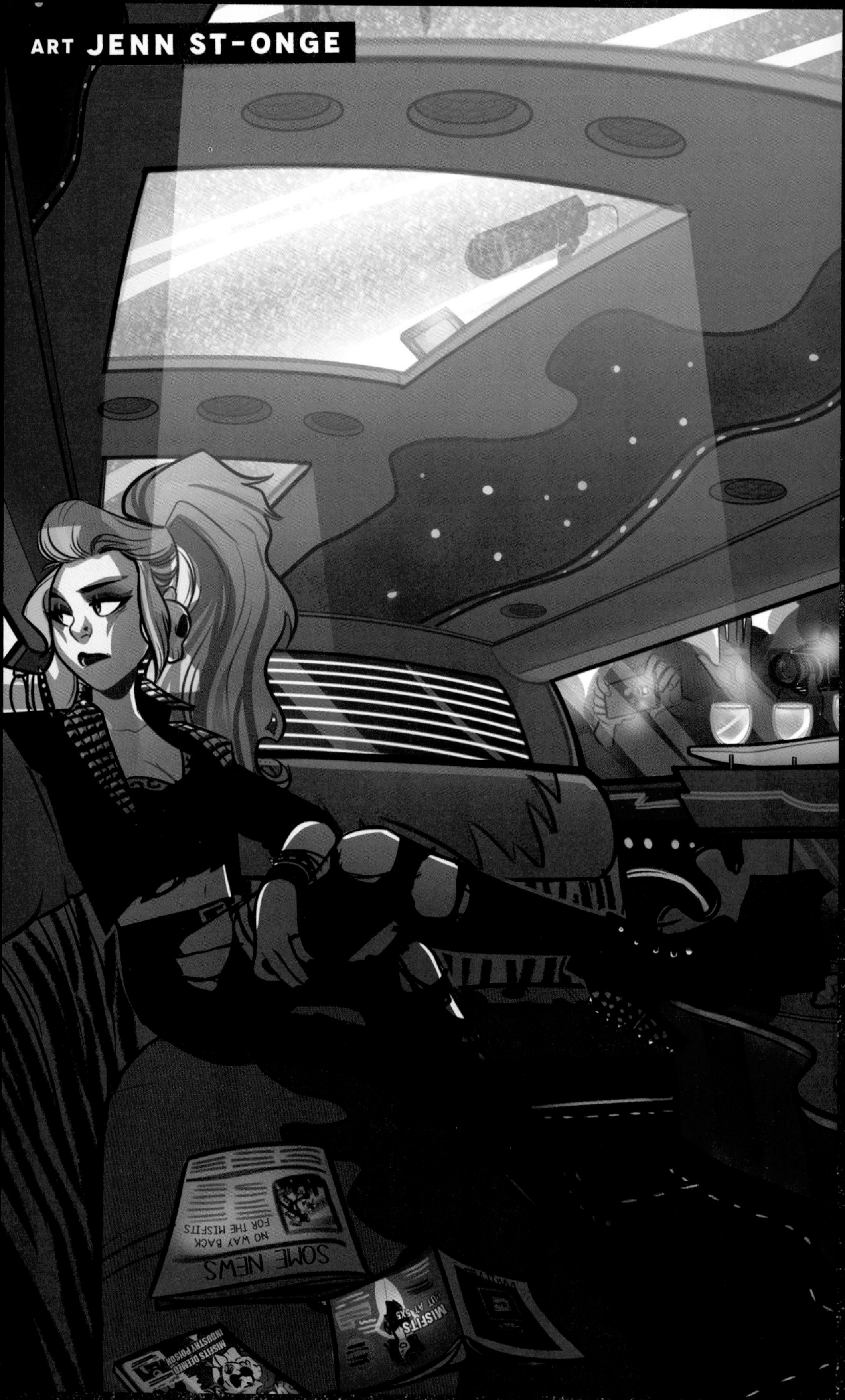

SOME NEWS
NO WAY BACK FOR THE MISFITS
MISFITS CUT AT 5X5
MISFITS DEEMED INDUSTRY POISON

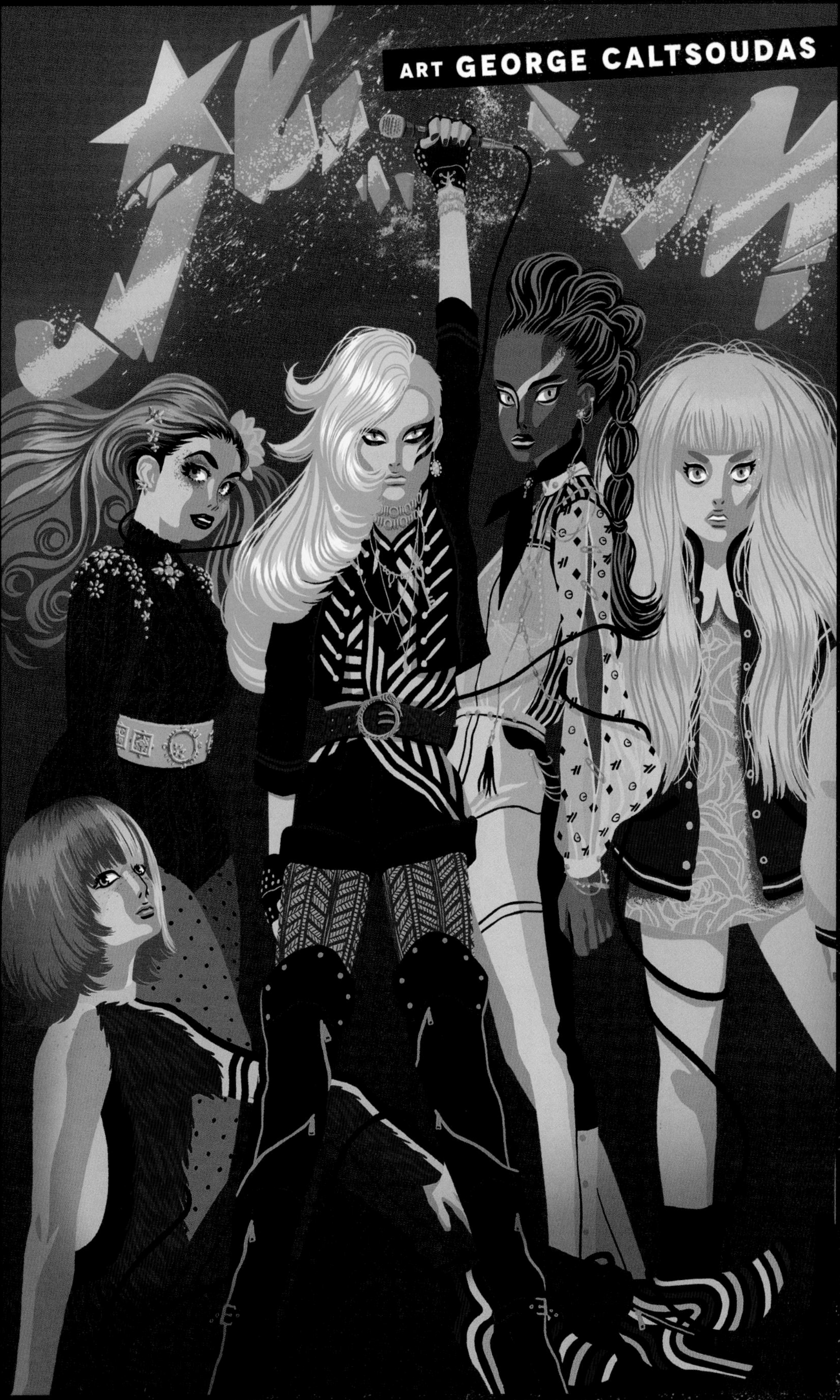
ART GEORGE CALTSOUDAS

ART JENN ST-ONGE

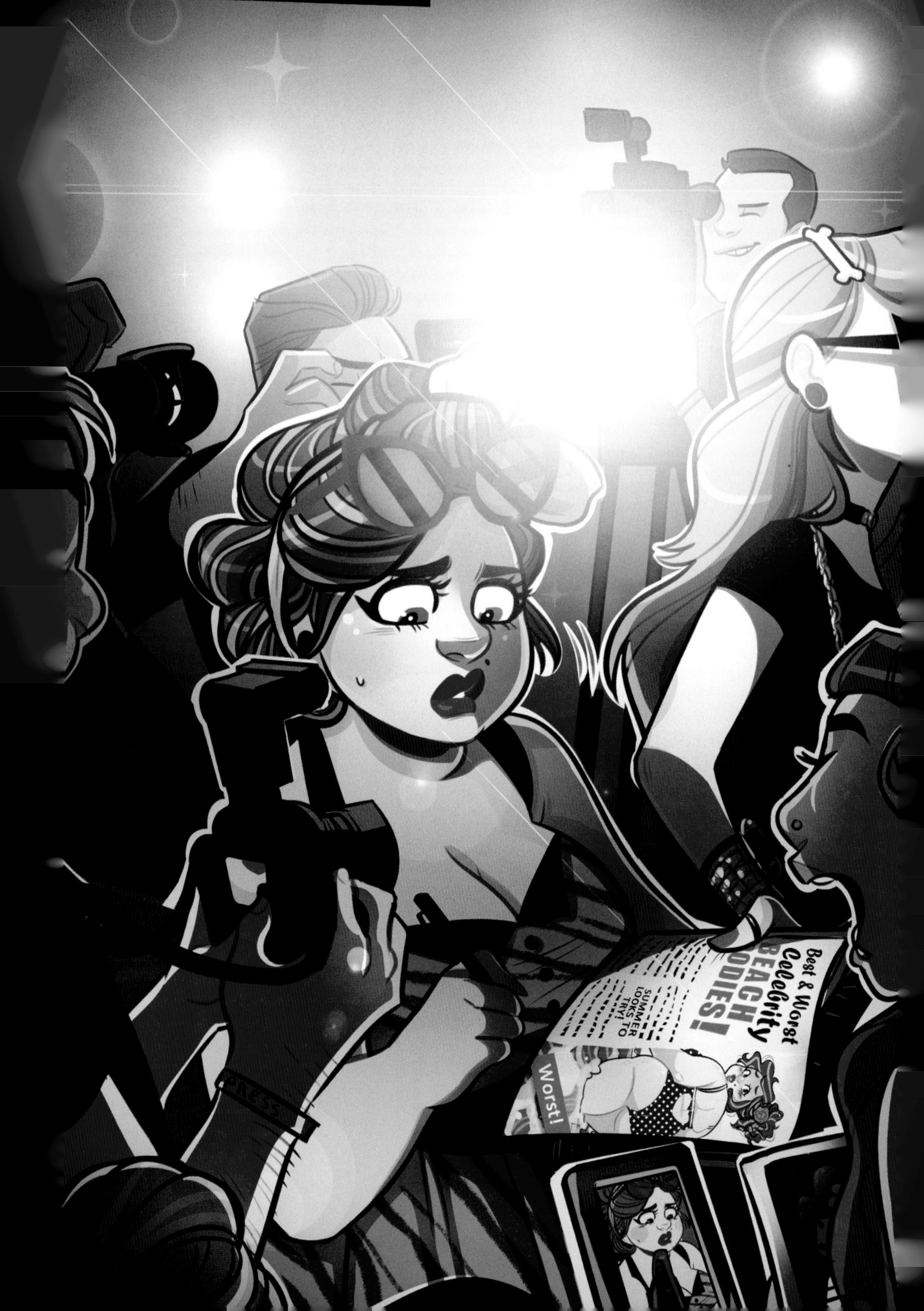
PRESS
Best & Worst
Celebrity
BEACH
ODIES!
SUMMER
LOOKS TO
TRY!
Worst!

ART DEREK CHARM

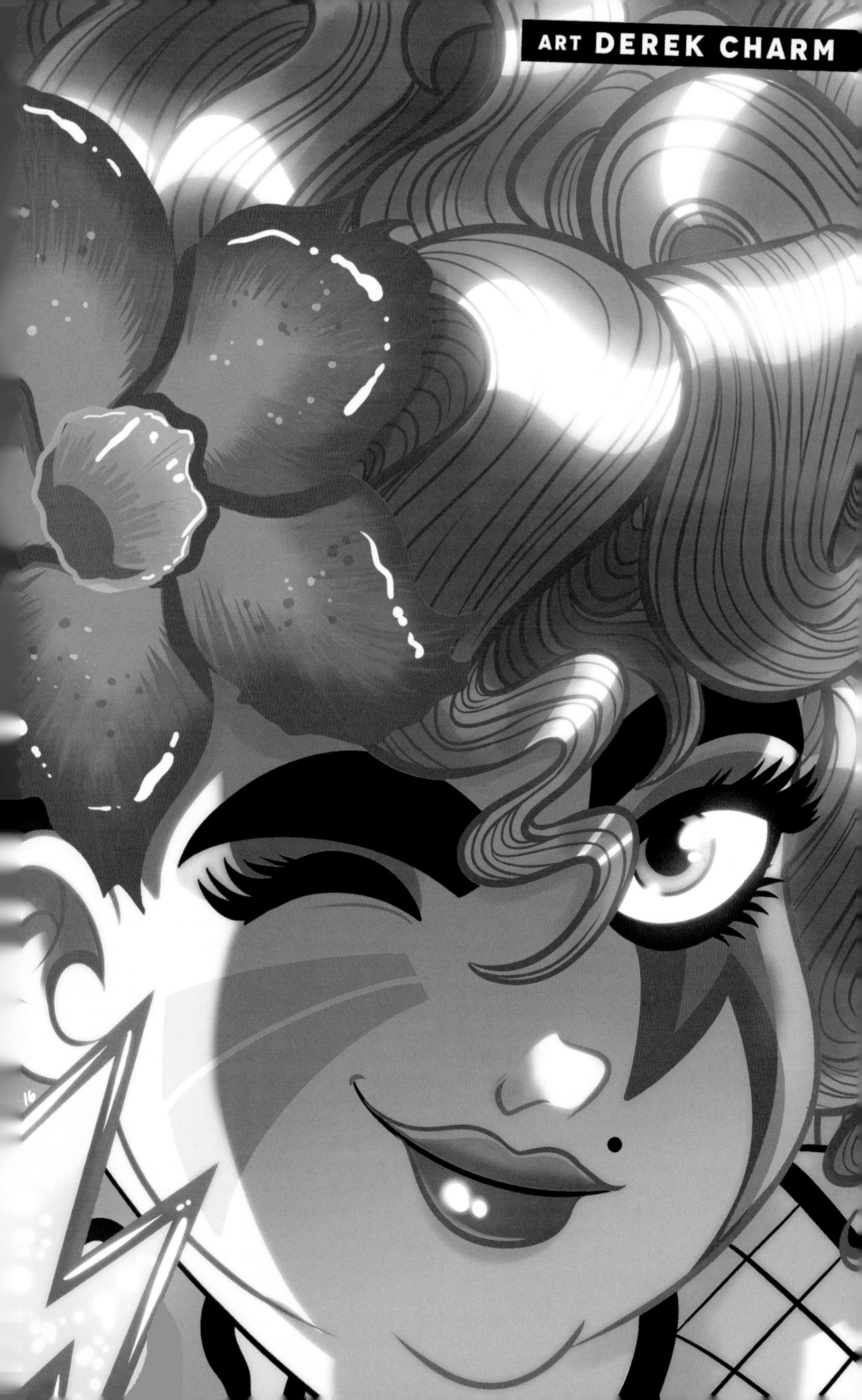

ART JENN ST-ONGE

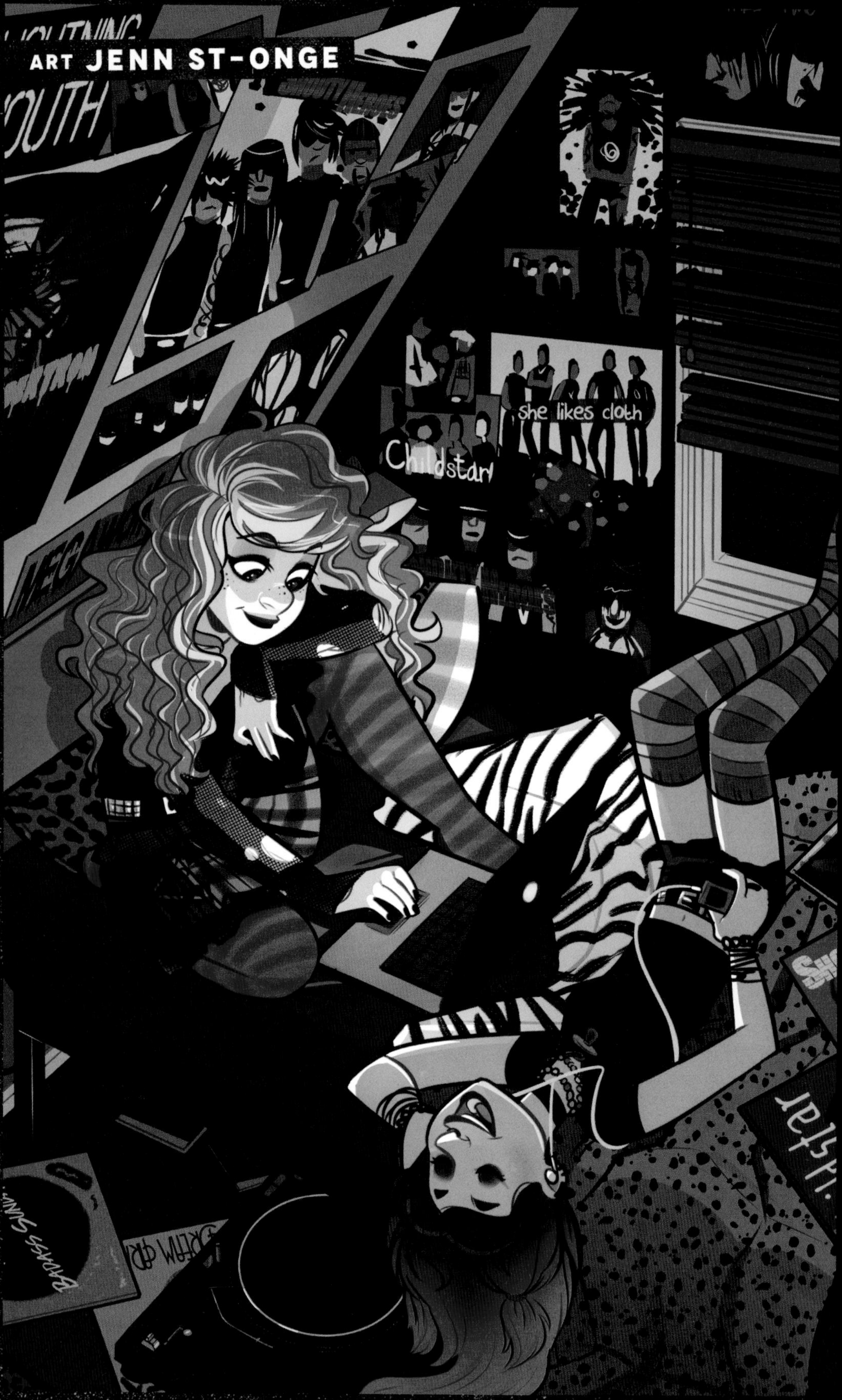
she likes cloth
Childstar

ART SOPHIE CAMPBELL

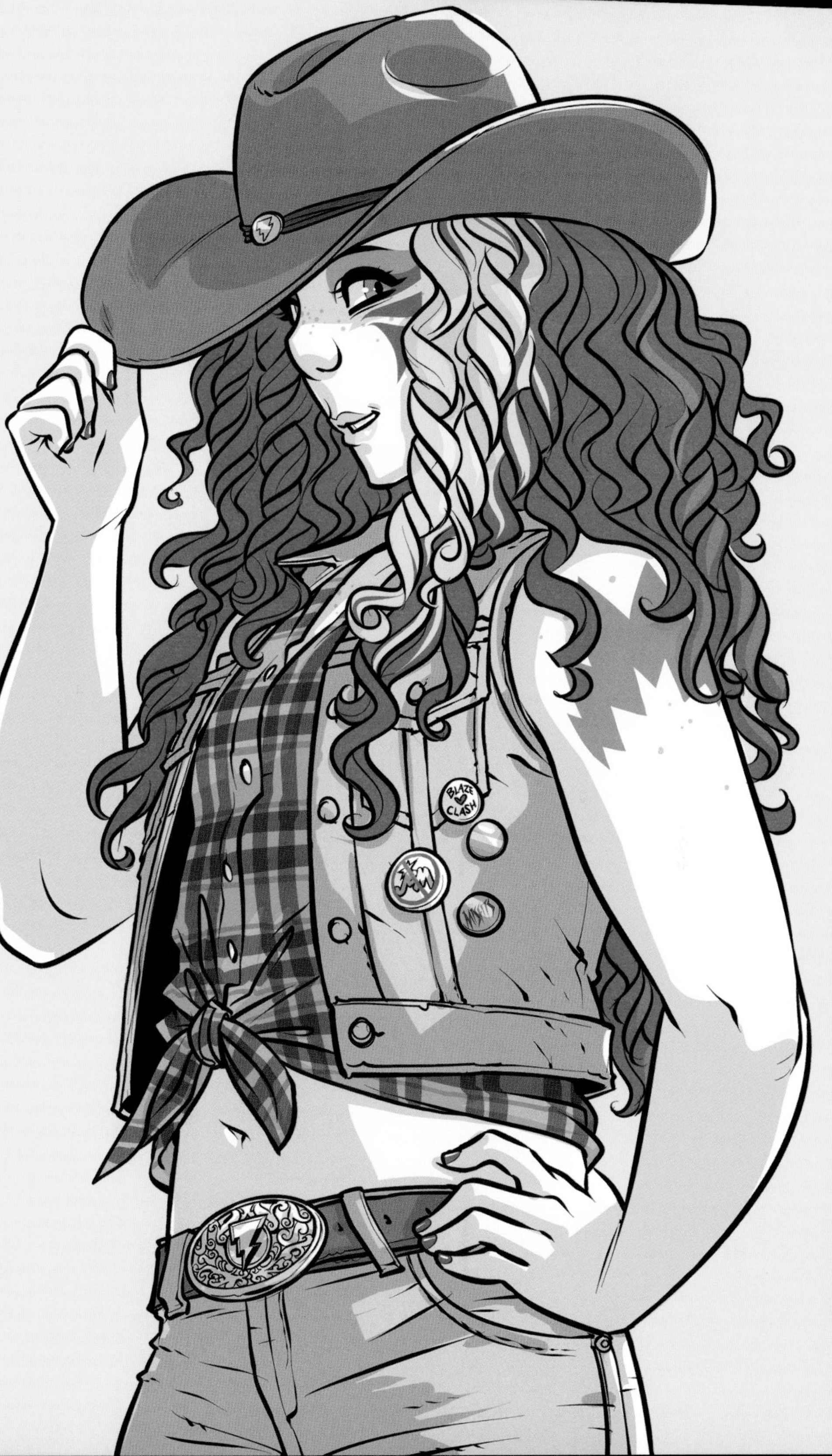
BLAZE
CLASH

ART JENN ST-ONGE

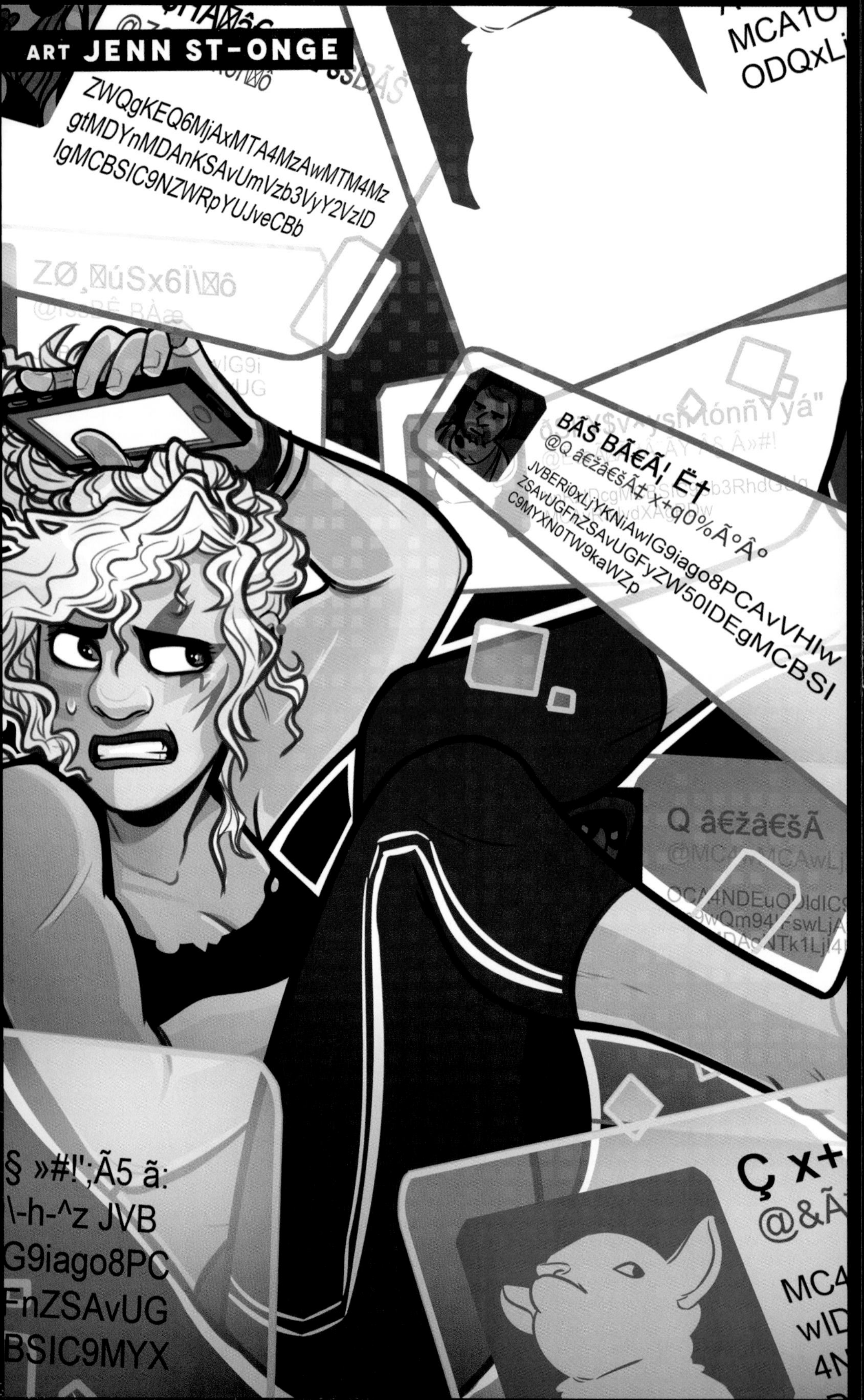
ZWQgKEQ6MjAxMTA4MzAwMTM4Mz
gtMDYnMDAnKSAvUmVzb3VyY2VzID
lgMCBSIC9NZWRpYUJveCBb
MCA1O
ODQxLj
BÃŠ BÃ€Ã¦ Ët
@Q â€žâ€šÃ‡ x+q0%Ã°Â°
JVBERi0xLjYKNiAwIG9iago8PCAvVHlw
ZSAvUGFnZSAvUGFyZW50IDEgMCBSI
C9MYXN0TW9kaWZp
Q â€žâ€šÃ
§ »#!';Ã5 ã:
\-h-^z JVB
G9iago8PC
FnZSAvUG
BSIC9MYX
Ç x+

ART MEREDITH McCLAREN

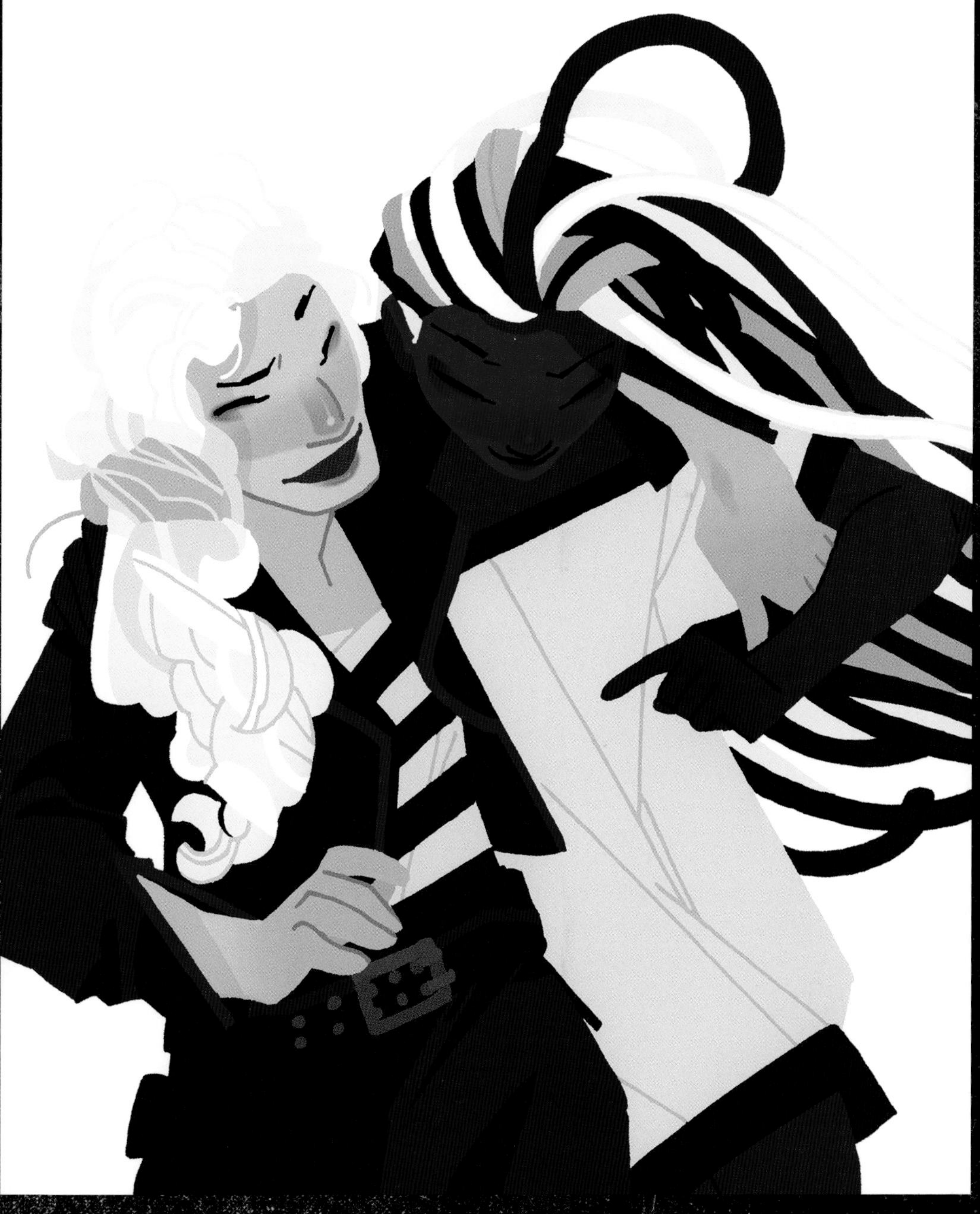

ART **JENN ST-ONGE**

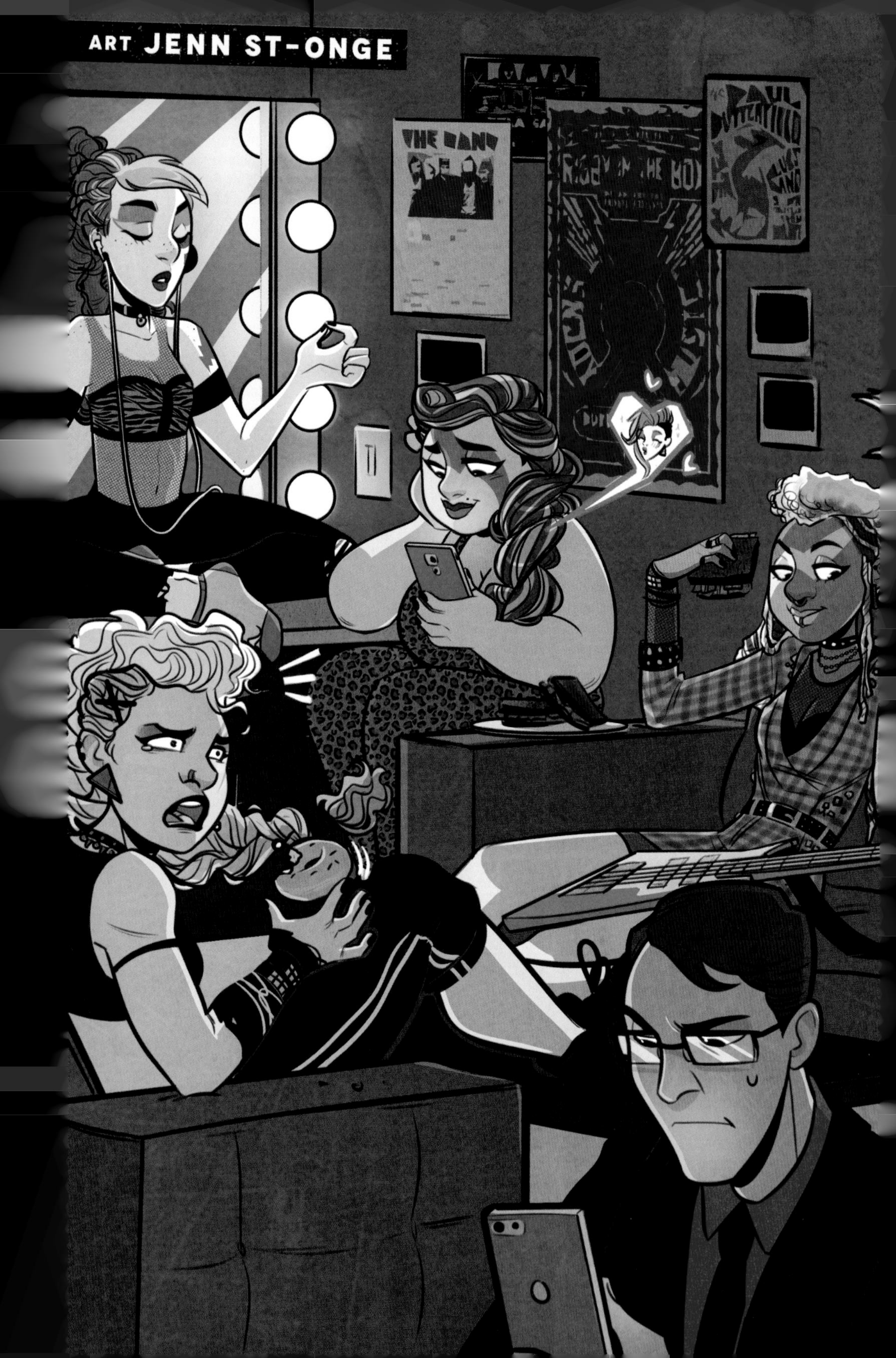
THE BAND
PAUL

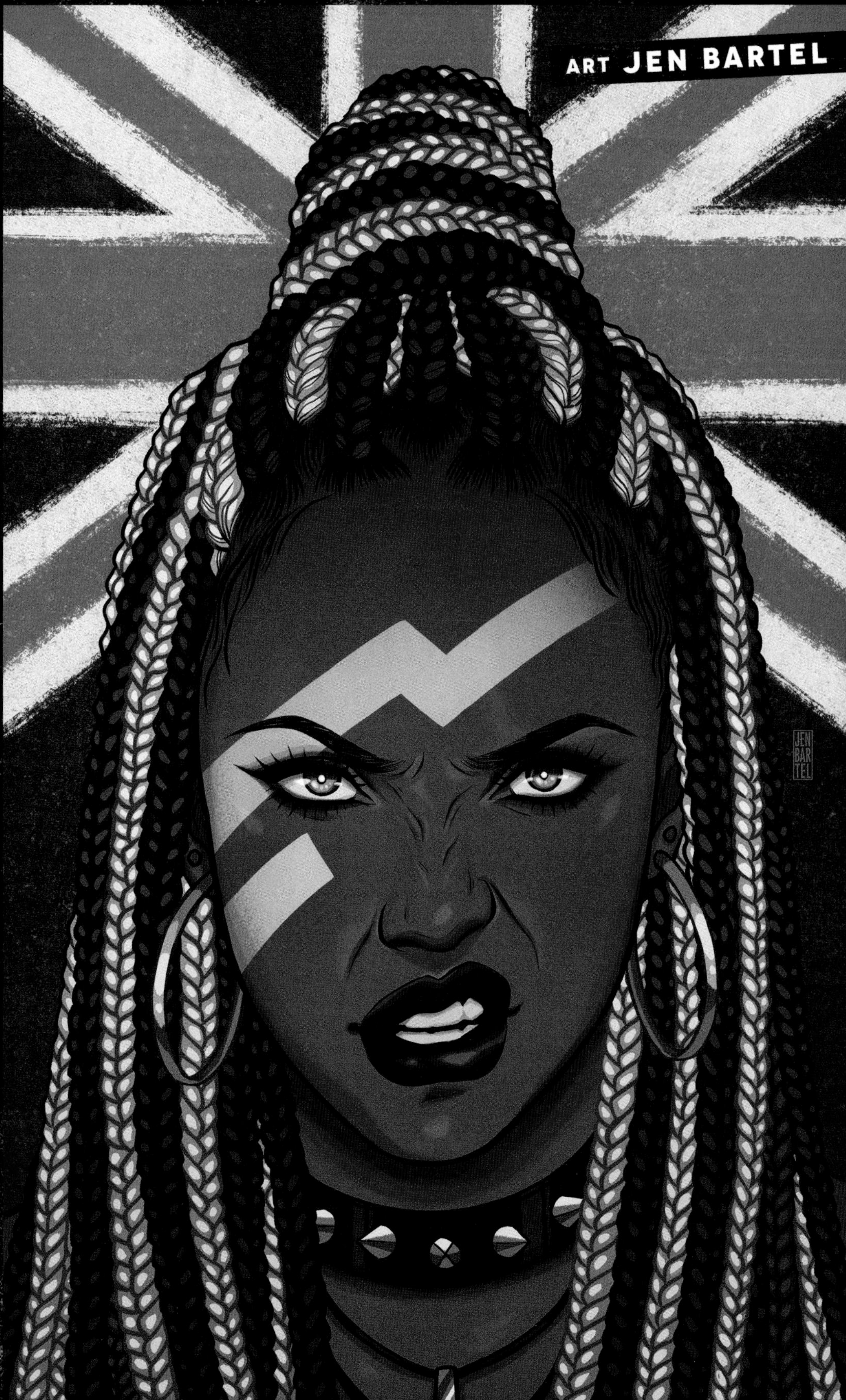
ART JEN BARTEL
JEN
BAR
TEL

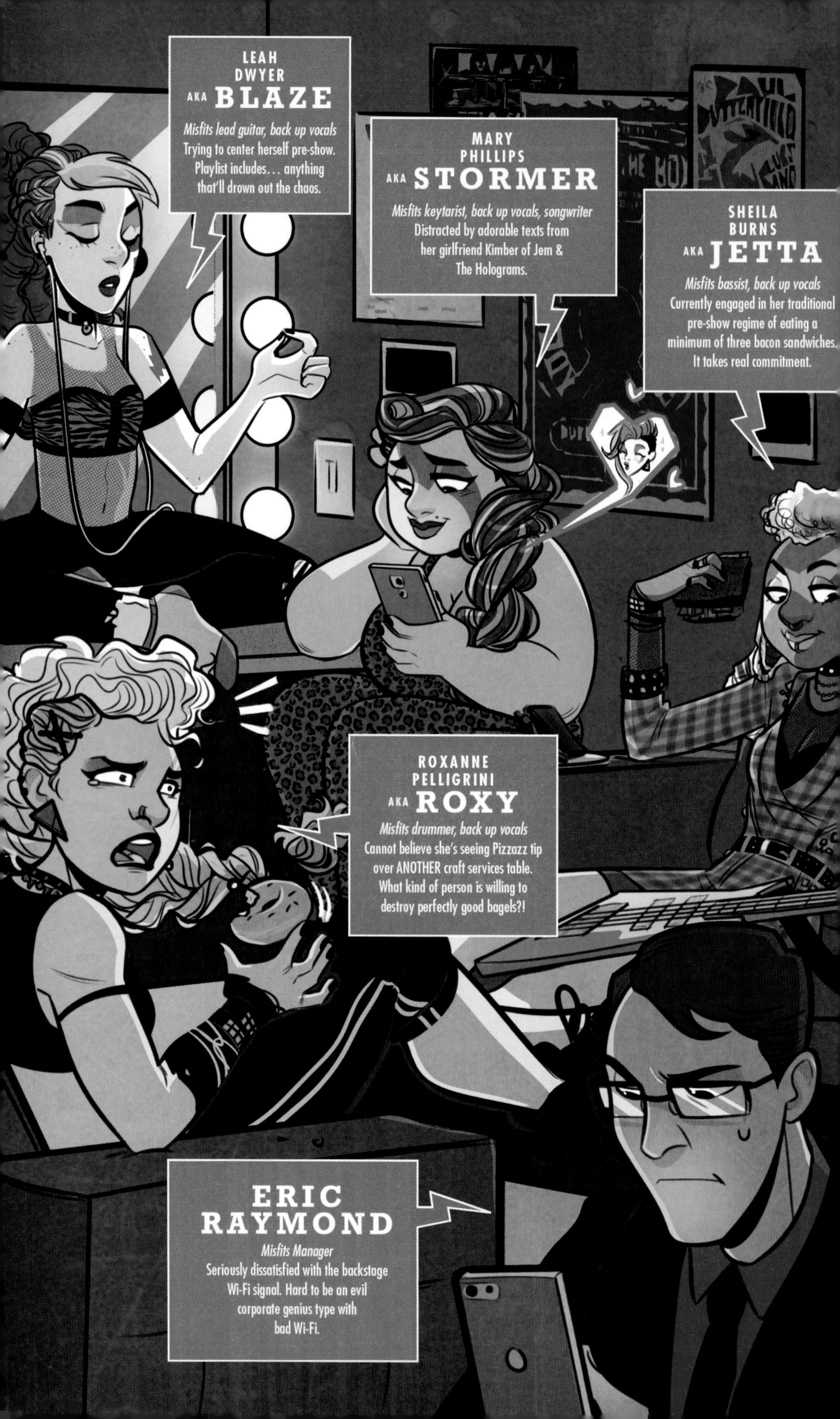
LEAH DWYER AKA BLAZE
Misfits lead guitar, back up vocals
Trying to center herself pre-show. Playlist includes… anything that'll drown out the chaos.
MARY PHILLIPS AKA STORMER
Misfits keytarist, back up vocals, songwriter
Distracted by adorable texts from her girlfriend Kimber of Jem & The Holograms.
SHEILA BURNS AKA JETTA
Misfits bassist, back up vocals
Currently engaged in her traditional pre-show regime of eating a minimum of three bacon sandwiches. It takes real commitment.
ROXANNE PELLIGRINI AKA ROXY
Misfits drummer, back up vocals
Cannot believe she's seeing Pizzazz tip over ANOTHER craft services table. What kind of person is willing to destroy perfectly good bagels?!
ERIC RAYMOND
Misfits Manager
Seriously dissatisfied with the backstage Wi-Fi signal. Hard to be an evil corporate genius type with bad Wi-Fi.

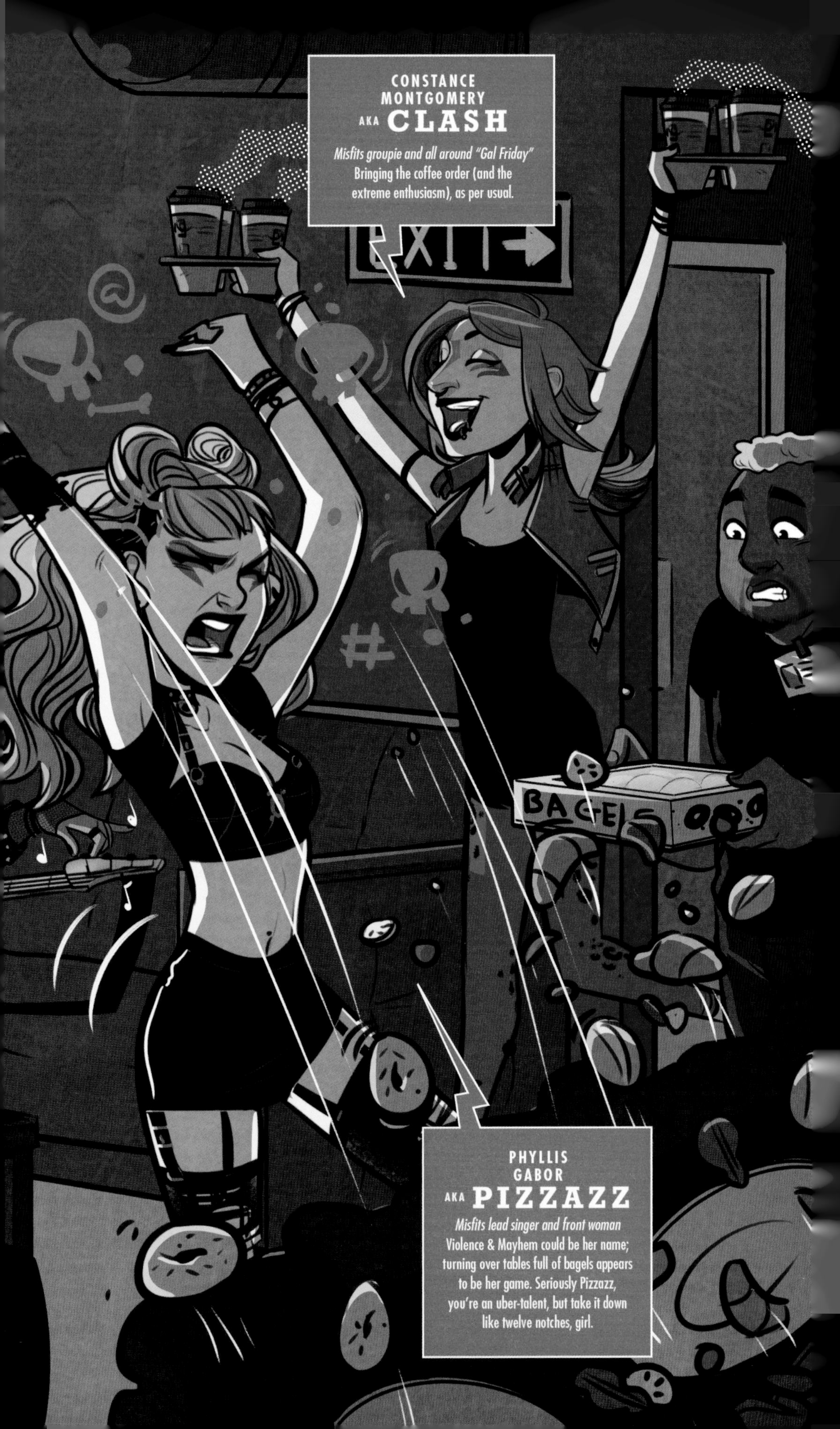
CONSTANCE
MONTGOMERY
AKA CLASH
Misfits groupie and all around "Gal Friday"
Bringing the coffee order (and the extreme enthusiasm), as per usual.
EXIT
BAGELS
PHYLLIS
GABOR
AKA PIZZAZZ
Misfits lead singer and front woman
Violence & Mayhem could be her name; turning over tables full of bagels appears to be her game. Seriously Pizzazz, you're an uber-talent, but take it down like twelve notches, girl.

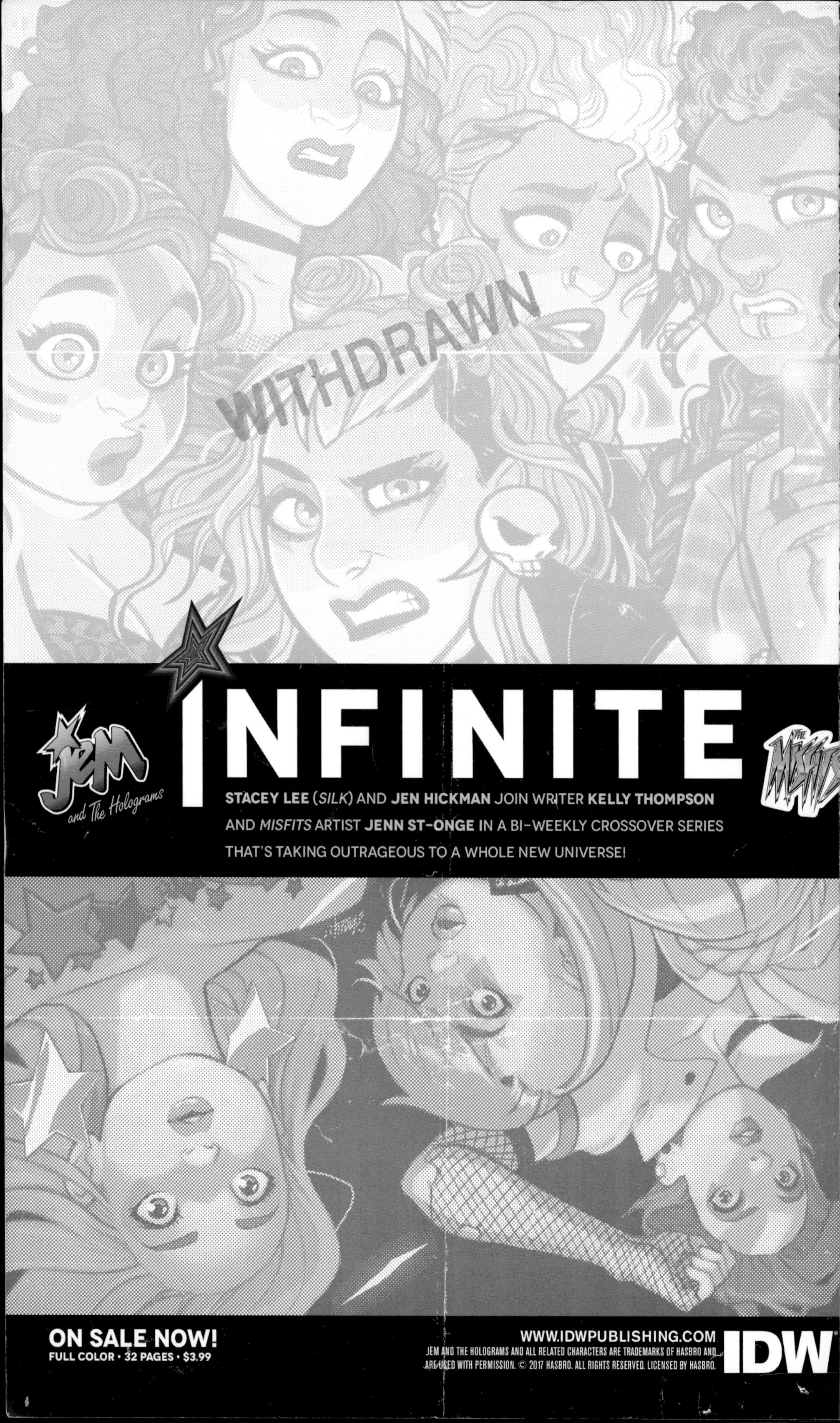
WITHDRAWN
JEM and The Holograms
INFINITE
THE MISFITS
STACEY LEE (SILK) AND JEN HICKMAN JOIN WRITER KELLY THOMPSON
AND MISFITS ARTIST JENN ST-ONGE IN A BI-WEEKLY CROSSOVER SERIES
THAT'S TAKING OUTRAGEOUS TO A WHOLE NEW UNIVERSE!
ON SALE NOW!
FULL COLOR • 32 PAGES • $3.99
WWW.IDWPUBLISHING.COM
JEM AND THE HOLOGRAMS AND ALL RELATED CHARACTERS ARE TRADEMARKS OF HASBRO AND ARE USED WITH PERMISSION. © 2017 HASBRO. ALL RIGHTS RESERVED. LICENSED BY HASBRO.
IDW